W9-COS-544

FLORIDA STATE
UNIVERSITY LIBRARIES

JUN 14 2001

TALLAHASSEE, FLORIDA

EXTERNAL ECONOMIES AND COOPERATION IN INDUSTRIAL DISTRICTS

External Economies and Cooperation in Industrial Districts

A Comparison of Italy and Mexico

Roberta Rabellotti
Lecturer in Economics
Department of Economics
University of Padua
Italy

HC
310
.D5
R3
1997

First published in Great Britain 1997 by
MACMILLAN PRESS LTD
Houndmills, Basingstoke, Hampshire RG21 6XS and London
Companies and representatives throughout the world

A catalogue record for this book is available from the British Library.

ISBN 0–333–69387–6

First published in the United States of America 1997 by
ST. MARTIN'S PRESS, INC.,
Scholarly and Reference Division,
175 Fifth Avenue, New York, N.Y. 10010

ISBN 0–312–17580–9

Library of Congress Cataloging-in-Publication Data
Rabellotti, Roberta.
External economies and cooperation in industrial districts : a
comparison of Italy and Mexico / Roberta Rabellotti.
p.   cm.
Includes bibliographical references and index.
ISBN 0–312–17580–9 (cloth)
1. Industrial districts—Italy.   2. Industrial districts—Mexico.
3. Footwear industry—Italy.   4. Footwear industry—Mexico.
I. Title.
HC310.D5R3 1997
338.945—dc21   97–9326
                                                                   CIP

© Roberta Rabellotti 1997

All rights reserved. No reproduction, copy or transmission of this publication may be made without written permission.

No paragraph of this publication may be reproduced, copied or transmitted save with written permission or in accordance with the provisions of the Copyright, Designs and Patents Act 1988, or under the terms of any licence permitting limited copying issued by the Copyright Licensing Agency, 90 Tottenham Court Road, London W1P 9HE.

Any person who does any unauthorised act in relation to this publication may be liable to criminal prosecution and civil claims for damages.

The author has asserted her right to be identified as the author of this work in accordance with the Copyright, Designs and Patents Act 1988.

This book is printed on paper suitable for recycling and made from fully managed and sustained forest sources.

10   9   8   7   6   5   4   3   2   1
06   05   04   03   02   01   00   99   98   97

Printed in Great Britain by
The Ipswich Book Company Ltd
Ipswich, Suffolk

To Giulio

Contents

List of Tables

List of Maps and Figures

Acknowledgements

This book was researched and written with the financial help of grants from several institutions: in Italy the Fondazione Luca D'Agliano and Fondazione Einaudi in Turin, in Mexico the Istituto Tecnologico de Monterrey and finally, in Geneva, the International Institute for Labour Studies. Financial support was also granted by two research projects, sponsored by the Regional Government of Emilia-Romagna and by the Italian National Research Council (CNR).

The research would not have been possible without the cooperation of the many people in firms and institutions in Mexico and Italy, who gave generously of their time. I am particularly grateful to Rosa Maria Sanchez Cantu of the Istituto Tecnologico de Monterrey and to Octavio Paredes Miranda of the Istituto Tecnologico del Calzado in Guadalajara; their enthusiasm in supporting this research project made possible my fieldwork in Mexico. Both the Camara de la Industria del Calzado in Guadalajara and in Leon were always very supportive. Finally, I have a debt of gratitude to the Mexican entrepreneurs, who always participated in my research with great enthusiasm.

In Italy, I am grateful to the Unione Industriale del Fermano, to the Associazione Calzaturifici della Riviera del Brenta and to all the entrepreneurs interviewed in Marche and Brenta. A thank-you goes also to the Dipartimento di Scienze Economiche of the University of Padua and to the Istituto di Economia Politica of Bocconi University of Milan, which kindly allowed me to use their facilities.

A number of people made constructive comments and suggestions on earlier drafts: Gioacchino Garofoli, John Humphrey, Stefano Kluzer, Bernard Musyck, Khalid Nadvi, Roberta Capello and Werner Sengenberger. Paolo Giudici and Valeria Severini helped me in the statistical analysis.

Special thanks go to Frances Stewart: she strongly encouraged me to undertake this project and her constant involvement in my research has always been a great support. I am also gratefully indebted to Roberto Camagni, who constantly supported my scientific interests, inspiring me with his enthusiasm and creativity. Finally, the intellectual stimulus of Hubert Schmitz has given me continuous encouragement since the start of the research. Without him this book would never have been possible.

ROBERTA RABELLOTTI

1 Introduction

The aim of this study is to explore the potential of the industrial district 'model' to analyse two footwear clusters in Italy, the 'land' of districts, and two other clusters in a less developed country (LDC), Mexico. Through empirical research we assess the extent to which the core characteristics of the 'model' correspond to the clusters considered. The investigation focuses upon external economies and cooperation which stem directly from the key stylized facts of the industrial district 'model', with particular emphasis upon the intense linkages within the clusters examined.

This introductory chapter first discusses how this research originated, then it presents the main questions addressed and outlines the structure of the book.

1.1 THE ORIGIN OF THE RESEARCH

Research on industrial districts originated in the second half of the 1970s in Italy, where a widespread phenomenon of industrial development based on geographically concentrated and sectorally specialized small and medium sized enterprises (SMEs), was identified by a number of scholars.[1] The increase in the number of employees, production, exports, and per-capita income in north-central and north-eastern Italy, also known as the 'Third Italy',[2] increasingly attracted the interest of Italian and foreign economists and sociologists,[3] trying to understand the reasons for this 'economic miracle'. During the 1980s a great amount of research, both at the empirical and theoretical level, was carried out in Italy and in other Western countries, where many agglomerations of small firms, similar to the original Italian districts, were identified. A great deal of discussion went on about whether a certain agglomeration could be assimilated to the ideal–typical industrial district or not. Several definitions were suggested in the literature emphasizing different aspects of the same general phenomenon: Becattini proposed the Marshallian notion of 'industrial district' (1979) while, for instance, Garofoli (1981 and 1983) introduced the concept of 'system area'.

In more recent years industrial districts also generated a great deal of interest among development economists (Schmitz, 1989). Traditionally, in less developed countries small firms were seen as socially desirable, but their viability remained in doubt. The role of small firms was to create jobs, to be a seed-bed for indigenous entrepreneurship, to use predominantly local resources, to produce for local markets satisfying the basic needs of the poor, to contribute to a more equitable distribution of income, but rarely were they seen as able to become internationally competitive. The success of industrial districts in the West was thus taken as a sign that small firms could be economically viable and strongly contribute to the industrial growth of their country. The concept of the industrial district was then introduced in the study of industrial development in the Third World, both at the empirical and theoretical level (Rasmussen *et al.*, 1992).

The initial objective of this research was to contribute to understanding the adequacy of the industrial district model for analysing clusters of firms in less developed countries, through a comparative study. Originally, we planned to compare two Italian industrial districts in the footwear sector, expected to match the ideal–typical model, with two clusters[4] of spatially concentrated and sectorally specialized enterprises in Mexico, in the same industrial sector.

The ideal–type of industrial district, as described in the literature, may be summarized by stressing four key stylized facts:

1. a cluster of mainly small and medium spatially concentrated and sectorally specialized enterprises;
2. a strong, relatively homogeneous, cultural and social background linking the economic agents and creating a common and widely accepted behavioural code, sometimes explicit but often implicit;
3. an intense set of backward, forward, horizontal and labour market linkages,[5] based both on market and non-market exchanges of goods, services, information and people;
4. a network of public and private local institutions supporting the economic agents in the clusters.

Widespread availability of external economies and cooperation effects, stemming from the above features and particularly from the last two characteristics, is commonly seen as the key stylized fact making small firms in the districts economically viable and internationally competitive; in other words allowing the districts to reach a high degree of collective efficiency (Schmitz, 1992a, 1995b).

Research on the Italian case was to provide the reference point for the comparison with Mexico. More precisely, the intention was to document the characteristics of an ideal–typical district for a particular sector, footwear, and to identify the reasons why firms within industrial districts produce external economies and cooperate, the functions involved and the economic advantages deriving from these collective activities. The purpose of the comparison with Mexico was to allow us to investigate similarities and differences in the quantity and quality of linkages and to compare the degree of collective efficiency between the two cases. In other words, the Italian case was to provide the empirical reference point (that we expected would match the district model) against which to compare the Mexican situation, hence possibly its adherence to the model itself.

Nonetheless, empirical work brought to our attention some significant differences between the Italian reality and the 'model'. Among others, some of the main discrepancies identified are: the modest development of forward linkages, the relatively little importance attached to informal relationships among firms in the districts analysed and the decreasing availability of a skilled labour force. These findings led us to extend the comparison to a third level: the study became a threefold comparison of the industrial district model, as it is defined in the literature, the reality in Italy and that in Mexico.

The next section sets out the issues addressed in the book and the main research questions which are analysed through a review of the available evidence and the presentation of some original empirical material drawn from field work in Italian and Mexican footwear clusters.

1.2 THE MAIN RESEARCH QUESTIONS

The main overall question addressed in this book refers to the adequacy of the model of industrial organization proposed by the literature on industrial districts in representing the real situations analysed in Italy and in Mexico. Given that the first key factor of spatial concentration and sectoral specialization is the initial condition explicitly satisfied by the selection of the case studies, our analysis investigates the intensity and the quality of backward, forward and horizontal linkages, linkages in the labour market and institutional linkages as well as the collective effects which derive from them. Moreover, although cultural and social background are not explicitly investigated in the empirical research, they are implicitly considered in our analysis through their interconnections with the economic aspects of the system.

Therefore, this study is focused on the collective effects generated by the implicit and the explicit interactions of economic agents within the industrial districts. Those effects are classified according to the following typology:

(a) static and dynamic external economies which are the by-product of some activities undertaken within the districts. Their static effect is the reduction of production and transaction costs for local firms. From a dynamic viewpoint, we can refer to the increase in the collective learning, namely the accumulation of know-how and knowledge, taking place in a spontaneous and socialized way within the district, and freely available to allow every firm to grow and innovate;

(b) cooperation effects are the results of explicit and deliberate cooperative behaviours among economic actors. Examples are: the sharing of specific information within groups of firms, joint projects on technology, market, product development and training carried out by the members of the entrepreneurial associations or by other groups of firms which explicitly decide to collaborate. Cooperation effects may be either static or dynamic and therefore contribute to increasing the efficiency or the innovation capability of the system.

The empirical investigation identifies the various linkages among the economic actors within the clusters. The collective effects emerging from these linkages are classified following the above typology and then compared to identify similarities and differences in the collective efficiency of the cases investigated.

To explain the differences that emerged from the empirical investigation, in intensity and quality of the collective economic effects between the 'model', the Italian districts and the Mexican clusters, two dimensions neglected by the traditional industrial district model are stressed:

1. the impact which the external conditions (in the case studies these are the trade policy regime and the characteristics of the international market) may have on the core characteristics of the districts, on the behaviour of the economic actors and on the degree of collective efficiency;

2. the heterogeneity of economic actors within the districts and therefore the possibility that the linkages and the collective effects deriving from them vary in intensity and quality according to the different actors involved.

With the first dimension, the following question is investigated: how much of the differences between diverse clusters of firms may be explained by reasons external to the districts? In the case studies, the question may therefore be formulated as follows: how much of the lower degree of collective efficiency in the Mexican clusters, in comparison with the Italian districts, may be explained by factors which are unrelated to the internal functioning of the district model?

In Mexico, the long closure of the domestic market limited the division of labour within the industry, favouring vertical integration. In Italy a long period of expansion driven by excess demand in the international market favoured a process of export-led growth, without the need to invest in marketing and commercialization and to build up a commercial capability inside the firms. To address the second dimension, we introduce the hypothesis that within districts the economic actors may behave differently. In the empirical investigation the stratification of the sample of enterprises by size allows the analysis of the possibly heterogeneous characteristics and behaviours of different groups of firms within the clusters studied. We investigate whether small, medium and large firms behave differently within each district. In particular, the existence of different strategies and different ways of 'using' the collective effects of the districts by the different groups of enterprises is analysed. The objective is to understand to what extent the behaviour of the different types of firms depends on their being part of a district and how the different behaviours influence the development of the district.

In the Italian and Mexican clusters there are three diverse profiles, which characterize three different groups of firms, classified by size. Medium enterprises appear in both countries as the best performing, characterized by an intense use of the institutional support available in the districts. Small firms rely extensively on informal solidarity networks, which allow them to survive in the market, notwithstanding their poor performance. Finally, large firms, mainly characterized by stable performance, tend to be more self-sufficient and vertically integrated, behaving in a rather independent way from the institutions existing in the districts.

A further important issue that came to the fore during the undertaking of this study is the question of change of the districts. The importance of this aspect emerged clearly when radical changes in technologies and/or market made evident the crisis and transformation of many Italian industrial districts. The most common reactions to this were either to question the efficacy of the whole model to explain a particular way of organizing production or to firmly believe in the capacity of the model to reproduce itself adapting to the new situation, without really introducing any radical change in the system's structure.

Moving from a static to a dynamic approach, in other words from snapshots of given district characteristics at a given point in time to a study of the development process through which those characteristics have been generated, is crucial to an understanding of the differences between districts. In fact, districts may differ because they are in different stages of development or follow different development trajectories. This is a fundamental issue to analyse if industrial districts are to be recommended as one of the possible approaches to industrial development in LDCs. This need for a dynamic approach to industrial districts emerged in the course of this study but did not guide the data collection and is therefore not directly addressed in the empirical investigation. Nevertheless, the issue of change is discussed to derive some lessons for further research.

Finally, some policy lessons for industrialization are derived from the comparative study. The question addressed here is to what extent collective efficiency can be enhanced by public and private sector institutions.

1.3　THE STRUCTURE OF THE BOOK

The book is structured in three parts. Part I sets out the analytical framework for the empirical analysis and contains the following chapters:

(a) Chapter 2 summarizes the debate about industrial districts in Italy and its diffusion in the other industrialized countries;
(b) Chapter 3 has two main objectives: to review the stylized facts of the 'model' and to introduce two analytical concepts for the analysis of the collective effects deriving from linkages. The first part of the chapter therefore presents an overview of the industrial district literature about spatial factors, socio-cultural components, economic elements, institutions and policies. The second part discusses the concepts of external economies and cooperation effects;
(c) Chapter 4 discusses the relevance of the industrial district debate in less developed countries. It is an overview of some of the most relevant empirical material available on the identification and the existence of clusters in LDCs, on their economic and social characteristics and on the role played by the institutions in their process of development.

Part II presents the empirical results in the two following chapters:

(a) Chapter 5 comprises the Italian case study on two shoe districts: Brenta and Marche. The chapter includes some background information on the Italian footwear industry and the results of the empirical investigation on the linkages among the economic actors. The methodology adopted for the field work is presented in Appendix 1;

(b) Chapter 6 is structured like Chapter 5 and presents the results from the empirical investigation in two footwear clusters in Mexico: Guadalajara and Leon.

Finally, Part III contains the threefold comparison using the 'model' and the Italian and Mexican cases, and presented in the two following chapters:

(a) Chapter 7 includes the comparison of the collective effects identified in the cases analysed and the discussion about the impact of external conditions on the clusters' structure. Furthermore, it provides the results of the statistical analysis of our survey data, based on factor, correspondence and cluster analyses; these statistical methods help to unravel the issue of heterogeneity within the districts;

(b) Chapter 8 contains the discussion about change in the districts and some policy considerations. It ends with a summary of the major findings of the study and the presentation of their implications for future research.

Part I

The Debate on Industrial Districts

2 The Origin of the Debate

2.1 INTRODUCTION

This chapter presents an overview of the Italian debate which originally prompted the research on industrial districts. Behind this debate and the ensuing research stood the structural transformation of the Italian economy which took place during the 1960s and 1970s. As shown in section 2.2, some previously backward regions of the country experienced a rapid industrialization process. The traditional dualist structure of the Italian economy was deeply altered, leading to the perception of the existence of a 'Third Italy' and of the key role of SMEs in its development.

Section 2.3 presents the main steps in the conceptualization of the 'Third Italy' model of industrialization. It does this by referring to some of the main contributions which sparked the subsequent discussion on the industrial districts.

Along with the identification of the new model of industrial development, a great deal of interest was also generated by the issue of the most appropriate unit of analysis. Some of the concepts suggested in the literature, including that of industrial district itself, are discussed in section 2.4.

Finally, section 2.5 analyses how the debate spread outside of Italy and, in particular, it discusses how the literature about flexible specialization deals with the industrial district model.

2.2 THE ECONOMIC PERFORMANCE OF THE THIRD ITALY

Until the 1950s and 1960s the Italian economic system was characterized by a clear-cut dualism between the industrially developed regions in the Northwest and the backward, mainly rural areas in the South, Centre and Northeast. By the late 1960s some important structural changes began to take place, with the Centre and the Northeast of the country experiencing a rapid process of industrialization. The figures that follow provide a summarized description of such changes.

A first indicator of structural change is the share of agricultural

11

employment. This shows a significant decrease during the 1960s and the 1970s in the regions which later came to be known as the Third Italy (Table 2.1 (numerals in bold characters) and Figure 2.1). The share of agricultural employment in 1961 was greater than 30 per cent in Emilia-Romagna and Trentino, and above 40 per cent in Marche and Umbria; it was 24 per cent in Piedmont and 12 per cent in Lombardy, the two core regions of the industrialized North. Within two decades the share of agricultural employment in the regions of the Third Italy became very similar to that of northern regions.

The reduction in regional disparities which took place during the 1960s and 1970s is also confirmed by the growth rate of non-agricultural employment in some of the regions of the Third Italy in comparison with Lombardy and Piedmont. As shown in Table 2.2, the Third Italy regions register a higher growth rate than Lombardy and Piedmont, particularly if we consider the growth rate of employment in firms with less than 100 employees. Table 2.3 shows the impressive growth of the industrial value added during the 1970s in the regions of the Third Italy, where the registered growth rate is higher than in Lombardy and Piedmont. The figures for Marche are particularly impressive: in 1973 the industrial added value was twice as much as in 1963.

To analyse the impact of the economic structural changes on the degree of attractiveness of the different regions we suggest the regional balance of population migration as an indicator. From Table 2.4 one can see that from 1973 Veneto and Marche, traditionally characterized by a negative balance, began to attract migrants from other regions. In 1980 Emilia-Romagna, Veneto and Tuscany showed a higher positive balance than Piedmont and Lombardy and this may be considered as a signal of greater attractiveness of the Third Italy regions compared to the old industrialized northern areas.

The figures given in these tables show that since the mid-1970s a process of industrialization, largely based on SMEs, was taking place in some regions of the Centre and Northeast of Italy. These structural economic changes attracted a great deal of interest among economists and sociologists, who tried to understand their characteristics and origins. Some of the most interesting interpretations of this phenomenon of industrial growth are presented in the next section.

Table 2.1   Share of agricultural employment in some Italian regions (%)

Regions	1961	1971	1981
Piedmont	24.1	16.0	10.7
Lombardy	11.9	5.8	3.8
Trentino-Alto Adige	**34.4**	**17.2**	**13.2**
Veneto	**29.3**	**16.0**	**10.7**
Friuli-Venezia Giulia	**22.2**	**11.3**	**6.5**
Emilia-Romagna	**33.2**	**21.2**	**13.7**
Tuscany	**25.5**	**13.1**	**9.4**
Umbria	**45.8**	**24.7**	**12.4**
Marche	**49.6**	**30.5**	**18.3**
Italy	29.7	18.4	12.8

Source: ISTAT (a)

Map 2.1   The Third Italy.

Table 2.2   Growth rate of non-agricultural employment (%)

Regions	1961–71		1971–81	
	All firms	SMEs*	All firms	SMEs*
Piedmont	11.4	12.8	8.8	10.7
Lombardy	10.2	26.9	7.2	7.5
Veneto	**13.7**	**42.0**	**10.3**	**27.0**
Emilia-Romagna	**11.8**	**35.0**	**12.4**	**65.0**
Tuscany	**7.3**	**22.6**	**10.9**	**20.0**
Marche	**15.7**	**42.0**	**16.5**	**40.0**
Italy	10.3	22.5	13.3	10.0

Source: ISTAT (a)

* SMEs: < 100 employees

Table 2.3   Value added at factor costs, millions of Lira (1963 prices)

Regions	1963		1973		1963–73	
	Industry	Total	Industry	Total	Industry growth rate %	Total growth rate %
Piedmont	1 646 783	2 980 341	2 359 610	4 606 934	43.3	54.6
Lombardy	3 154 183	5 886 321	5 205 368	9 395 270	65.0	59.6
Trentino	**168 828**	**428 922**	**298 060**	**717 961**	**76.5**	**67.4**
Veneto	**762 774**	**2 000 685**	**1 393 039**	**3 310 870**	**82.6**	**65.5**
Friuli	**241 220**	**649 481**	**425 821**	**1 069 185**	**76.5**	**64.6**
Emilia	**869 778**	**2 355 112**	**1 530 180**	**3 637 284**	**75.9**	**54.4**
Tuscany	**766 199**	**1 911 359**	**1 361 158**	**3 017 566**	**77.7**	**57.9**
Umbria	**136 103**	**370 898**	**256 003**	**573 756**	**88.1**	**54.7**
Marche	**161 341**	**584 404**	**348 771**	**952 596**	**116.2**	**63.0**
Italy	10 757 000	27 679 000	18 374 000	43 835 000	70.8	58.4

Source: UNIONCAMERE

2.3   FROM DUALISM TO THE THIRD ITALY

During the 1950s and 1960s studies on industrial development in Italy were dominated by discussions on the dualism between the North and the South. The argument may be summarized by referring to Graziani (1972), who stressed the difference between the large firms in the North, competing in the open market, and the small firms in the South, pro-

Table 2.4   Balance of internal migration among regions

Regions	1961	1966	1973	1980
Piedmont	91 855	25 508	24 383	2 250
Lombardy	110 353	18 437	39 832	6 529
Trentino-Alto Adige	811	-2 716	-762	-109
Veneto	-34 243	-11 360	8 282	7 232
Friuli-Venezia Giulia	-2 063	-4 437	2 148	2 774
Emilia-Romagna	1 850	-8 698	15 052	14 004
Tuscany	8 842	2 327	13 987	13 814
Umbria	-11 449	-6 973	-743	1 843
Marche	-16 617	-9 936	214	4 548

Source: ISTAT (b)

ducing mainly for the local market, protected by the idiosyncratic tastes of the southern population. In the North, competition brought efficiency, unionization and high wages, while in the South the lack of it generated inefficient, non-unionized firms and wages remained low.

Later on, Graziani (1975) shifted the focus of his analysis from the dualism between North and South to the dualism between large and small firms. Together with Graziani, Paci (1973) and Brusco (1975), among others, investigated the wave of decentralization that took place in Italy at the end of the 1960s. Paci and Graziani wrote about the dependent subcontractors characterized by inefficiency, low technology and poor working conditions. Brusco, on the contrary, stressed the potential for small firms to adopt modern technologies and thus reach efficiency levels comparable to those found in large enterprises.

A number of studies published in a book edited by Garofoli (1978) stressed the evolution from a model of industrial development dominated by dependent and inefficient small firms to a system characterized by autonomous firms working directly for the final market and capable of pursuing their own independent strategy of investment and growth. This was the beginning of a new perception of small firms as independent and efficient economic actors, actively contributing to the process of the country's industrial development.

Goglio (1982) further articulated this change through his analysis of the different roles played by small firms in industrial development. He proposed a classification of small firms according to their degree of autonomy from large firms: the marginal small firms exploiting small niches of the market neglected by the large firms; the peripheral small firms specialized in labour-intensive sectors and characterized by high flexibility; and the dependent small firms strongly linked to the large firms, without a direct market contact.

In the same period other scholars challenged the existence of a dualism between North and South. In our opinion, the studies by Bagnasco (1977) and Fuà (1983) are the most significant contributions to the debate on the interpretation of Italian economic growth. In his book *La Terza Italia* (1977), Bagnasco coined the term 'Third Italy', contrasting the traditional dichotomy between North and South with a threefold differentiation among a central economy, dominated by large firms in the industrialized north-western regions, a peripheral economy in the central and north-eastern areas, characterized by a predominance of small firms and, finally, a marginal economy in the underdeveloped South.

Fuà (1983) identified a model of development, named NEC from Nord-Est-Centro (North-East-Centre), characterized by locally specific factors like the rural and artisan traditions, the common social origins of workers and entrepreneurs, the role played by the family and the small size of firms. According to Fuà, these factors represented a mix with a high potentiality for development, which exploded in a rapid process of industrialization in the NEC area, thanks to the joint effect of some generic factors like the reduction of transport costs and the increase in demand of diversified goods, and some factors specific to those areas, like the return of migrants willing to invest their skills and capital and the spin off of industrialization from neighbouring areas.

Both Bagnasco and Fuà stressed the important role of non-economic factors in the industrialization process, particularly the social, political and spatial characteristics of the areas under investigation. Moreover, according to both studies, the main economic actors in the process of industrial development in the Third Italy are clusters of small spatially localized and sectorally specialized enterprises.

These clusters of small firms attracted the interest of other researchers who studied them, identified their characteristics and suggested diverse definitions, emphasizing different aspects of the same general phenomenon. The discussion about the most appropriate unit of analysis is the content of the next section.

2.4 THE LOCAL PRODUCTIVE SYSTEMS: SOME DEFINITIONS

Giacomo Becattini is one of the scholars who has made the greatest contribution to the definition, identification and interpretation of the industrialization process which took place in Italy from the 1970s. His first significant contribution in this field was the introduction of the concept of 'urban countryside' (*campagna urbanizzata*) (Becattini, 1975). Analysing the process of development in Tuscany, Becattini emphasized the crucial role played by small urban centres tightly linked with the surrounding countryside. According to him, the industrialization process in the 'urban countryside' took advantage of the existence of a large pool of rural labour force, willing to work at low cost and in a flexible way.

Some years later, Becattini (1979) introduced the concept of industrial district for which he drew some inspiration from the works of Alfred Marshall. He defined the industrial district: 'as a socio-territorial entity which is characterized by the active presence of both a community of people and a population of firms in one naturally and historically bounded area' (Becattini, 1990, p. 38).

In the elaboration of his theory of industrial districts Becattini emphasized the socio-economic origin of the concept. He stressed the importance of the existence of a local community characterized by a relatively homogeneous system of values and views, which constitutes one of the preliminary requirements for the development of an industrial district. These common values are spread throughout the districts and are transmitted across generations thanks to the existence of a system of institutions, like the family, the church, the school, the dominant political party or the firm.

He also introduced the concept of 'population of firms' to stress the importance of the existence of a spatial concentration of firms, highly specialized in different phases of the same production process and strongly interacting with each other. According to Becattini, firms within industrial districts are strongly rooted in the territory and from this it follows that: 'any single unit of production which operates within a district is to be considered at one and the same time both as an entity possessing its own history which in principle is disconnected from its territorial origin and as a specific cog in a specific district' (Becattini, 1990, p. 40).

According to Marshall, industrial districts are characterized by the development of economies external to the firms but internal to the districts.[1] Marshall, in fact, in the *Principles of Economics* stressed the importance of: 'those very important external economies which can often be secured by the concentration of many small businesses of a similar character in particular localities: or, as is commonly said, by the localization of industry'. (8th edition, 1920, p. 221)

A further important feature of industrial districts, that Becattini borrowed from Marshall, is the concept of 'industrial atmosphere', which he did not define but which seems to refer to:

(a) the concentration of a large number of skilled and specialized people which favours a process of mutual training and learning by doing. Quoting the words of Marshall (1920): 'the mysteries of the industry become no mysteries; but are as it were in the air, and children learn many of them unconsciously'. (p. 225);

(b) the existence of very strong specialization, spatial proximity and cultural homogeneity which aids the fast diffusion of innovations and know-how.

In brief, the Marshallian industrial district is identified by the following features:

(a) with regard to its economic structure: (1) spatial proximity of firms; (2) specialization in the same sector or *filière*;[2] (3) division of the production cycle in phases; (4) differentiation and customization of the products;

(b) with regard to the social structure: (1) existence of a system of common values like labour ethic, high risk and saving propensities; (2) sense of community; (3) existence of an institutional network favouring the diffusion and transmission of values.

The concept of Marshallian industrial districts elaborated by Becattini was adopted by Sforzi (1987, 1990) in an empirical exercise aimed at identifying the districts in the Italian reality. Sforzi developed a three-stage method through which in the first step he identified some local labour market areas, defined as self-contained areas in terms of the supply and demand of labour: in other words, these are areas where the majority of the population can find a job locally. The second stage consisted of identifying some socio-economic characteristics of the areas such as the number of entrepreneurs and workers in small and medium enterprises, the existence of extended families and the availability of infrastructures. Following these lines, the local labour market areas identified were categorized according to their socio-economic characteristics.

One of these categories fits the socio-economic features of the typical model of light industrialization introduced by Becattini (1978). In the final stage, the areas characterized by light industrialization were analysed according to their sectoral characteristics, selecting those systems dominated by manufacturing. Following this procedure Sforzi identified 61 Marshallian industrial districts, mainly localized in north-eastern and central Italy and specialized in traditional sectors like textiles and clothing, footwear and tannery, ceramics, musical instruments, toys and sporting goods.

An alternative unit of analysis – the system area – was proposed by Garofoli at the beginning of the 1980s. Garofoli (1981, 1983) introduced a typology of models of local development in which he identified three different types of areas dominated by SMEs and classified according to their degree of division of labour: the first type of areas is characterized by little interaction among firms specialized in the same products, the second type by some interactions with suppliers and, finally, the system areas by a high degree of division of labour and by intense interactions among firms specialized in some stages of the production process. According to Garofoli, the system areas are mainly located in the peripheral areas and are characterized by: a tendency to specialize in traditional sectors; high availability of skilled workers; high density of 'face-to-face' relationships among economic actors and high social mobility. From a statistical point of view, some of the system areas were also identified on the base of indexes such as the location and specialization indexes, the mobility rate and the turnover rate of enterprises (Garofoli, 1981).

What really distinguishes Garofoli's system areas from other units of analysis presented in the literature is the emphasis on change. Garofoli (1983, 1992) stressed the possibility that a change in external conditions (for instance a technological innovation or a change in the international market) and/or in internal conditions (for instance a lack of skilled labour force, an increase in wages or a lack of infrastructures) may induce a crisis in the system area and possibly a radical change in its structure. As shown later in section 8.2, the question of change and of the capability of industrial districts to elaborate a strategy of transformation has become crucial in the most recent years due to crises occurred in some districts (Bianchi, 1994).

From what we have said so far, we can conclude that the local productive systems characterized by a high concentration of specialized SMEs represent a diffused model of production organization in Italy. In the literature different definitions of the unit of analysis have been proposed and several identification exercises have been conducted.[3] They share a double emphasis on:

(a) the social structure, characterized by social mobility, the existence of a common system of values and the transmission of specialized skills among people within the areas;
(b) the economic structure, characterized by the high division of labour and specialization, the existence of economies external to the firms and internal to the area, as well as the high rates of firm creation and mortality.

All these aspects, characterizing the territorial systems of small enterprises, will be analysed in greater detail in Chapter 3.

2.5 THE DIFFUSION OF THE DEBATE OUTSIDE ITALY

At the beginning of the 1980s Charles Sabel, in collaboration with authors such as Brusco, Piore and Zeitlin, introduced to the literature the concept of flexible specialization. In 1984 Piore and Sabel published *The Second Industrial Divide*, in which this notion was extensively discussed, based on empirical material from Italy, West Germany and Japan.

The starting point in Piore and Sabel's book was the economic crisis of the capitalist system which took place in the 1970s and 1980s in most industrialized countries. They adopted a historical-sociological approach to explain the reasons for this crisis, how it developed and how it could be overcome.

The origin of the crisis was identified in the profound changes occurring in the international system of competition. This involved a move away from rigid mass production and standardized goods towards a more innovative and flexible production system.

Mass production was identified by the existence of large firms with highly specialized equipment and narrowly trained workers, profitable only with markets large enough to absorb huge quantities of standardized goods. In contrast with the traditional mass-production paradigm, a model of industrial development based on small spatially concentrated flexible firms came to the attention of the international public thanks to Piore and Sabel's book.

In the flexible specialization system a large number of small enterprises engage in small batch production, adopting flexible production procedures which require close collaboration between the factory and the client. The diffusion of professional know-how allows skilled workers to leave the factory and become small entrepreneurs, guaranteeing a high degree of social mobility within the areas characterized by flexible specialization (Sabel & Zeitlin, 1985).

In their study Piore and Sabel highlighted the Italian experience of industrial development based on clusters of specialized technologically advanced small firms, manufacturing a wide range of products to suit the needs of highly differentiated markets.

In line with the definition of industrial districts and system areas proposed by Becattini and Garofoli, the flexible specialization system is characterized by spatial proximity and sectoral specialization of SMEs linked among themselves by very strong ties, by the production of highly customized products and by a stable social structure in which the family plays an important role as a source of low cost and flexible labour, specialized skills and diffused entrepreneurship. Nevertheless, in comparison with Becattini and Garofoli's approach the flexible specialization literature puts more emphasis on presenting this way of organizing production as an alternative that has achieved strength because of the crisis of the mass production system.

Outside the flexible specialization approach the success of small firm agglomerations has attracted the interest of a large number of scholars, among whom Best (1990) saw it as an aspect of the 'new competition' paradigm. Several definitions and conceptualization of the phenomenon have also been suggested in the literature: Storper, Harrison and Scott introduced the concept of 'regional production systems' (Storper & Harrison, 1991; Scott & Storper, 1992); Colletis, Courlet and Pequer (1990) the 'local industrial systems' and the research group of GREMI Européenne (Groupe de Recherche sur les Milieux Innovateurs) (Aydalot, 1986; Camagni, 1991).

Many empirical studies have also been carried out, identifying successful agglomerations of small specialized firms in Denmark, Germany, Spain, Canada, among others (Pyke & Sengenberger, 1992). Extending the model of industrial districts to other countries beyond Italy, Sengenberger and Pyke (1992) aimed at emphasizing that these organizational principles could be borrowed for use in other places by stating: 'Of course it is not being suggested that somehow the total experience of one country such as Italy could be simply transferred to another one; rather, what is being suggested is that other countries could learn from what has happened in the Third Italy or Denmark or Germany, and consider how the sorts of principles that we have highlighted could be successfully applied, or adapted to, local circumstances'. (p. 27)

The shift of the approach to industrial districts from theoretical and empirical phenomena to policy instruments for industrial development assumes a particular relevance, introducing the model into the debate on developing countries (see Chapter 4).

3 The Industrial District Model

3.1 INTRODUCTION

In the literature, the industrial district model is not presented as an analytical model, but rather as a list of stylized facts useful to organize empirical investigation and to confront it with reality. We propose to define industrial districts in terms of four key elements:

(a) a cluster of mainly small and medium enterprises that are spatially concentrated and sectorally specialized (locational and spatial factors);
(b) a strong, relatively homogeneous, cultural and social background linking the economic agents and creating a common and widely accepted sometimes explicit but often implicit behavioural code (social and cultural factors);
(c) an intense set of backward, forward, horizontal and labour linkages, based both on market and non-market exchanges of goods, services, information and people (organizational and economic factors);
(d) a network of public and private local institutions supporting the economic agents in the clusters (institutional and policy factors).

The above features of the industrial district model, and particularly the last two key facts, bring about some collective economic effects – external economies and cooperation effects – whose exploitation makes up the efficiency gains for the economic agents located in the cluster and increases the system's innovative capability.

This chapter has a twofold objective:

1. section 3.2 presents an overview of the literature on the four key stylized facts of the model, bringing together the empirical evidence which represents the 'model', taken as a reference point in the comparison with the Italian footwear districts and the Mexican clusters that follows (see sections 5.6, 6.6 and 7.7);
2. section 3.3 discusses the concepts of external economies and cooperation effects, which are the two analytical tools used in this study for analysing the degree of collective efficiency of the clusters selected for the empirical research (see section 7.2).

23

3.2   THE INDUSTRIAL DISTRICT MODEL: AN OVERVIEW OF THE LITERATURE

In this section an overview of the literature organized around the four key elements of the industrial district model stressed above is presented. The aim is to bring together a stylized picture of the districts, which is adopted in this study as a reference point in the comparison with the realities investigated.

3.2.1   Locational and spatial factors

Industrial districts have been defined as a socio-territorial entity as well as an economic concept (Becattini, 1979; Bellandi, 1982). Space is therefore embedded in the definition of the district, defined as localized thickening of the network formed by relationships among economic actors, comprising the area shared in common and delimiting it (Sforzi, 1990). Moreover in industrial districts geographical proximity is always associated with sectoral specialization, so that clusters of firms belonging to a specific industry as well as an assortment of ancillary industries and services are located in spatially bounded areas.

Spatial proximity has some evident positive effects in reducing transport and transaction costs and favouring the circulation of information and face-to-face contacts among the economic actors located in the same area. These aspects were first stressed by Marshall in his analysis of the advantages of the 'localized industries' (Marshall, 1920) and then underlined in the most recent analysis on industrial districts (Bagnasco, 1977; Fuà & Zacchia, 1983; Piore & Sabel, 1984).

One of the spatial characteristics of industrial districts stressed in the Third Italy literature is the small urban dimension (Bagnasco, 1988; Bagnasco & Trigilia, 1984). The positive effects of this spatial condition have been identified in lower labour and land costs, strong integration between local banks and industry, social cohesion and common cultural background. Another important spatial aspect which often characterizes industrial districts is the existence of strong urban–rural linkages that has some positive effects in terms of labour force availability, flexibility and costs (Camagni & Capello, 1990).

To conclude, spatial agglomeration and sectoral specialization are common conditions stressed in most of the literature; moreover, as shown in section 4.2, clustering is a rather diffused phenomenon in less developed countries as well. Although clustering *per se* brings few benefits (Schmitz, 1992a), nonetheless it is a necessary condition for a number of subsequent developments, which are related to the other three factors addressed below.

3.2.2 Social and cultural factors

Most of the Italian industrial districts are characterized by a process of transformation from rural to industrial areas, which took place without breaks, through a progressive transfer of the rural labour force to industry. This process, described in Fuà (1983), generated some social features, common to most Italian districts, with important implications for the economic and organizational system of the districts.

First, in rural society the family played a very important role in the organization of economic activities. In the case of Italian industrial districts this also remained true during the industrialization process, guaranteeing the persistence of a strong social unit within which rural and industrial jobs were shared among all the family members, including young people and women. Moreover, the family provided support and security to its members and represented an important place for the transfer of skills from one generation to the other and for transmitting a very strong labour ethic (Paci, 1973, 1980). As Trigilia (1990) writes, working hard seems to be the rule in industrial districts and this takes the form of long working hours and flexible organization of labour.

Second, the common rural origin of most of the people working in industrial districts made it easy to maintain a certain social homogeneity, facilitating the relationships among workers and entrepreneurs, linked by common social values and origins. The existence of a common social background has not favoured the kind of militant unionism and conflictual relations that has prevailed in Italy in large firms and industrial cities (Trigilia, 1989).

Moreover, relationships within the industrial districts are facilitated also by high social mobility which makes it possible to move easily from one job to the other or to an independent entrepreneurial position, creating new firms as well as shutting them down and going back to work as employees. Bagnasco and Trigilia (1984 and 1985) stress the role played by this particular social model in the process of industrialization of two industrial districts: Bassano in Veneto and Valdelsa in Tuscany. Specifically, Trigilia (1990) writes: 'Workers enjoy a low degree of proletarianization, not only with reference to the organization of labour and chances for mobility, but also in relation to a working experience that does not entail a sharp uprooting from their original communities'. (p. 177)

Another important aspect to consider is political homogeneity, which characterized many of the Italian industrial districts; the central regions particularly tend to be left orientated while in the regions of the North East there is a deeply rooted catholic culture.[1] According to Trigilia (1986), the existence of a strong political subculture has contributed to preserving the specific socio-economic fabric described earlier. In the two case studies quoted above, Bagnasco and Trigilia (1984 and 1985) analyse how different political subcultures may influence the process of industrial development, studying two districts: one dominated by the catholic culture (Bassano) and the other, Valdelsa, by a socialist culture. They conclude that both the socialist and catholic movement have contributed to defending the local society, cutting across class boundaries and assuming a wider community dimension. Moreover, this tendency to strengthen the local culture may also be useful in explaining the localist approach to political economy, analysed in greater detail in section 3.2.4. Finally, the dominant political subcultures contribute to the high degree of legitimacy of entrepreneurship and to the diffusion of a labour ethic which has been very important for the growth of small firms (Trigilia, 1990).

To conclude, it may be worthwhile to stress the relevance of these social features for industrial district performance. In industrial districts the organization of economic relations tends to be intertwined with social relations, and economic behaviour is likely to be at least in part shaped by social norms and by the organization of the social structure. So community rules influence ways of doing business and relationships between entrepreneurs and their labour force and generally speaking between economic actors belonging to the community. According to Dei Ottati (1986), the family ties or the common social origins of the entrepreneurs also contribute to creating a sort of moral reputation, which implies the existence of moral in addition to economic sanctions in case of opportunistic behaviour.

Deriving from the social characteristics of industrial districts, trust is often considered as the guiding principle in business relationships and in explaining cooperative behaviour in the districts. On this issue, the industrial district literature feeds into a wider debate on the social embeddedness of economic relationships (Granovetter, 1985; Platteau, 1994; Sabel, 1992). The general argument is that a strong social common identity facilitates trust and helps explain cooperative behaviour. Moving on from this static line of reasoning, in his study on a footwear cluster in Brazil, Schmitz stresses that the increasing differentiation within the community and the key role of external export agents have begun to change the foundation of trust, from being ascribed, to being earned (Schmitz, 1995a). It seems that the new critical ties are based on conscious investments in inter-firm relationships. A question for future research arises: is the cluster capacity of investing in linkages a crucial asset for increasing competitiveness?

3.2.3 Economic and organizational factors

Economic and organizational factors are central to this study. In this section, we present some key facts emphasized in the literature as characterizing the typical industrial district. Moreover, the concepts of external economies and cooperation effects, adopted in the empirical study as analytical tools useful for classifying the collective effects deriving from clustering in the footwear industry in the Italian and Mexican cases, are elaborated in greater detail in section 3.3. Drawing from a synthesis of the structural characteristics of industrial districts presented in Garofoli (1993), we can identify the following key economic and organizational factors:

1. an outstanding productive specialization at the local level. The specialized production of the local system contributes significantly to total national, and sometimes international, production in that sector or industry;
2. a high level of division of labour between firms. With regard to this Becattini (1990) writes: 'Each of the many firms which constitute the population tend to specialize in just one phase, or a few phases, of the production processes typical of the district. In short, the district is an instance of a localized realization of a division of labour, which is neither diluted in the general market, nor concentrated in one firm or in just a few firms'. (p. 40)

Some advantages derive from the high degree of division of labour and they were already stressed by Marshall in his *ante litteram* description of industrial districts: 'With regard to many classes of commodities it is possible to divide the process of production into several stages, each of which can be performed with the maximum of economy in a small establishment. If there exist a large number of such small establishments specialized for the performance of a particular stage of the process of production, there will be room for the profitable investment of capital in the organizing of subsidiary industries adapted for meeting their special wants'.[2]

Marshall defines the advantages depending on the possibility to split the production process into specialized phases, which allow firms to fully utilize highly specialized instruments and skilled labour, as external economies, which are static, and their effect is to lower the cost of production within the districts;[3]

3. the existence of a large number of local agents, without a leading or a dominant firm. Among firms the relationships are characterized by a balance between competition and cooperation (Brusco, 1990). Competition occurs horizontally among equal firms, in other words firms specialized in the same product or the same activity, and it is based on a range of dimension, not just on price. In the literature, competition on quality, design, choice, speed and flexibility of adjustment has been stressed as typical of industrial districts (Sengenberger & Pyke, 1992). Cooperation concerns the relationships between firms and their subcontractors and suppliers and inter-firm relationships through specially established institutions providing collective services and advice;

4. specialization and skills of workers represent a resource which contributes to determining the common knowledge available to the district as a whole, as explained by Becattini (1990): 'The specialization of the worker – which is sometimes firm-specific and sometimes district-specific – is lost only to a very limited extent, from the point of view of the district, when the workers move from one firm to another. His specialization remains part of that "public good" which Marshall labels "industrial atmosphere". When, to quote Marshall, "the secrets of industry are in the air", the transmission of the skills acquired through the canonical channels (technical schools and factory training), is powerfully integrated by a spontaneous exchange and reorganization of notions and opinions by "face to face" and "conviviality" relationships which daily life in the district offers with unusual frequency'. (p. 42);

5. the existence of an efficient system of 'face-to-face' relationships between economic actors, which facilitates the circulation of information about technology, market, suppliers and components, and decreases transaction costs;

6. the existence of specialized and well-established networks of economic agents, who place the products of the districts on their final markets. A well-known case, often quoted in the literature, is Prato, a textile district where there is a network of middlemen, known as *impannatori*, who book the orders in the international market and divide them among the local producers (IRPET, 1980).

3.2.4 Institutional and policy factors

This section discusses the role of the institutional intervention in the development and growth of industrial districts. A key question is to understand if industrial districts may be considered the result of a planned action or rather if institutional interventions can play a role only in the consolidation of the districts' growth. Brusco (1990) distinguishes between an industrial district model Mark I and Mark II. Mark I refers to the initial, largely spontaneous, phase of growth. While, in the Mark II industrial district, Brusco identifies a need for institutional intervention which either did not exist before or was at least less evident. Schmitz (1992b), referring to the case of Baden-Wurttemberg, writes: 'although regional government policy did not create the industrial organization which led to the observed collective efficiency, it would be hard to entirely dismiss claims that it has helped industry to cope with the challenges of the 1990s'. (p. 116)

The main policy implication which emerges from Brusco and Schmitz's studies is that industrial districts can not be created *ex novo* with policy interventions but, when a critical mass of specialized and geographically concentrated enterprises exists, institutions can play a role in supporting industrial growth and innovation.

The question is therefore to analyse the characteristics and the actors involved in the institutional interventions aimed at fostering and sustaining the growth of industrial districts. In the Third Italy the first important issue to stress concerning industrial policy is the absence of any specific interventions addressed towards industrial districts on a national level. In fact, only in 1991 was the existence of industrial districts ratified by a national law, recognizing them as potential units of specific intervention. On the base of indexes like manufacturing industrialization, entrepreneurial density of the manufacturing industry, specialization, employment in the manufacturing sectors in which the area is specialized, and employment in SMEs, more than 100 districts have been identified.

Nevertheless, there is some evidence that the growth of the Italian small-firm sector, and consequently the small-firm industrial districts, may have benefited from a national legal and regulatory framework which provides financial facilities and exemptions from regulations and administrative burdens for artisans[4] (Parisotto, 1991).

However, the most significant interventions in Italian industrial districts have always taken place at the local and regional levels, involving public as well as private actors. An important role is definitely played by the regional financial agencies and development boards, which were created at the beginning of the 1970s in almost all the Italian regions with the aim of promoting and supporting the local manufacturing sector, mainly through financial incentives (Bianchi *et al.*, 1986).

Since the beginning of the 1980s in many regions, particularly those with large concentrations of small and medium-sized enterprises, these regional agencies have promoted and sponsored the creation of business service centres. Emilia-Romagna is probably the most interesting case because its regional development agency ERVET has promoted the creation of a vast network of service centres, some of them dedicated to specific sectors, like CITER for the textile and clothing sector, CERCAL for the footwear industry or CESMA for agricultural machinery construction, and others like ASTER (technology development) and CERMET (quality upgrading) aimed at providing services to the industry in general (Bellini *et al.*, 1990; Pyke, 1992). Other examples of service centres include: ISELQUI in Marche providing a quality control service to the main sectors of specialization of the region (musical instruments, furniture and shoes), and TECNOTEX in Biella (Piedmont) providing professional training, research and technological experimentation to the wool industry.

Together with business service centres, the entrepreneurs' and artisan associations are best known as providers of collective services in the Italian industrial districts. Examples of the services provided are the supply of information, quality control and testing facilities for raw materials, entrepreneurial and managerial training, translation of tenders, consultation on fiscal and legal matters, book-keeping and research on foreign markets (Pyke, 1992).

Other agencies providing real services are consortia of firms, trade associations, bodies sponsored by local or provincial council, or organizations that involve local authorities, associations, trade unions and individual business people (Brusco, 1992). The crucial lesson which can be drawn from the Italian experience, as well as from the experience of other European countries as documented in Schmitz and Musyck (1994), is that real services were rarely provided by the public sector itself. The main reasons are expertise and finance: 'A great deal of sector and sometimes even product specific expertise is required for an effective delivery of real services. Also, the financial sustainability of such programmes requires that the private sector itself makes a major and generally growing contribution to their existence' (Schmitz & Musyck, 1994, p. 900).

This is confirmed by Bianchi *et al.* (1986) who conclude that among the business service centres, the most successful ones are those created to satisfy very specific and peculiar sectoral needs; while other experiences originated through the initiative of the public sector generically aimed at technology transfer without real direct involvement of the local enterprises, have very often failed to reach their objectives.

It is anyway extremely difficult to offer a precise and substantial assessment of the performance of these initiatives. Schmitz and Musyck propose the self-financing of the centres as a performance indicator. However, it must be stressed that, although self-financing can be an incentive to make the centres more efficient and orientated to satisfy market needs, it can also become an incentive not to opt for innovative and inevitably risky activities from the financial point of view (Bellini *et al.*, 1990). In other words, self-financing may be in contradiction with the 'public' nature of some of the services, like training and innovation development, provided by the centres. The emphasis on localness also emerges when we analyse the specificity of the provision of credit in industrial districts. Becattini (1990) stresses the relevance of local credit provision in the Third Italy introducing the 'theory of the local bank': 'The local bank is an organism born and bred in the district, that is very closely linked with local entrepreneurs (and often with other local social and political lobbies), and deeply involved in local life, which it knows in detail, and to which it gives direction to a considerable extent'. (p. 47)

Signorini (1992) in his study on Prato concludes that local banks tend to lend more easily to local firms because they have access to information which is usually too costly for national banks to obtain on SMEs. The existence of local banks, therefore, helps overcome the usually very strong difficulties to credit access faced by small firms. However, according to Signorini the positive effect of local banks is more concerned with the quantity of credit than with its price.

With regard to credit, other local institutions common in industrial districts are the loan guarantee consortia providing mutual credit guarantees to the members. The loan consortia have a very positive rate of repayment records, far superior to similar loans in the Italian banking sector as a whole (Murray, 1991).

To conclude, notwithstanding the difficulties in systematically assessing the effective role played by public and private institutions in industrial districts, a few policy lessons can be drawn:

1. industrial districts can not be created by a top-down policy intervention. The Third Italy districts, as well as other European experiences, have been characterized by an industrial policy 'from below', at local or regional level;
2. in many cases entrepreneurial associations and other institutions close to the enterprises have played a significant role in the provision of services;
3. collaboration between public and private bodies in the definition of firms' needs and in the implementation of institutional initiatives is a solution frequently adopted.

3.3   TWO USEFUL INSTRUMENTS OF ANALYSIS

This section discusses two analytical concepts – external economies and cooperation effects – used in this study to identify those collective effects whose interplay is supposed to bring about efficiency gains for firms in the district and to increase the capability of the system, as a whole, to innovate and grow. This entails investigating whether industrial districts can be defined as systems characterized by a total efficiency which is greater than the pure sum of the efficiency of the economic actors working within them and by an innovation capability which is greater than the innovation capacity of each individual firm.

The distinction between external economies, defined as the by-product of some activities undertaken within the districts and cooperation effects, defined as the result of explicit and voluntary cooperative behaviours, is similar to what Schmitz (1992a) captures in the concept of collective efficiency. He distinguishes between unplanned or incidental effects and planned or consciously pursued collective efficiency and defines collective efficiency as the sum of local external economies and joint action (Schmitz, 1995b). This study takes this a step further by distinguishing between static and dynamic external economies and between static and dynamic cooperation effects.

3.3.1   External economies

External economies can be defined as positive or negative unpaid, out of the market rules, side-effects of the activity of one economic agent on other agents. External economies therefore imply that market prices in a competitive market economy will not reflect marginal social costs of production. Hence a market failure arises, meaning that the market economy cannot attain a state of efficiency on its own. Specifically, in an otherwise perfect market economy, an economic agent producing external economies (positive external effects) for other agents would not extend his externality-generating activity to the point where marginal cost of production equals marginal social benefits of production (Mishan, 1971).

The concept of external economies was first introduced by Alfred Marshall in his *Principles of Economics* (1920) when analysing industry production costs as a function of output: 'We may divide the economies arising from an increase in the scale of production of any kind of goods, into two classes – firstly, those dependent on the general development of industry; and secondly, those dependent on the resources of individual houses of business engaged in it, on their organization and the efficiency of their management. We may call the former external economies, and the latter internal economies'. (p. 266)

The latter concept is now recognized as economies of scale in the individual firm, when it concentrates on an increasing scale of production. Marshall elaborated the meaning of the former concept using several examples: the increased knowledge about markets and technology accompanying the expansion of industrial output, the creation of a market for skilled labour, for specialized services and for subsidiary industries, the possibility to split the production process into specialized phases and, finally, the improvement of physical infrastructures such as roads and railways.

Thus external economies essentially turn into cost reductions for individual firms as a consequence of industry growth; in other words they are economies external to the firm but internal to the industry. These externalities remain firmly within the framework of a static analysis, as they refer to the allocative efficiency of given resources and express collective efficiency as a positive function of the district's size and of the density of interactions which occur within the cluster.

Remaining in a static framework, the Marshallian aggregation of a large number of small firms into one district also favours the reduction of transaction costs among economic actors operating therein. According to Williamson (1975) transaction costs vary depending on:

(a) the specific item being exchanged;
(b) the frequency with which they recur;
(c) the uncertainty which they are subject to;
(d) the degree to which they are supported by investments in durable, transaction-specific assets.

In situations characterized by high uncertainty, complexity and opportunism transaction costs tend to be very high. In industrial districts the reduction in transaction costs can be explained by geographical proximity and socio-cultural homogeneity: economic actors tend to interact mainly with partners who are located in their own area, with whom therefore they can have 'face-to-face' contacts. The stability of many relationships and the importance of building a reputation decrease the risk of opportunistic behaviour. In the districts a delay in delivery or bad quality production immediately becomes common knowledge and a bad reputation negatively influences future relationships.

Moreover, in industrial districts, firms facing some problems with their partners can easily find a new enterprise able to satisfy their needs. This is possible because of the large concentration of similar firms in a small geographical area and the intense diffusion of information which reduces costs involved in finding a suitable replacement partner.

Another important aspect characterizing transactions in industrial districts is the possibility of easily recycling investments in transaction-specific assets, like specific knowledge or machines (Dei Ottati, 1986). Investments can, in fact, be used in similar transactions with different partners or sold to other firms without excessive losses. Easy recycling of investments decreases their specificity, without reducing their specialization.

Moving from static to dynamic external economies, reference may again be made to Marshall. In fact, some of his examples alluded to the dynamic effects of industrial growth, which promote a kind of 'industrial atmosphere', capable not only of reducing the cost disadvantage of small firms compared to large ones, but mainly helping them in their growth and innovation strategy. This is particularly obvious when he referred to external economies as being dependent on the general progress of industrial environment. Examples of dynamic externalities suggested by Marshall are the accumulation of skills, know-how and knowledge taking place in a spontaneous and socialized way within the district.

Stewart and Ghani (1991) identify three types of dynamic external economies: changing attitudes and motivations, skill formation and changing knowledge about technologies and markets. The first type of externalities refers to a sort of demonstrative effect on attitudes which induces economic agents to adopt new technologies or introduce new products or new forms of organization.

The second type, human capital formation, is generally acknowledged to be an important source of externalities. In an industrial district where a mass of skilled and specialized workers is concentrated, the training process takes place in a spontaneous and socialized way, both at the formal and informal level (on-the-job learning), generating an overall positive incentive to work. The last type of dynamic externalities is related to technology transfer through interactions between firms outside of the market, which can generate technological upgrading in many different forms. Spatial proximity facilitates the movement of skilled labour bringing knowledge of new, improved technologies. Besides, the availability of skilled workers has important effects on the mastery of an industry's actual know-how. Finally, the adoption of innovations can be also favoured by the easy interactions between firms in meetings and informal gatherings.

The effects generated by dynamic external economies can be interpreted as increases in collective learning. Referring to the concept of 'learning by doing' incorporated by Arrow (1962) in the theory of growth to make technical progress endogenous; each firm learns not only from its own activities but also from those of other firms. According to Arrow's model, if a firm increases its capital this has an impact on its product as well as on the level of knowledge of the economic system, therefore justifying the existence of increasing returns at the level of the economy as a whole. In industrial districts the investments of each economic actor in product and process innovations, in information collection or in marketing generate a collective learning effect which increases the rate of growth of the entire system's collective efficiency.

A further effect of dynamic external economies has been introduced by Camagni (1991), who stresses the role played by the districts in the reduction of uncertainty in innovation processes, due to imperfect information, difficulties in precisely defining the effects of innovative decisions, problems in controlling the reactions and behaviour of economic actors. According to Camagni the local environment performs a function of gathering and screening information through informal interchanges between firms and a process of collective learning through the mobility of skilled labour force, customer-supplier interchanges and imitation processes.[5]

From what has been said so far it is possible to conclude that externalities have been widely used as a concept to capture several economic effects of clustering, both in a static and a dynamic perspective. The next step is to understand under which conditions an economic system, and specifically an industrial district, produces externalities.

According to economic theory (Brosio, 1993), the largest production of external economies is in the case of public goods which are characterized by:

(a) non-rivalry of consumption, in other words they can be consumed by one individual without detracting from the consumption opportunities still available to others from the same unit;
(b) non-excludibility of benefits, in other words goods or services whose benefits cannot be withheld costlessly by the owner or provider. Such benefits are therefore available to all once the good or service is provided.

Given that in a private good there is full rivalry and excludibility, in this case the production of externalities is at its minimum. In between public and private goods, there is a *continuum* of cases displaying different degrees of excludibility and rivalry and characterized by different intensities of external economies.

At least two consequences relevant for our discussion stem from this understanding of external economies. First, because external benefits cannot be readily captured and because external costs can be easily avoided (free-rider problem), activities generating external economies will not be undertaken to any significant extent. Therefore within a pure market economy, there will be a tendency to underinvest in areas subject to a high degree of external economies, because every economic actor will have some incentives to behave like a free-rider. Then, the problem is to explain why is it that such a large number of collective effects is produced by economic actors within industrial districts. The answer lies in the introduction of the concept of cooperation above and beyond external economies, to explain, to some extent, the degree of collective efficiency in industrial districts.

The other consequence of the public good nature of externalities is related to the heterogeneity among economic actors within the districts: non-excludibility of externalities implies equal access to the district advantages by every economic actor located within it. This clashes with heterogeneity of performance, behaviour and ways of 'using' the districts which can be observed in industrial districts and is one of the main results of the empirical work in the Italian footwear districts and the Mexican clusters (Chapter 7). Again by referring to the concept of explicit cooperation, the next section shows how some collective benefits of the districts may in fact be restricted to specific groups of economic actors, leading to the heterogeneity detected in the districts analysed.

To conclude, external economies are only one category of the possible collective effects of industrial clusters explaining the efficiency gains and the innovation capability of firms within the districts. The problem of under-investment in activities generating external economies and the existence of different behaviours and performances among firms in the same district suggest the necessity to consider other types of collective effects, specifically the cooperation effects.

3.3.2 Cooperation effects

The notion of cooperation can help explain the extensive production of collective effects in the industrial districts. Some concepts of game theory are useful for an understanding of how and why economic actors may cooperate within a system to generate collective benefits, overcoming conflicts of self-interest and the free-rider problem.[6]

Referring to a simple Prisoner's Dilemma game, the only Nash equilibrium in a one-shot game is the mutual non-cooperative behaviour. The cooperative behaviour – even if its payoffs are Pareto-superior to the non-cooperative strategy – will not be pursued, because each player knows that the best reply to the other player's cooperation is defection.

One way of enforcing cooperation is to rely on an external authority that can penalize non-cooperation or reward cooperation, but this case is not relevant for explaining cooperative behaviour in industrial districts. An alternative way is self-enforcement in repeated games (Wilkinson & You, 1992). The key to self-enforcement is the importance of the future: if the game is repeated infinitely or the terminal date is uncertain, the players may find it in their self-interest to cooperate for fear of later retaliatory defection by the other players (Platteau, 1994).

In a sufficiently stable environment, where the relationships among the agents are characterized by a certain degree of continuity, rational agents develop a mutual interest in cooperation (Brugnoli & Porro, 1993). The key mechanisms are individual reputations and path-dependency of cooperation. A similar situation has been discussed in the game theory literature as a 'tit for tat' strategy. According to Axelrod (1984), a player decides to cooperate on the first move and then does whatever the other player did on the previous move. This policy means that 'tit for tat' will defect once after each defection of the other player. The problem in 'tit for tat' strategy is 'forgiveness': if one individual defects, s/he can always tries to renegotiate (this means 'forget the past, let's start again'). This possibility can destroy the credibility of any punishment scheme, raising doubts about the self-enforcement of cooperation based exclusively on a rational self-interest-maximizing behaviour.

Wilkinson and You (1992) propose that: 'where rational self-interest falters, social norms can come to the rescue. If it is a social norm to punish the cheaters and if a sufficient number of people follow these norms, the threat of retaliation can once again become an effective deterrent to non-cooperative behaviour'. (p. 27)

According to Axelrod (1984), if in an economic system there exists a critical mass of norm-followers, whose interactions among themselves represent a large proportion of their total interactions, there is a tendency to follow the norms and to adopt cooperative behaviour.

The analogy with industrial districts is straightforward. From the point of view of the relationships going on within them, industrial districts can be seen as rather stable systems, characterized by well-established and accepted social norms, by frequent, long-term interactions among a large number of economic actors, who know each other very well and by the rapid and pervasive dissemination of information (for instance, see in section 5.5.1, the stable and long-standing linkages between Italian shoe producers and their suppliers). Besides, in industrial districts one usually finds institutional arrangements, such as long-term trading relationships, long-lived organizations and well-functioning communication networks, through which the self-enforcement of cooperation takes place more easily (Wilkinson & You, 1992). Within districts reputations for fairness are highly valued and the sanctions for enforcing the limits of commonly accepted business behaviour may be very heavy, the ultimate sanction being social exclusion from the community. Ultimately, in industrial districts economic actors can have a self-interest to adopt a cooperative behaviour (Brugnoli & Porro, 1993).

It must be also stressed that the stability of the systems and the social norms which regulate the relationships among the economic actors cannot be taken as eternal; changes in external and/or internal elements can impact it and consequently the self-interest in cooperation within the district. This is a crucial point to address when moving from a static to a dynamic approach to districts, which is considered in section 8.2 of this study.

Examples of the products of cooperative behaviour, enforced by self-interest and induced by the existence of a critical mass of norm-followers, are cooperation on process or product innovations between the producers and their suppliers (for instance, in section 5.5.1 the cooperation between Italian shoe firms and the manufacturers of components or the producers of machine tools for the sector), the diffusion of information and the collective learning effects among groups of firms linked for instance by family ties or friendship. Cooperative effects can be either static or dynamic, therefore enhancing the system's efficiency and its innovation and growth potentiality. Cooperation effects differ from externalities because the latter are the spontaneous by-product of economic activities within the district, while the former are the product of an explicit and voluntary cooperative behaviour among economic actors.

In the case of externalities the non-compensation mechanism explains the tendency of under-investment and the lack of self-interest among economic actors. On the other hand the existence of a mechanism for compensation accounts for the rational interest of economic actors to cooperate among each other, producing cooperation effects and increasing the collective efficiency of the system. In a long-term perspective, compensation can assume various forms, such as monetary exchange, exchange of information, technology, know-how or human capital, or building up a reputation which can become useful in future interactions.

Besides, the existence of a mechanism for compensation allows the introduction of excludibility in the exploitation of collective advantages deriving from cooperation effects, which can be defined as club goods.[7] A club is a voluntary group deriving mutual benefit from sharing production costs, information, commercial networks or any good or service characterized by excludable benefits.[8]

Club goods, because they are excludable, are produced by the market and this explains why in industrial districts, where cooperation behaviour is induced by self-enforcement and by the existence of a critical mass of norm-followers, cooperation effects tend to be particularly important to explain collective efficiency. In fact in industrial districts it is possible to identify several groups whose activities generate cooperation effects shared among the members of the clubs. Some examples are entrepreneurial associations, export consortia, groups of firms linked by family ties or friendship, other groups cooperating on some product or process innovation projects. The existence of selection mechanisms to exclude economic actors from the benefits of cooperation effects contributes to explaining heterogeneity within industrial districts.

Finally, differences among economic actors can also be explained by differences in their capability to assimilate and exploit district benefits and therefore cooperation effects as well as external economies.

Bearing in mind the new evolutionary approach to technological change (Nelson & Winter, 1982; Dosi *et al.*, 1988),[9] the firms' ability to exploit district advantages differs according to their past history, the previously accumulated know-how and their cumulative learning processes. Therefore, in the industrial districts firms are not all equal in relation to externalities and cooperation effects; what really matters is their capability to transform generic resources into specific comparative advantages with respect to other firms. So, for instance, the existence of a large reservoir of skilled labour in the district becomes a crucial asset for a firm's strategy of growth when the firm employs a skilled worker, who brings along accumulated knowledge which can be usefully assimilated into the firm's structure.

To conclude, it is worth summarizing the different categories of collective effects contributing to collective efficiency in industrial districts:

(a) static and dynamic external economies are the by-product of some activities undertaken within the districts. They tend to be characterized by non-rivalry and non-excludibility which can lead to underinvestments in a market economy. Moreover, external economies are part of a common pool from which every economic actor can freely draw. In industrial districts a typical example can be the circulation of information about markets or technologies, freely available to every economic actor located in it, who can use the same information, adapting it at her/his potentially different needs. Other examples of external economies are the creation of a collective market reputation of the district and the diffusion of a common professional and managerial culture;

(b) cooperation effects are the result of explicit and voluntary cooperative behaviours which differ by external economies because of two important characteristics: excludibility and compensation. An example of the effects of cooperative behaviours in industrial districts is the sharing of specific information within groups of firms linked by formal or informal agreements, but in any case explicit. Other examples are projects on technology, marketing, training, and design, carried out jointly by the members of the entrepreneurial associations or by groups of firms which explicitly decide to cooperate.

3.4 IS THERE AN 'INDUSTRIAL DISTRICT' MODEL?

The enthusiasm generated by the successful experience of industrial districts in some European countries, and particularly in Italy, has sometimes induced social scientists and practitioners to believe in the existence of a clearly defined model, with very precise characteristics and definite components, that could be reproduced elsewhere. However, as we said before, the industrial district framework is not an analytical model, but rather a list of stylized facts, useful for organizing empirical investigation and comparing it with reality. As pointed out in section 3.2, the main features of industrial districts emphasized in the literature can be presented by stressing four key elements:

1. the spatial concentration of sectorally specialized enterprises, which is the necessary condition for the development of the clustering effects, related to the other three elements listed below (3.2.1);
2. the existence of a common cultural and social background, which influences ways of doing business, labour relations and inter-firm relationships within the districts (3.2.2);
3. the existence of an intense set of backward, forward, horizontal and labour linkages based on competition, cooperation, flexibility and specialization (3.2.3);
4. the existence of a network of local public and private institutions, which, although they cannot create industrial districts *ex novo*, may support their growth and enhance the degree of collective efficiency.

The above features of the stylized model, and particularly the last two key facts, bring about some collective economic effects. Section 3.3 presents two concepts proposed for classifying those economic effects and adopted in the empirical investigation in Italy and Mexico (7.2):

(a) external economies which are the unintentional by-product of economic activities undertaken within the districts (3.3.1);
(b) cooperation effects which are the result of explicit and voluntary cooperative behaviours of the economic agents acting within the districts (3.3.2).

The second part of this discussion assesses the usefulness of the 'model' to represent the realities of two Italian footwear industrial districts and two Mexican clusters. The stylized facts presented in this chapter, with particular evidence for the economic and institutional factors, therefore represent the reference point for the comparison. Moreover, external economies and cooperation effects are the two analytical tools adopted to analyse the collective efficiency in the clusters investigated and to classify the collective effects detected.

The threefold comparison stresses the existence of different degrees of intensity and quality of the collective effects deriving from clustering (Rabellotti, 1995). The attempt to understand the reasons for the discrepancies between the ideal–typical industrial district, the Italian and the Mexican real cases bring into view three shortcomings of the 'model', which answer the following questions:

1. how much of the differences in the intensity and quality of collective effects can be explained by reasons external to the districts?
2. is it possible to identify heterogeneous behaviours and different ways of 'using' the district among the economic agents within the same cluster?
3. are districts different because they are in different stages of their development path or because they follow different trajectories of growth?

The first two questions are addressed in Chapter 7 through an analysis of the empirical results of the field work in Italy and Mexico, while the question about dynamics was not directly considered during the data collection; nevertheless, some related aspects are highlighted in Chapter 8 as issues for further research. Finally, before presenting the results of the empirical investigation, the next chapter is a brief overview of some of the empirical material available about clusters in LDCs to identify similarities and differences of behaviour and structural characteristics between the stylized facts presented in this chapter and some cluster realities in developing countries.

4 The Relevance of the Industrial District Debate for Developing Countries

4.1 INTRODUCTION

For several decades the role played by small and medium-scale enterprises in the development process has attracted a great deal of interest among scholars and practitioners. One of the milestones was a report from an ILO Kenya Mission (ILO, 1972), which first introduced the label of 'informal sector'. The report was driven by concern about the role played by SMEs in alleviating poverty, but it also made some assertions on their growth potentiality. Since then, many more studies have been produced on small and medium enterprises and on the impact they have on the economic systems.[1]

Most of these analyses concentrate on the economic characteristics and behaviour of SMEs and on the obstacles that hamper their development (Anderson, 1982; Schmitz, 1982). Much debate has centred around the static efficiency or productivity of small enterprises (Little, 1987).

SMEs are described as highly labour-intensive, flexible in responding to changes in the market and technologies, capable of taking advantage of local skills and resources, in catering to the local market, and in satisfying the basic needs of the poorest. SMEs are also believed to contribute to a more equitable distribution of income and to improving economic and social democracy by promoting participation and fostering diffuse entrepreneurship.

Overall the focus of the literature about SMEs is, therefore, on their social desirability rather than their economic efficiency and viability. SMEs are always seen as a necessary initial stage of the industrialization process, bound to disappear or at least decrease in importance in favour of an increasing presence of large firms in the economic structure of the industrializing countries.

Recently, a new approach towards small-scale industry in developing countries has been stimulated by the successful experience of the industrial districts in the developed world. The capability of small

43

clustered firms to be economically viable and strongly contribute to the growth process in industrial districts attracted a great deal of interest in development studies (Schmitz, 1989; Rasmussen *et al.*, 1992; Pederson *et al.*, 1994).

This shifts the emphasis of the research on SMEs from analysing whether they have growth and employment potential to studying under what conditions they can grow. Moreover, the new approach places the cluster of small firms and the behaviour of the enterprises within it at the centre of the analysis, dealing with the characteristics of interfirm linkages and with the relationships of SMEs with their environment.

In their survey on industrial districts carried out in developing countries Nadvi and Schmitz (1994) write that: 'A deliberate focus on clustering in research on small enterprise development in LDCs is relatively recent, going back no further than 1989'. (p. 5) This chapter presents an overview of some of the main empirical material available addressing the question of the identification and the existence of clusters in less developed countries, their economic and social characteristics and, eventually, the role institutions play in their growth.

4.2   INDUSTRIAL CLUSTERS IN LDCs

Sectoral specialization and geographical concentration of small and medium-scale enterprises are rather common phenomena in developing countries. A wide range of cases[2] are documented in the literature, including Argentina, Brazil, Ghana, India, Indonesia, Kenya, Mexico, Pakistan, Peru, Tanzania, South Korea and Zimbabwe. The most common sectors of specialization are textiles, clothing, footwear, leather, carpentry, furniture, electrical appliances and metal products. In many cases such small firm clusters have a long historical tradition in self-employment and in craft or artisan manufacture of specific products.

In many of the clusters analysed there is a critical mass of specialized enterprises, forward- and backward-linked economic activities and specific supporting institutions. In the shoe sector Schmitz (1995a) studied a cluster in the Sinos Valley in Brazil where over 500 shoe firms, a hundred tanneries, 200 component manufacturers, 700 domestic workshops and 45 leather and footwear machinery producers are concentrated. In the same sector a cluster of approximately 1000 small-scale and micro firms including a number of tanneries and component manufacturers was documented in the Peruvian city of Trujillo by Villaran (1993). Moving to Asia, in India Knorringa (1995) ana-

lysed a footwear district in Agra counting about 5000 small workshops and household units and Cawthorne (1995) studied another case
in Tiruppur, where, in 1986, 80 per cent of all factories were specialized in the textile sector.

In Pakistan Nadvi (1992) documented a number of cases in the Pun-
jab region in several sectors: sporting goods, surgical equipment, textiles, electrical appliances, metal products, steel utensils and machine
tools. In South Korea, also, known for its large conglomerates
('chaebols'), the existence of a textile industrial district, where two-
thirds of all Korean textile firms are concentrated, is reported by Cho
(1994). Finally, in Africa a few agglomerations of specialized enterprises have been reported in metalworking and furniture-making activities, although in most cases they are less spatially concentrated and
sectorally specialized in comparison with the other cases mentioned
above and are more limited as to number and range of firms (among
others see McCormick, 1997; Rasmussen, 1991; Sverisson, 1992).

On the basis of the available empirical evidence, we agree with Nadvi
and Schmitz (1994) who conclude that in developing countries: 'sectoral
and spatial small firm clusters are neither infrequent nor insignificant.
They are found across a wide range of developing countries'. (p. 12)

Obviously, the existence of a critical mass of specialized and concentrated activities, in many cases with strong historical roots, does
not necessarily imply that those clusters show dynamic and sustained
growth. Nonetheless, clustering can be considered as a major facilitating factor for a number of subsequent developments (which may or
may not occur): division of labour and specialization among small
enterprises; the emergence of suppliers who provide raw materials,
components, machinery and spare parts; the emergence of agents who
sell to distant national and international markets; the emergence of
specialized producer services; the emergence of a pool of skilled workers;
the formation of associations providing services and lobbying for their
members (Schmitz, 1995b).

4.3 THE SOCIAL ENVIRONMENT

The role of socio-cultural factors in the development of industrial districts has been particularly stressed in the European debate (see section 3.2, above). In LDCs knowledge about this important aspect is
still very limited and the few available studies dealing with social environment come to different conclusions.

Although there is agreement on the importance of a social environment characterized by strong family ties, sense of community, caste and ethnic identities, there are cases in which the socio-cultural factors seem to play a negative role instead of promoting social cohesion and facilitating the relationships among the economic actors located in the clusters. This happens, for instance, in the Agra footwear cluster where the caste divisions hamper the development of cooperation between producers, largely of lower caste Hindus and poor Muslims, and traders of upper caste Hindus and rich Muslims (Knorringa, 1995).

On the other hand, in other cases socio-cultural identity plays a positive role in promoting cooperation and trust and providing a commonly accepted set of codified rules. This is reported, among others, in the Sinos Valley in Brazil where a strong community spirit developed based on a common German heritage (Schmitz, 1995a); in Cyprus where there is a strong civic and national cohesion based on being Greek and Christian in contrast to Turkish and Muslim (Murray, 1992) and in Mexico where in rural clusters in the clothing sector strong social networks are formed around male migrants who shared a common experience of life in the US (Wilson, 1992).

A very interesting result which comes out in a few studies is that social environment changes with time. So, for instance in the Mexican rural knitwear clusters social links have weakened over time due to increasing differentiation within the cluster (Wilson, 1992). Rapid growth caused a similar effect on social networks in the Sinos Valley, weakening trust relationships among firms (Schmitz, 1995a). Nadvi and Schmitz (1994) rightly question: 'the ability of existing socio-cultural networks to not only regulate the functioning of social norms of behaviour, but effectively survive as the cluster's economic structure changes'. (p. 36)

In his study on the Sialkot surgical instruments cluster in Pakistan, Nadvi (1995) emphasizes that the importance of strong family ties was eroded by growth and replaced by an increase in 'weaker' social ties, based on being local and on 'knowing and being known'. In a dynamic approach, it seems therefore that building up a social reputation becomes a crucial asset for interacting within the cluster, with the foundation of trust changing from being ascribed to being earned (Schmitz, 1995b).

4.4 THE ECONOMIC EFFECTS OF CLUSTERING

Sectoral specialization and spatial concentration alone bring few benefits if they do not favour the growth of different types of inter-firm linkages from which collective efficiency gains develop. The spatial proximity of a group of firms specialized in making the same or similar products *per se* in fact does bring few benefits. However, it is a major facilitating factor for division of labour among specialized producers, for the emergence of suppliers, buyers and institutions aimed at providing specific services, and for the circulation of information about technology and market. The density, quality and type of these linkages are crucial to explaining the real economic advantages from clustering. To this end section 3.3 suggests a distinction between external economies and cooperation effects.

In the literature on industrial districts in LDCs the analysis of the economic effects of clustering is mainly concerned with some cases of static external economies. There are, in fact, a few cases in which an organization of production based on a high division of labour, similar to the situations described by Marshall is reported (see section 3.3.1). Examples are the footwear sector (Levy, 1991) and the machine tool industry (Amsden, 1985) in Taiwan, the clothing industry in Lima, Peru (Visser, 1997), and the previously mentioned cases of the Sinos Valley in Brazil (Schmitz, 1995a), and Agra (Knorringa, 1995) and Tiruppur (Cawthorne, 1995), in India.

However, with regard to the degree of the division of labour in developing countries, it may be important to note that a division of the different phases of a production process among specialized firms can be hampered by high transaction costs (Rabellotti, 1990). The limited development of suppliers, the poor quality of their products, the unreliability of their services, increase the costs in gathering information and coordinating transactions with suppliers. Therefore, a firm may regard vertical integration as a way to avoid potential supplier problems like delays in delivery or instability in product quality (Meyanathan & Munter, 1994). This is also the case in the two footwear clusters analysed in Mexico (see section 6.5.1).

A different form of inter-firm relation identified in some LDCs industrial clusters is subcontracting between large and small firms. This is not typical of the Third Italy but it has been reported for instance in Southern Germany (Schmitz, 1992b), where in some clusters large firms play a leading role in organizing production of small subcontracting firms located in the same area.

In developing countries the existence of large–small firm relations within clusters contributes to overcoming the traditional polarization of the economic systems, frequently characterized by a net separation between the large and the small firms, which often work in different sectors and for different markets with very few occasions for contact (Rabellotti, 1994).

Some signs of interaction between large and small firms have been reported by Schmitz (1995a) in the Sinos Valley and in South Korea by Cho (1994). In the Korean case two types of subcontracting relations have been identified: a hierarchical linkage driven by cost reduction motives and a more collaborative relationship based upon trust and long-term reputation driven by the search of quality, specialization and flexibility. Villaran in Peru (1993) and Knorringa in India (1995) have also reported a similar differentiated typology of large–small firm relations.

Another type of relation found in some LDCs clusters is the linkage between traders and producers. This has been particularly stressed by Weijland (1994) who, in a study on rural industry in Indonesia, shows the key role played by traders in linking the producers to distant markets. Other clusters in which the existence of trader–producer linkages have been reported are the Sinos Valley in Brazil, Agra in India and some of the Pakistani clusters.

Producer–trader relations can differ very much in quality. This result is stressed by Knorringa (1995) in Agra and it is also evident in the Mexican footwear clusters analysed in this study (see section 6.5.2). Basically, there are two types of linkages: a first, probably more common, hierarchical relation in which traders exploit producers buying at the lowest possible price, without paying too much attention to quality and a second more cooperative linkage based on common effort to produce and sell good quality products. In this latter case the cooperation between producers and traders often favours product and process innovation.

The last type of linkages taken into consideration are horizontal linkages among similar firms. In the literature some cases of firms sharing large orders by pooling their production capacity are reported by Dawson (1992) in the carpentry and metalworking sectors in Ghana, by Nadvi in steel utensil manufacturing industries in Pakistan (1992) and by Sandee (1994) in the roof tiles sector in Indonesia.

A different case of horizontal cooperation is described by Murray (1992) in Cyprus where a group of firms in the furniture industry agreed to open a joint retail shop, for which they would make products on a specialized basis. So, for instance, one firm was assigned kitchen furniture, another bedroom suites and so on. Murray reports of striking successes of the group, which has opened other shops in each of the major towns in Cyprus and has also begun joint export operations. Similar experiences of product specialization, with every firm specializing in one product to make up within a group a full range of items, sold with a common brand, have been promoted by UNIDO in Bolivia, Honduras, Jamaica and Nicaragua. The groups of small enterprises following this strategy of cooperation are mainly specialized in clothing, metalworking and agro-industry (Rabellotti, 1996).

From the empirical evidence available a conclusion can be drawn that industrial clusters in LDCs show a wide range of inter-firm linkages within the same clusters. The clearest lesson from these studies is that linkages differ in depth, quality and intensity and this generates different degrees of collective efficiency in the clusters.

4.5 THE INSTITUTIONAL SUPPORT

In developing countries the active promotion of small-scale enterprises has a relatively long tradition. Specialized institutions exist in many countries and development programmes addressed towards SMEs are rather diffused. While macro policies have generally discriminated against small producers, a battery of direct assistance programmes have sought to compensate for the negative effects of these broader policies. In this framework, the emphasis is on SMEs' role in reducing unemployment and underemployment and in redistributing income; SMEs are therefore assisted for social reasons through financial programmes.

There are some evaluations of these support programmes (Liedholm & Mead, 1987; Webster, 1991), from which it is evident that small firms often have difficulties in accessing these initiatives because they are highly centralized and bureaucratized, too generic and not flexible enough to satisfy the very diversified needs of their potential users.

With regard to industrial clusters, no targeted support interventions are reported in the available literature, either at central and local level. At the macro level, it is important to emphasize that the state influences the workings of industrial districts through macroeconomic policies.[3] Cawthorne (1995) in her study on the cotton knitwear industry in Tiruppur concludes that: 'Tirappur was an industrial cluster for a long time before it was a dynamic, expansionary, industrial cluster and the change was almost purely a function of export success. This suggests perhaps a more general point, that it is not clustering *per se* which makes for industrial success but clustering in a propitious macro-economic context'. (p. 46)

Our empirical investigation in the Mexican footwear clusters emphasizes the role that the trade policy regime can have on the intensity and quality of linkages among economic actors. In Mexico the long closure of the market has not favoured the development of cooperative backward and forward linkages among the shoe producers, suppliers and buyers (see section 6.5). Among the measures most commonly adopted in LDCs' industrial clusters, there are schemes for encouraging subcontracting or initiatives for creating quality control centres, training institutions or research and technology centres.

A recent World Bank study on subcontracting (Meyanathan & Munter, 1994) documents several specific policies adopted in some East Asian countries. These include tax incentives (in Malaysia and Singapore) and programmes designed to enhance the flow of information to small subcontractors (in Taiwan and Thailand). In Indonesia the study reports an initiative named 'foster-father' linkage and partnership programme, in which large companies market the products of small enterprises and help them overcome production and financing problems. The World Bank study also tries to evaluate the effectiveness of the described policy initiatives and the main conclusion is that the countries which used a multi-agency approach failed to produce the desired results, because they did not have the institutional capacity in place for providing really focused assistance.

Sectoral and business associations also play a role in introducing support initiatives in industrial clusters. In LDCs' clusters a number of sectoral associations are active: some of them have only lobbying aims but others provide a wide range of specific real services like training, quality control, information collection, legal and labour counselling. In their survey Nadvi and Schmitz (1994) conclude that: 'Not all such bodies serve the collective interest of the cluster, some becoming the preserve of more powerful elements within the clusters. A few, however, stand out either for their role in providing what Brusco (1990) terms "real services", or a lobbying body articulating the cluster's collective interests'. (p. 25)

Apart from the activity of sectoral and business associations, private institutions play a very minor role in supporting small firms in LDCs' clusters and experiences of joint private/public initiatives are very rarely reported in the literature. Private institutional interventions and cooperation between private and public bodies have proved to be rather successful in industrialized countries in the provision of real services through the establishment of joint initiatives, where public institutions may play the role of catalyst and sometimes make important financial and infrastructural contributions, while the private sector supplies specific expertise and often contributes on the financial side too (Schmitz & Musyck, 1994). The importance of private channels is also confirmed by a World Bank comparative analysis on the support systems for SMEs in Indonesia, Korea, Japan and Colombia, which comes to the conclusion that the leading source of support comes from buyers and traders, from suppliers and subcontracting principals, from banks and from the joint efforts on SMEs themselves[4] (Levy, 1994).

On the whole, it seems that in developing countries most industrial strategy is elaborated and managed at the central level, while there are few local level initiatives and these are often hampered by a centralized decision-making process and a lack of financial independence. Referring to industrialized countries Zeitlin (1992) writes: 'Hence promoting industrial districts does not mean the dissolution of national policy-making, but rather a new distribution of tasks between different levels of government – local, regional, national and even supranational'. (p. 292)

These considerations may well apply also to LDCs, where the redistribution of tasks and a new more decentralized approach to industrial policy are an important condition for the success of industrial clusters.

4.6 SOME FINAL CONSIDERATIONS

The aim of this chapter has been to present an overview of the main literature available on industrial clusters in less developed countries. The first finding is that clustering is not an uncommon feature in LDCs. In Asia and Latin America particularly there is evidence of clusters, characterized by deep concentrations of specialized industries, with a long historical tradition. Second, various types of inter-firm linkages have been identified in the clusters investigated. Sometimes they involve explicit cooperation behaviour and more frequently they consist of informal sharing of information, know-how, tools and equipment among firms. Consequently, clustering in developing countries sometimes generates external economies and cooperation effects, which increase the degree of collective efficiency of the cluster as a whole and improve the working conditions of individual firms. Third, the existence of a common social identity playing an active role in providing the basis for inter-firm linkages has also been emphasized in some of the available studies. Finally, some forms of institutional interventions assisting small firm clusters in LDCs have been documented in the literature. Nevertheless it must be emphasized that there is a profound lack of studies specifically focused on analysing the clustering phenomenon in LDCs. Most of the studies mentioned above are in fact only partially or indirectly based on the industrial district approach. There is, therefore, a need for analyses which take the stylized model of the Third Italy as a reference point and evaluate if and how its core characteristics are in evidence.

The distinct feature of this study is the direct comparison of two footwear clusters in Mexico and two districts in Italy with the 'model'. The aim is to assess to what extent the reality of two clusters in a less developed country is coherent with the reality of two districts, specialized in the same sector in an industrialized country and with the 'model'. The comparison confronts the effects deriving from clustering in Mexico and Italy in an attempt to understand the similarities and differences in the intensity and quality of linkages among the economic actors. The 'model' manifests some important shortcomings in representing these realities and in explaining the differences identified. Some dimensions in addition to the elements of the ideal–typical district, namely the impact of the external environment on the districts' structure, the internal differentiation of the economic actors and the need to move from a static to a dynamic approach, are therefore introduced in the analysis (see Chapters 7 and 8).

Part II

The Empirical Analysis

5 The Italian Districts of Brenta and Marche

5.1 INTRODUCTION

This chapter presents the results of the empirical investigation carried out in two Italian footwear districts: Marche and Brenta. The areas analysed are two of the most important districts specialized in the shoe industry in Italy. Marche is the largest concentration of footwear firms and Brenta is an area with a long tradition in the production of high quality women's shoes.

The aim of the investigation in these areas was initially to provide sectoral empirical material about two ideal–typical districts as a reference point for the study in Mexico. However, as stated in Chapter 1, the empirical work immediately brought to our attention some significant discrepancies between the 'model' and these Italian districts. The study was therefore extended to include a third dimension and became a threefold comparison between the Italian, the Mexican realities and the 'model'.

Accordingly, the objective of this chapter is to present the analysis of the different types of interactions among the economic actors going on in Brenta and Marche and then to compare these results with the 'model'. It is organized as follows:

(a) in 5.2 some background information about the performance and the structure of the Italian footwear industry is presented;
(b) in 5.3 there is a presentation of the economic characteristics of the two districts – Brenta and Marche – selected for the empirical investigation;
(c) the results of the survey on backward, forward, horizontal, labour and institutional linkages are presented in 5.4;
(d) in section 5.5 the discrepancies between the case studies and the stylized model are finally discussed.

5.2 THE ITALIAN FOOTWEAR INDUSTRY

In this section some background information on the Italian footwear industry is presented: first the performance of the sector from the 1960s to the 1990s is analysed, second the structure of the industry is examined considering the number of firms, size distribution and spatial concentration, third the different phases of the production process and their technological features are investigated and finally an overview of the main Italian footwear areas is presented.

5.2.1 The performance

At the beginning of the 1960s the Italian footwear industry ranked fourth in Europe, after France, Great Britain and Germany. At that time the production was mainly directed towards the domestic market and the sector was dominated by small, artisan enterprises. In the following three decades the European geography of the footwear industry changed profoundly, due to a severe reduction of activity in France, Great Britain and Germany and an impressive growth of the sector in Italy (Table 5.1).

The outstanding growth of the Italian footwear industry, begun in the 1960s, went on continuously until 1985, led by exports. At the beginning of the 1950s, exports represented a mere 3.7 per cent of total production; in 1970 the proportion of exports increased to 63 per cent; in 1985 it was 83 per cent and, in 1993, 84 per cent (ANCI,[1] 1994).

The competitive factors explaining the success of the Italian footwear industry have followed a rather typical evolutionary pattern. In the first phase of development, during the 1960s, Italy exploited a labour cost advantage with respect to other European competitors. Subsequently, the high specialization of the Italian footwear system, based on the division of the production cycle among several enterprises, specialized in the different phases of production, and on the existence of a very well-developed network of backward-linked firms, producing components and raw materials for the sector, became the main source of comparative advantage. The organization of production among manufacturers and suppliers within a number of specialized areas, allowed the Italian industry to become highly flexible and adaptive to market changes. In the international market, the Italian shoe firms began to be considered highly reliable and able to quickly satisfy different size orders and consequently they could progressively increase their export share.

Table 5.1   Production, import and export of leather shoes, 1972–1990
(millions of pairs)

Country	1972–1974 average	1980	1985	1990
Italy				
–production	249.9	276.5	371.6	320.2
–import	1.4	5.4	7.5	19.3
–export	152.7	200.4	292.6	245.2
France				
–production	91.0	92.0	86.1	76.9
–import	16.7	44.8	55.9	80.1
–export	26.0	23.9	27.3	19.4
Germany (W)				
–production	96.3	70.1	66.3	53.6
–import	74.2	116.5	138.8	184.6
–export	10.8	15.6	25.3	32.4
UK				
–production	83.8	61.7	53.5	56.2
–import	20.4	47.4	64.9	50.6
–export	9.4	12.1	9.5	8.6

Source: FAO, 1992

More recently during the 1980s, other European countries like Spain,
Portugal and the former Yugoslavia, some newly-industrializing south-
east Asian countries (NICs) like Taiwan and South Korea and also
other developing countries like Brazil, India and China became very
competitive in the international market and greatly increased their export share. In order to face this increasing competition, the Italian footwear
system strengthened its advantage in terms of image, fashion content
and design in order to reduce the price elasticity of demand for its
products, trying to increase the exports in the medium-high and high
segments of market. From 1987 to 1993 exports in the low price market decreased from 6 to 2 per cent, in the low to mid price range from
33 to 21 per cent, while in the medium price segment the exports
increased from 44 to 57 per cent, in the mid to high price range from
11 to 13 per cent and in the high price segment from 6 to 7 per cent
(ANCI, 1994).

Notwithstanding its attempt to counter this increasing competition by upgrading its exports, the Italian footwear sector had to start competing in a market where a large increase in the quantity of shoes supplied faced a stable demand. The competition became stronger because the new producers could exploit a labour cost advantage in comparison with Italy. Besides, a change in consumer habits favoured a shift from classical leather shoes, in which Italy is strong, towards synthetic athletic shoes, in which countries like Korea, Taiwan and Hong Kong tend to be specialized.

From the Second World War onwards, Italian exports gradually increased, to peak in 1985. However from 1986 on, exports decreased continuously, except for 1990 when there was a small increase and in 1993 when, thanks to the devaluation of the Lira,[2] exports increased consistently (Table 5.2). On the international market, Italy shifted from second place in 1986 to third place in 1993, among the world leading exporters, after China and Hong Kong (ANCI, 1994).

Concerning leather footwear only, which represents 67 per cent of total Italian exports, in 1990 Italy was still the leading exporter, but its share of world exports decreased from 43.2 per cent in 1970 to 19.9 per cent. In the same period, the second and the third most important exporters, South Korea and Brazil, increased their share from 1.9 per cent and 0.5 per cent to 15.7 per cent and 12.3 per cent respectively (Table 5.3) (UNIDO, 1992).

The European Union is traditionally the most important market for Italian shoes. In 1993 sales to EU countries accounted for 62 per cent of all exports in quantity and 59 per cent in terms of value. Despite a significant decline in its Italian imports, Germany continues to absorb the largest proportion of Italian shoe exports (28 per cent in quantity and 27 per cent in value) (ANCI, 1994).

After the EU, the US is the second most important market, although since the end of the 1980s until 1992, the Italian exports have been penalized by the revaluation of the Lira against the dollar. From 1985 to 1993 the share of exports to this market decreased from 17 per cent to 9 per cent in quantity and from 22 per cent to 12 per cent in value[3] (ANCI, 1994).

The difficulties on the international market were compounded by some difficulties in the domestic market due to a large increase in imports. From 1980 in Italy shoe imports increased continuously, the only exceptions being 1989 and 1990, due to the introduction at EU level of a temporary quota on imports from south-east Asia and 1993, due to the effect of the Lira's devaluation (Table 5.2). In fact, from 1980, imports

Table 5.2 The Italian footwear industry, 1970–1993

Year	Employees	Pairs 000's	Production value £ mill.*	Production value Index**	Exports 000's pairs	Imports 000's pairs
1970	132 608	345 898	2 974.27	100.0	217 666	3 370
1971	141 360	372 878	3 243.19	109.0	235 848	3 081
1972	135 923	380 834	3 346.47	112.5	246 704	5 650
1973	130 050	356 967	3 299.22	110.9	226 412	7 472
1974	135 791	383 601	3 530.84	118.7	251 483	7 398
1975	130 791	366 306	3 685.17	123.9	232 424	6 977
1976	130 806	410 581	4 462.75	150.0	264 701	9 512
1977	120 806	398 129	4 551.68	153.0	264 986	13 543
1978	127 967	429 344	4 740.69	159.4	294 803	20 044
1979	142 819	515 388	5 548.98	186.6	374 351	27 384
1980	132 475	415 743	4 899.70	164.7	314 609	36 761
1981	139 636	468 692	4 654.78	156.5	338 581	42 032
1982	142 288	531 300	5 048.37	169.7	387 325	38 389
1983	135 128	487 718	4 645.27	156.2	374 237	54 318
1984	134 317	496 198	4 838.72	162.7	393 134	53 359
1985	133 914	524 509	4 994.71	167.9	434 753	56 073
1986	128 825	499 285	4 799.67	161.4	411 022	63 917
1987	122 513	464 581	4 526.62	152.2	383 872	89 048
1988	115 886	436 162	4 086.47	137.4	378 191	100 675
1989	114 123	406 935	4 338.50	145.9	339 858	92 207
1990	113 980	424 916	4 330.29	145.6	360 022	73 668
1991	111 701	410 894	4 258.97	143.2	347 820	104 006
1992	108 350	418 827	4 065.77	136.7	338 657	127 524
1993	108 000	451 702	5 038.49	169.4	380 566	101 699

Source: ANCI, 1994

* At 1980 prices   ** 1970 = 100

increased from 36.8 million pairs to 127 million pairs in 1992 (46 per cent from Asian countries and 35 per cent from other EU countries), decreasing to 101 million in 1993 (ANCI, 1994).

It is important to emphasize that in recent years there was a significant increase in leather shoe imports, traditionally the production domain of the Italian industry, from 9.2 million pairs in 1986 to 32.7 in 1993 (ANCI, 1994). In 1994, the breakdown of imports according to product was the following: 38 per cent fabric shoes, 22 per cent slippers, 32 per cent leather footwear products and the remaining 8 per cent rubber and synthetic shoes (ANCI, 1994). Furthermore, the average price of imported footwear increased by 68 per cent from 1987 to

Table 5.3   Some of the world's largest exporters of leather footwear (1970 and 1990)

Country	Exports 1990 (000's pairs)	Share of world exports 1970	1990
Italy	**245.2**	**43.2**	**19.9**
South Korea	193.2	1.9	15.7
Brazil	152.3	0.5	12.3
Taiwan	108.1	0.9	8.8
Spain	77.7	9.0	6.3
Portugal	69.4	0.8	5.6
China	41.8	0.4	3.4
Hong Kong	39.3	0.3	3.2
Mexico	**4.6**	**0.2**	**0.4**

Source: UNIDO, 1992

1993, while in the same period the average price of exports only increased by 34 per cent (ANCI, 1994). This increase boosts concern about competition in the high-price product range.

Considering domestic consumption, in Italy per capita consumption of shoes is low if compared with other developed countries: in 1992 the average per capita consumption rate was 3.4 pairs, while the European average was 4.5 (SATRA, 1993). Moreover, the trend of consumption decreased slightly from 157.8 million pairs in 1985 to 152.1 in 1990, with some increases in 1987 and 1989 and finally it increased to 194.1 million in 1993. Concerning the breakdown by upper materials, in 1993 61 per cent of domestic consumption was in the leather/hide category, 12 per cent in synthetics, 11 per cent were slippers, 1 per cent rubber shoes and the remaining 15 per cent mainly fabric shoes (ANCI, 1994).

Therefore, after 30 years of continuous growth the Italian footwear industry is now going through a difficult period. In both the domestic and the international market, it has to face increasing competition from countries with a clear advantage in terms of labour cost. In this study the particular form of organizing production which has been so successful in a situation characterized by demand surpassing supply is analysed and moreover we explore how this system reacts to the new external situation, in other words if and how these specialized systems of production are able to adapt and change their internal rules in order to cope with an international market dominated by an increasing supply facing a stable demand.

5.2.2 The structure of the sector

The most evident features of the Italian footwear industry are as follows: high number of producers, small average company size and spatial concentration in a few specialized areas.

In 1993 the total number of producer companies was 8100 and the total industry workforce was 108 000. Considering the trend, the number of firms grew continuously from 2145 companies in 1951 to 9682 in 1985 and then declined. Concerning the workforce, the highest level was reached in 1979 with 142 819 employees and then a negative trend began, with the only exception being 1982 (ANCI, 1994) (Table 5.2).

Including the industries backward-linked with the footwear sector, in 1993 the Italian footwear system accounted for 2265 producers of components and accessories (36 620 employees), 2173 tanneries (23 000 employees) and 315 producers of machinery for the sector (5000 employees) (Table 5.4) (ANAC, 1994; UNIC, 1994; ASSOMAC, 1994).[4]

The footwear sector is characterized by a very low level of concentration: only 0.7 per cent of companies have more than 100 employees and firms with a workforce of less than 50 employees account for 74.8 per cent of all employment. There is a considerable number of firms employing fewer than 10 people, representing 72 per cent of all companies in the sector and 23 per cent of all employees (Table 5.5 and Table 5.6). According to some estimates of the entrepreneurial association, small family enterprises account for 75 per cent of all companies with fewer than 20 employees and employ a total of 17 220 people (ANCI, 1993).

Concerning changes in the size breakdown of the footwear industry, Table 5.5 shows that in the decade 1951–1961 very small firms with fewer than 9 employees increased considerably, while in the next decade (1961–1971) small enterprises employing between 10 and 49 people registered the highest rate of growth, and finally in the period 1971–1991 the situation remained stable.[5] The trend is confirmed by the average size per firm, decreasing from 21.5 employees in 1951 to 16.7 in 1981 and 9.3 in 1991. The small average size prevails also in the related sectors: in the component sector it is 14.4 employees, in the tanning sector is 10.6 and in the mechanical sector 15.4 employees.

A strong spatial concentration is a common feature of the shoe industry in many countries[6] and in Italy this phenomenon is particularly evident. Terrasi (1988) has calculated the location indexes[7] in every province and has identified 7 regions in the country where the sector

Table 5.4   The Italian footwear *filière* (1993)

Industry	No. of firms	Employees	Production (£.mill.)
Shoes	8 100	108 000	11 531
Components	2 265	32 620	2 515
Leather*	2 173	23 000	7 600
Machine tools	315	5 000	920

Source: ANCI (1994); ANAC (1994); UNIC (1994); ASSOMAC (1994)

* The leather industry includes the whole production of the sector, not only products reserved for the shoe industry

Table 5.5   The size structure of the Italian footwear industry, no. of firms (1951–1991)

Breakdown by number of employees (%)	1–9	10–49	>50	100–499	>500	Total no. of firms	Average size
1951	54.8	34.7	6.3	3.9	0.3	2 142	21.5
1961	63.3	29.1	5.0	2.5	0.1	5 784	18.0
1971	59.5	32.9	4.8	2.7	0.1	7 882	17.5
1981	59.3	33.8	4.4	2.4	0.1	7 820	16.7
1985	74.8	22.2	1.9	1.0	0.0	15 036	9.7
1991	72.1	25.6	1.5	0.7	0.0	15 890	9.3

Source: Gaibisso, 1992 (based on industrial census data and Cerved data bank for 1985 and 1991)

Table 5.6   The size structure of the Italian footwear industry, no. of employees (1951–1991)

Breakdown by number of employees (%)	1–9	10–49	>50	100–499	>500	Total no. of employees
1951	12.8	35.5	17.7	29.9	4.1	46 153
1961	16.1	35.7	19.3	25.0	3.9	104 401
1971	13.6	38.7	18.6	25.8	3.3	137 755
1981	14.0	41.3	18.0	23.8	2.9	130 924
1985	20.5	43.5	13.8	16.0	6.3	145 611
1991	23.3	51.5	10.8	12.7	1.8	147 660

Source: Gaibisso, 1992 (based on industrial census data and Cerved data bank for 1985 and 1991)

is concentrated; these are, in order of importance: Marche (23.6 per cent of total production value), Veneto (23.4 per cent), Tuscany (19.1 per cent), Lombardy (10.3 per cent), Apulia (7.5 per cent), Emilia-Romagna (6.4 per cent) and Campania (4.9 per cent). Together these regions account for 96 per cent of the total number of enterprises and 95 per cent of the industry's workforce (Table 5.7) (ANCI, 1994).

In these regions the footwear sector is geographically concentrated in some restricted areas, comprising a few small towns and villages, the main ones being: Fermo and Civitanova in Marche, Vigevano and Parabiago in Lombardy, Verona and the Brenta area in Veneto, San Mauro Pascoli in Emilia-Romagna, Naples in Campania, Casarano and Barletta in Apulia (Figure 5.1).

Considering the changes in the geography of the Italian footwear sector, Lombardy has declined in importance: in 1951 it employed 54 per cent of the total workforce in the industry, in 1992 it accounted for only 9 per cent, whilst Marche rose from 4 per cent in 1951 to 25 per cent in 1992. During the 1970s Tuscany grew in importance but recently this growth process has slowed down. In contrast, the footwear industry in Campania has recently expanded (ANCI, 1994).

Concerning product specialization, leather and hide footwear represent about 72 per cent of total output, followed by synthetic shoes at 19 per cent. Street shoes and athletic shoes, manufactured mainly in Apulia, account for 79 per cent and 14 per cent of total production respectively. According to their market segment, women's shoes are 49 per cent of total production, men's shoes are 23 per cent and children's shoes are 5 per cent[8] (ANCI, 1994).

From what has been said so far it is possible to conclude that the Italian footwear industry is structured in very specialized, geographically concentrated and integrated production systems. Within each district there are many small and medium sized firms, specialized in different phases of the production cycle, backward- and forward-linked enterprises, services and institutions to support the sector.

5.2.3 The production process

In this section the different phases of the production cycle of the leather shoe industry[9] are described, analysing their technological features with particular emphasis on the most recent innovations brought into the sector. Five main phases can be distinguished in the shoe production cycle:

Table 5.7 Footwear producing regions (1993)

Regions	No. of firms	(%)	Employees	(%)	Production value (£.mill.)	(%)	Export value (£.mill.)	(%)
Marche	**2 511**	**(31.0)**	**27 756**	**(25.7)**	**2 720.4**	**(23.6)**	**1 421.4**	**(18.2)**
Tuscany	1 677	(20.7)	19 008	(17.6)	2 201.6	(19.1)	1 698.2	(21.8)
Veneto	**1 337**	**(16.5)**	**21 384**	**(19.8)**	**2 703.0**	**(23.4)**	**2 221.7**	**(28.6)**
Lombardy	761	(9.4)	9 504	(8.8)	1 190.7	(10.3)	954.3	(12.3)
Campania	591	(7.3)	8 100	(7.5)	566.3	(4.9)	100.1	(1.3)
Apulia	591	(7.3)	11 880	(11.0)	867.8	(7.5)	621.0	(8.0)
Emilia-Romagna	300	(3.7)	5 184	(4.8)	738.2	(6.4)	426.5	(5.5)
Rest of Italy	332	(4.1)	5 184	(4.8)	543.4	(13.8)	327.5	(4.3)
Total	8 100	(100.0)	108 000	(100.0)	11 531.4	(100.0)	7 770.7	(100.0)

Source: ANCI (1994)

Map 5.1 The main Italian footwear districts.

1. the creation of samples which includes designing, development of sizes and selection of materials;
2. the production of uppers, including the cutting and stitching phases;
3. the preparation of bottoms: soles, insoles and heels;
4. the assembly of pieces which is the process of stretching the upper over the last and attaching it to the bottom;
5. the finishing phase which consists of ironing and polishing edges and bottoms to improve both appearance and wearability.

The production process can be vertically integrated in one firm or, as happens in most of the cases in the Italian footwear industry, can be separated among several enterprises specialized in one or two phases of the cycle. Normally, in Italy shoe manufacturers design their own shoe styles, then models are often developed by specialized service firms, uppers are cut and stitched in some other specialized firms and bottoms are made by specialized enterprises which buy the soles, insoles or heels. Finally, the different components come back to the shoe firm where they are assembled and finished. In section 5.5.1 the tendency of shoe producers to decentralize the different phases of the production cycle is discussed in greater detail and the reasons for decentralization according to the firms interviewed in Brenta and Marche are presented.

Regarding the footwear industry technology, and specifically the production of leather shoes, the advances are quite limited. Only in large mass production firms, specialized in the low-price segment of the market, has automation considerably increased during the last few years. The most far-reaching development in shoemaking is regarded as the introduction of computer-aided design (CAD) for creating samples. It is now possible to design a shoe on the computer screen and thus draw up the components and develop the different sizes. In some of the most advanced firms it is then possible to download the data generated from the CAD onto the production machines on the shopfloor for guiding the cutting and stitching processes. These developments are leading to computer integrated manufacturing (CIM) which, however, is still relatively rare and in the experimental stage in the footwear sector (World Bank, 1990). CAD systems can save time, reduce unit labour and material requirements, and improve product quality by allowing designers to modify the existing styles on the computer, without having to construct many models; it also ensures accuracy in grading patterns by size.

Notwithstanding these very evident advantages, however, the adoption of CAD systems is still limited to only a few firms in Italy. The limited diffusion can be explained by a number of factors: first many firms cannot afford to pay the cost of adopting the system; second the potential of CAD is still rather unclear to many entrepreneurs, who very often lack the necessary background to understand them; and finally the introduction of CAD requires a requalification of designers and pattern makers. This last point is crucial. It is not only a question of understanding how to use these new systems but, rather, it is a matter of the skills required with the adoption of CAD, which are completely different from those traditionally associated with the modelist's job. According to a specific study on this topic by Gottardi (1991) it appears that the successful adoption of the system is very often negatively correlated with the age of the people who have to use it. This means that it is very difficult to convince designers and modelists, with a long experience of working in the traditional way, to use these new systems, while young people are more open to using new instruments in their activity.

Moving on to the other phases of the production cycle, the cutting phase is crucial from the standpoints of both product quality and production costs. In the majority of the Italian firms cutting is generally done by hand or with the help of hollow punches and requires highly skilled workers because there are great risks of wasting material if mistakes are made at this stage. The characteristics of the leather itself, which being a natural material can present imperfections and irregularities, make it very difficult to convert cutting into an automated procedure.

In the stitching phase, when products are standardized and rather simple, it is possible to introduce advanced numerically-controlled machines, which can automatically perform several required operations. However, automated machines have limited capacity when it comes to handling frequent design changes or to carrying out complicated processes and therefore their diffusion remains limited.

Finally, in the assembling and finishing phases a number of machines exist to automatically execute one or more operations, among them there are machines for pre-finishing, lasting and polishing.

Concerning technology, it can be concluded that the benefits from automation in the footwear manufacturing industry are associated with large volumes, long runs and mass production techniques and therefore automated machinery has so far been adopted mostly by large firms. This is very rarely the case in Italian footwear enterprises, which tend to be small and to produce a very diversified range of products, adopting a rather traditional technology which cannot act as an important barrier against the new comers on the international market. The footwear industry therefore still remains highly labour-intensive and this penalizes Italian shoe manufacturers that have to compete with producers from newly industrializing or developing countries where labour costs are lower. The heavy weight of labour costs is confirmed by the cost structure of the industry which, according to some estimates of the entrepreneurial association, in 1992 was 37.5 per cent raw materials and other inputs, 35 per cent labour costs and 27.5 per cent overhead charges (in other words fixed costs, expenditures in product development and in marketing)[10] (ANCI, 1993).

Finally, considering labour productivity, this varies more according to the quality of products than to the size of firms (Varaldo, 1988) and it is low in firms which produce high quality shoes, increasing with the decrease in quality. Differences in productivity are explained by the higher labour intensiveness to produce top-quality shoes in comparison with low-quality shoes, which can be produced with a higher degree of automation and with a shorter production cycle in the finishing phase.

5.2.4 The main Italian footwear areas

In this section a brief description of the main Italian footwear areas (Figure 5.1) as well as the two districts covered in the empirical survey (Brenta and Marche) is presented. Vigevano in Lombardy is the oldest footwear industrial district in Italy, where the production of shoes began at the end of last century. Its most impressive period of growth was during the 1950s and the 1960s when there was a concentration of more than one thousand shoe enterprises and about 400 firms in related sectors, producing more than one third of the total Italian output. After 30 years the number of firms has dramatically decreased to 300 and its share of national output has dropped to 5 per cent (6 per cent of total exports) (ANCI, 1993). The profound changes over the last 20 years have transformed the district, reducing the average size of firms and increasing the quality of products. Most of the largest firms, which produced standardized products, closed down, while small firms, highly specialized in specific phases of the production process, have survived and progressively increased their specialization and vertical disintegration.

In 1991, 66 per cent of the firms in the area had fewer than 10 employees and 75 per cent of the total employment was in enterprises with less than 50 people. In the district, vertical disintegration is very strong and about 62 per cent of the firms are specialized in the production of parts or components (Brusco *et al.*, 1987). The main products are high- and medium-high quality women's and men's shoes, while the production of children's shoes has almost disappeared. The shoes from Vigevano are well known for being really top quality both in terms of components and raw materials and in terms of the production process, thanks to the employment of a highly skilled labour force.

Aside from its shoes, the Vigevano area is also well known for the construction of machinery for the footwear sector. In this industry there are 315 firms with 5000-odd employees, which represents the most important concentration of firms in this sector in Italy and the world too. The development of the mechanical sector began during the 1970s, exploiting the know-how in the footwear sector accumulated in the district and partially alleviating the employment problems in the footwear industry (ASSOMAC, 1994).

In Veneto there are three main areas of specialization: the area around Verona, the Brenta area (discussed below) and Montebelluna. Verona is a rather unusual district in the Italian panorama of the footwear industry because it is specialized in the production of low-priced shoes and it is dominated by a few big enterprises subcontracting out part of the production to a large number of small firms. In 1989, in the area there were 815 enterprises which employed 9472 people and manufactured about 10 per cent of the total production in the sector (Ragazzi, 1992).

Montebelluna is specialized in the production of ski and after-ski boots, which is very different from the production of street and even athletic shoes in terms of technology and materials. About 70 per cent of the world's production in this particular segment of the market is concentrated in Montebelluna. The number of firms located in the area is about 500, employing 9000 people. Recently, some important changes have occurred in the area due to the arrival of large outside companies like Benetton and Rossignol, which have bought out some local firms (Camagni & Rabellotti, 1995).

In Emilia-Romagna the area specialized in the production of shoes is located around the small town of San Mauro Pascoli in the southern part of the region. The area is dominated by small artisan firms, representing 62 per cent of the total number of firms, specialized in the production of medium-high quality women's shoes. Around Ravenna there is another concentration of small footwear firms specialized in low-quality shoes. In the two areas there are about 750 enterprises which employ 8000-odd people (ANCI, 1993).

In Tuscany the growth of the shoe sector was favoured by the high concentration of the tanning industry in this region.[11] The most important areas are around Florence, Pisa and Pistoia. In Florence the footwear industry is specialized in women's shoes and in Pistoia in men's shoes in the medium-high quality segment, while in Pisa the production is rather diversified, above all in the medium-low segment of the market. The average size of the firms in the three areas is very small (8 employees) and the degree of division of labour among firms is very high (Ragazzi, 1992).

Moving to the South, in Campania there is a concentration of shoe enterprises around Naples. The district is dominated by a few medium enterprises, which produce women's shoes of medium-high quality and there are also a large number of very small artisan firms, which often work in the informal sector as subcontractors for the larger ones or they make very low quality shoes (Brusco *et al.*, 1987).

Finally, in Apulia there has been a recent boom in the footwear industry. There are two main areas: Barletta and Casarano. The Barletta area is specialized in the production of synthetic athletic shoes for the low segment of the market. Most of the firms located in the area were established in the late 1970s or early 1980s; there is a total of 300 enterprises employing 15 000 people. Many firms work as subcontractors for some large, foreign enterprises manufacturing athletic shoes. Finally, there is a very high degree of deverticalization of the production cycle among specialized enterprises in the area (Brusco *et al.*, 1987).

Casarano is a very peculiar district in the Italian panorama because it is characterized by very high vertical integration of the production cycle, both in the giant firm which dominates the area and employs 3000 people (the largest firm in the Italian footwear industry) and in the many medium and small firms of the area. The main products are low-quality leather shoes and moccasins (Ragazzi, 1992; Villa, 1990).

From this very general presentation of some of the most important footwear areas in Italy it is clear that the picture is not completely homogeneous: notwithstanding some commonalities, districts may differ in their history, in the histories of the economic actors comprising them and in their product or market specialization. The next section presents the results of the survey carried out in Marche and Brenta; the analysis is focused on assessing the adequacy of the industrial district model in representing these two specific cases.

5.3   MARCHE AND BRENTA: THE CRITICAL MASS

Two of the most important footwear clusters in Italy were selected for the empirical survey: Marche contains the largest concentration of firms producing leather street shoes and Brenta is an area highly specialized in the production of high- and medium-high quality women's shoes, with strong export-orientation. As shown below, in the two areas the first prerequisite identified by the industrial district model – the existence of a critical mass of spatially concentrated and sectoral specialized enterprises – is definitely satisfied. Moreover, the two areas are characterized by a long tradition of specialization in the footwear industry going back to the beginning of this century.

Marche

The shoe industry was established in Marche in the 1920s, when some people from Montegranaro, one of the main centres of the district, who had emigrated to Northern Italy to work in the footwear industry, came back to their villages to set up the first local enterprises. At first, the local industry worked mainly as subcontractor for the old-established enterprises, located in the North. Then, the sector started to grow, thanks to rapidly-increasing demand, with a first boom after the Second World War when some firms in the North closed down, and a second real boom during the 1970s when the footwear industry in Marche became the largest concentration of firms in Italy. From 1971–1981, the regional rate of growth of employment in the footwear industry was 91 per cent, while the average national rate in the sector was 38 per cent. From 1951 to 1993, the share of workforce in Marche over the national workforce in the sector rose from 4 per cent to 26 per cent (ANCI, 1994).

From Montegranaro the footwear industry progressively spread to the neighbouring rural areas and today the strongest concentration of firms is around Fermo, Montegranaro, Monte San Giusto, Monte Urano, Porto Sant'Elpidio, Sant'Elpidio a Mare and Civitanova Marche, an area located between two provinces – Macerata and Ascoli Piceno. All these are small towns with economies specialized in the footwear sector and some related industries. In the area more than one fourth of the total population works in the footwear industry, with a density of footwear enterprises of over 40 firms per 1000 inhabitants[12] (CENSIS, 1993). In 1989 the footwear industry together with the leather and textile industries contributed 35 per cent to the total value added

Table 5.8   Marche and Brenta: the critical mass

	Shoe firms	No. of employees	Pairs of shoes (millions)	% exported	Producers of components	No. of employees	Total no. of employees filière
Marche	2 410	25 437	108 536	52.2	772	9 600	35 037
Brenta	258	6 547	8 505	78.5	365*	2 373	8 920

Source: ANCI, 1994

* This figure includes modelists

and 47 per cent to the total employment in the Marche industry (Alessandrini & Canullo, 1994).

In Marche there is the largest concentration of shoe firms and producers of components and accessories in Italy: in 1993 it comprised 2410 footwear firms with 25 437 employees and 772 producers of components with 9600 employees. The value of their production was 2720 billion Lira, 24 per cent of the total value produced by the Italian footwear industry. Exports account for 52 per cent of total production and represent 18 per cent of total footwear exported in Italy (Table 5.8).

Brenta

In Brenta the origins of the footwear industry date back to the establishment of the firm Calzaturificio Voltan in 1898. It was founded by Giovanni Voltan, an artisan who, after spending some time in the United States to learn the trade, came back to his little village (Strà) with some machines for making shoes to set up his own business. In 1904, the firm employed 400 people, producing 1000 pair of shoes per day. It was the first shoe factory in Italy. At the beginning of this century, many workers from Voltan's enterprise began to set up their own independent businesses in Strà and other nearby villages, such as Vigonovo, Fossò, Fiesso d'Artico, Noventa, Saonara and Vigonza. This was the beginning of the Brenta shoe district, named from the river which flows through it.

During the footwear industry boom after the Second World War the sector progressively absorbed most of the rural workforce available in the area. In the 1960s, the local enterprises expanded, further increasing their penetration of the export market, specializing in the high and medium-high segments of the market.

Nowadays, 85 per cent of the shoes produced in the area are medium-high and high market segment women's shoes. This area has suffered from increasing competition in the international market and from 1986 to 1992 production decreased from 8,4 to 8,1 million pairs. Then, in 1993 production rose impressively to 8,5 million pairs, due to the strong devaluation of the Lira which favoured exports. Employment in the whole sector, including related industries, decreased from about 10 000 jobs in 1986 to 8900 in 1993. Finally, the number of firms remained stable at 775, after reaching a peak of 892 in 1989 (ANCI, 1994).

In 1993 the district accounted for 258 shoe enterprises, 132 of which were artisan firms,[13] 365 producers of components, 84 service firms specialized in the creation and development of models and 68 trading companies. The total value of shoe production is about 590 billion Lira, 4.5 per cent of the total production in Italy. The area is strongly export-orientated: 78 per cent of the production is in fact exported and this represents 5 per cent of total Italian exports in the sector (ACRIB, 1994) (Table 5.8).

5.4 RESULTS OF THE FIELD WORK

The field work was carried out in Marche and Brenta, two footwear districts where, as seen above, there is a critical mass of spatially concentrated and sectorally specialized shoe enterprises, backward- and forward-linked firms and institutions.

The objective of the inquiry is to study if and how firms interact with the other economic actors in the district, thereby identifying the collective effects described in section 3.3 and deriving from the district form of organization: external economies and cooperation effects. To this end the survey investigates the existence, the level of intensiveness and the quality of the linkages identified, the motivations behind them and the typology of actors explicitly or implicitly involved.

The survey is based on a questionnaire distributed to a sampling of 50 shoe firms, on a number of open interviews to key informers and on some in-depth network case studies.[14] The sample of 50 firms was randomly taken from the registry of members of the local entrepreneurial associations. The sample was also stratified by size: 24 enterprises employ fewer than 50 employees, 15 between 51 and 100 employees and 11 more than 100 people (Table 5.9).

Table 5.9   The sample

No. of firms	< 50 employees	51–100 employees	> 100 employees	Total firms
Marche	11	11	8	30
Brenta	13	4	3	20
Total firms	24	15	11	50

Source: author's survey

Before presenting a detailed picture of the linkages detected, some general characteristics of the sample firms are given below:

(a) 42 firms produce women's shoes, 12 men's shoes and only 6 children's shoes;

(b) 30 per cent of the sample firms were established before 1959, 32 per cent from 1960 to 1969, another 32 per cent from 1970 to 1979 and, finally, only 6 per cent after 1980. In Marche there is a larger concentration of recently established firms than in Brenta: 57 per cent of the sample firms were in fact created after 1970 while in Brenta 70 per cent were established before 1970. As seen in section 5.3, Marche is in fact a relatively recent district which enjoyed its boom during the 1970s while in Brenta the growth began during the 1950s and 1960s;

(c) the vast majority of firms in the sample are family firms, only 14 per cent of the firms interviewed are not managed at the family level. All the non-family businesses were established by people with some previous working experience in the sector in the districts;

(d) the totality of the entrepreneurs interviewed has local origins, at least from one generation.

5.4.1   Backward linkages

This section distinguishes between subcontractors, suppliers of raw materials, components and services, and suppliers of technology. In fact they all provide inputs and services but the distinction lies in the subcontractors being involved in a particular stage of the shoe production process, while the other categories of suppliers provide raw materials, components, services and technology.

Subcontracting

In the two areas analysed, Italian shoe producers may count on the existence of a wide network of small subcontracting enterprises specialized in one or two phases of the production cycle. According to a survey by Varaldo (1988), more than 80 per cent of the Italian footwear firms decentralize the production of bottoms, more than 70 per cent decentralize the phases of edging and sewing the uppers and more than 50 per cent subcontract the cutting phase.

Results from the sample firms confirm Varaldo's study (1988) that the production of bottoms is the phase most frequently decentralized. Table 5.10 shows that 78 per cent of the sample firms buy more than 90 per cent of soles, insoles and heels from other specialized firms. This happens because the production of bottoms is a separate phase from the rest of the process: it uses specialized machines, requires particular labour force skills and is characterized by larger scale economies than the rest of the shoe production. The producers of bottoms can therefore be considered more properly as suppliers than as subcontractors and the features of their relationships with shoe enterprises will be discussed in greater detail in the next section.

The stitching phase also tends to be decentralized to subcontractors, because it is highly labour intensive. Sometimes it is decentralized to homeworkers, who frequently are former employees of the shoe firm. In firms producing top quality products, stitching may be internalized to maintain a greater control over the process.

The cutting phase is important with respect to both the quality and cost of the final product, and it depends greatly on the labour force's abilities. As seen above in 5.2.3, there are high risks of wasting materials if mistakes are made at this stage and this can explain why cutting is less frequently decentralized than production of bottoms.

Finally, assembling and finishing are usually internalized because it is crucial to have strict control over these final phases. Decentralization to subcontractors is often adopted only as a temporary solution in case of large orders, too big for the internal capacity of the firm.

Considering the sample firms by size, in every phase, except assembling and finishing, small firms decentralize more than medium and large ones; specifically, more than 90 per cent of bottoms are bought outside by more than 90 per cent of the small firms interviewed.

Tendencies to decentralize also vary between the two areas analysed. In the cutting phase, 50 per cent of the sample firms in Brenta decentralize more than 90 per cent while in Marche the share decreases to

Table 5.10   The extent of externalizing production tasks (% of sample firms)

% of pairs externalized	0%	<50%	51%–90%	>90%
Cutting	26%	20%	20%	34%
Sewing	6%	16%	20%	58%
Bottoms	10%	10%	2%	78%
Finishing	96%	2%	2%	–

Source: author's survey

23 per cent. Moreover, the firms producing their own soles internally are all located in Marche. There are no major differences between Marche and Brenta as regards the decentralization of the edging and finishing phases.

According to the enterprises interviewed, the main reasons for decentralization are the reduction of costs (mentioned by 72 per cent of the firms), the increase in flexibility (54 per cent), the certitude of costs (28 per cent) and the increase in specialization (26 per cent). Considering firms by size, increased specialization and the certitude of costs are more relevant in small firms than in medium and large ones.

In a survey carried out by Varaldo (1988), very similar reasons for decentralization were emphasized by the firms interviewed; the main reasons being: cost advantages, possibility of increasing production while maintaining small size, high flexibility and specialization of 'stage' enterprises.

The cost advantages of externally decentralizing part of the production partly arise from greater tax evasion, higher exploitation of labour in small subcontracting enterprises and of course the freedom to break the relationship whenever sales decrease – but it is not only this. Being more specialized, subcontracting enterprises are better able to exploit the different economies of scale in the diverse phases of production, economies of scale which are relatively low in comparison with many if not most other manufacturing branches. The results are that they produce better products at lower costs, with a shorter lead-time. It may be worthwhile to point out that specialization is sometimes extreme: an example is a very small artisan firm specialized in cutting crocodile and other reptile skins that we interviewed in the network case studies in Brenta. The extremely high cost of these raw materials makes the cutting phase crucial, to avoid waste and exploit the skins to the fullest.

If these are the arguments in favour of decentralization, the firms interviewed also emphasized some problems: sometimes they have difficulties in controlling quality and obtaining punctual deliveries. This explains why the enterprises producing for the low segment of the market decentralize a large part of the production cycle to external subcontractors, while firms working for the top market are often more vertically integrated than average (Varaldo, 1988).

The shoe firms in Marche and Brenta tend to decentralize mainly within their area to facilitate the relationships with subcontractors, maintaining stable and continuous linkages with them and exerting a strict control over their work. According to the firms interviewed in the network case studies, the possibility of easy 'face-to-face' interactions helps to solve most problems rapidly and effectively.

Among the few firms which decentralize some production phases outside the districts, there are four enterprises in Marche which normally decentralize part of the edging phase to enterprises located in southern Italy. In four firms (three of them located in Brenta) edging is decentralized to eastern European countries and by one Marche firm to India. In the cases of decentralization to both southern Italy and abroad, firms have tried to exploit labour cost advantages; however, generally they mentioned many problems of quality control and deliveries. Nevertheless, decentralization of stitching and sometimes of leather cutting to eastern European countries has recently become an increasingly common strategy among Brenta firms to reduce labour costs. At the entrepreneurial association we were told about some middlemen, who have successfully begun to assist firms that want to decentralize to eastern Europe in managing quality control problems, selecting suppliers and contract compliance.

Analysing the relationships among the shoe firms and the producers of bottoms, these are very often based on a tight collaboration and, as said before, they will be described later on. Coversely, the linkages between other process specialized firms (for instance firms special-ized in the sewing or the cutting phases) and the final producers are mainly hierarchical, characterized by a strong dependence of the subcontracting firms on the shoe enterprises. Most of the subcontracting firms interviewed in the network case studies stress that their activity depends heavily on the demand of shoe producers, so that they move from periods of extra-work to periods in which they do not have enough work to occupy their workers. They are therefore obliged to demand extremely high flexibility in their workers. Often, they employ relatives or very young women, who are normally paid on a piece-rate basis. From the network case studies in Brenta, it is quite clear that most of the subcontracting firms suffer from their dependence on shoe producers, particularly during periods of crisis, because their workload can be significantly reduced and it becomes difficult to make any organizational plans; they can only wait and hope to be given work by the shoe producers.

More rarely, in these relationships there are also some aspects of cooperation. The footwear enterprises interviewed in the network case studies stated that they often supply raw materials, workforce training, technological assistance and sometimes even credit to some of their subcontractors. They have stable relationships with these subcontractors in order to have more guarantees in terms of quality and service. From the interviews, it appears that this strategy is common mainly among firms which produce a medium-high or high quality product; in this case the stability of the subcontractor relationships is an essential condition for maintaining the required quality level.

From what has been said so far we can conclude that decentralization is one of the main strategic assets of the Italian footwear industry and it is pervasive within the sample. Its extent depends on three main factors:

1. technological factors, because the different phases of the production cycle are characterized by different economies of scale;
2. structural factors, that can be represented as a trade-off between production and transaction costs: decentralization allows limits on the size of the firm and reduces labour costs but increases the costs of using the market;
3. strategic factors, such as the capability to control quality and to avoid the circulation of confidential information within the market.

Supplier relations

The existence of a very well developed system of suppliers working for the footwear sector represents one of the main assets of Italian shoe producers: it has allowed them to be competitive in a market recently characterized by stagnant demand. The ability of suppliers to manufacture a wide variety of products with short delivery times allows the shoe producers to postpone their purchases of inputs to the very last moment. This has several advantages: first of all, it reduces the inventories required for producing shoes; secondly, it leads to the progressive shortening of the period between order and delivery which characterizes the sector and, finally, it increases the capacity of shoe producers to diversify their products and satisfy market demand.

Table 5.11   Location of suppliers

		No. of firms buying inputs	
Type of inputs	Local area	Elsewhere in Italy	Abroad
Raw materials	28	47	8
Components	50	6	6
Machines	37*	25	4

Source: author's survey

* Both in Brenta and Marche, the local suppliers of machines are mainly dealers (see the section on technological linkage, p. 80)
Note: Firms interviewed gave multiple answers

This advanced system of production includes tanneries, producers of components and accessories, suppliers of machines and service firms. We will analyse the different components of the system in turn.

The tanning industry in Italy is very well developed; in 1993 there were in fact 2200-odd enterprises which employed 23 000 people and represented 50 per cent of the whole industry in Europe and 12 per cent on a global scale. The sector is concentrated in a few areas: S. Croce sull'Arno in Tuscany, Turbigo in Lombardy, Arzignano in Veneto and Solofra in Campania (UNIC, 1994).

Marche and Brenta are not among the areas of specialization in the tannery industry and in fact the sample firms buy leather directly from the producers (56 per cent) or from local retailers (34 per cent). Only a minority of them (10 per cent) sometimes import leather from abroad (Table 5.11).

Traditionally the collaboration between the tanning industry and shoe producers is very tight, based on regular twice-yearly meetings (in October and April) among some of the most important designers in the shoe sector and the main tanneries. In these meetings they define the main fashion trends and on the basis of these inputs, tanneries produce their sample collection, which is then presented at a specialized trade fair. After the presentation of the collection, the shoe manufacturers place their orders and production in the tanneries can finally begin.

Tanneries, therefore, play a very crucial role in determining the degree of competitiveness of the footwear sector. They have developed a capability of differentiating their products on the basis of their customers' specific requests. To be able to satisfy a very diversified demand in a short time, many tanneries produce semi-finished leather and store it waiting for orders to complete the production cycle. In other words, they create a warehouse of semi-finished products which are differentiated according to the market needs only in the finishing phase (Lanzara, 1988). In Brenta and Marche shoe producers usually express satisfaction about their relationships with tanneries, and these can be either direct or through a local agent. The firms interviewed in the network case studies declared that they can choose among a wide variety of products and even develop specific products for their needs with the tanneries. It may be important to stress that this possibility also exists for small orders.

Moving on to the manufacturers of components and accessories, as seen in section 5.3 (Table 5.8), there is a large concentration of these suppliers both in Marche and Brenta. In fact all the sample firms purchase at least part of their components locally. Only 24 per cent of the sample firms also purchase some of their components outside the district, in Italy or abroad (Table 5.11). The shoe firm–component producer relationship is very tight, based on continuous collaboration to develop the new fashion trends together. Both the footwear enterprises and the component firms believe that spatial proximity and the existence of long-term relationships (in many cases 15 to 20 years) are crucial factors which allow continuous interaction, facilitate comprehension and provide an important source of learning for all actors. All the component manufacturers interviewed asserted that their relationships with shoe firms external to their area are generally less collaborative and more market-orientated: they usually sell them products from their sample collection, without the possibility of developing customized products.

Altogether the relationships between shoe firms and their suppliers seem to be rather satisfactory and in fact 75 per cent of the sample firms have not encountered any particular problems and the remaining 25 per cent sometimes have to face some availability difficulties, namely delays in deliveries.

The firms interviewed declare that normally when there are problems with the suppliers they try to solve them together. In most cases it works because, as seen before, they usually have well established relationships, which due to physical proximity and the duration in time, have often become friendships. Moreover, if something goes wrong in either direction, in other words the producer of components does not supply the quality required or the shoe producer does not pay the orders, the information immediately circulates within the district. The consequence is a loss of reputation for the firm which has broken the agreement or ultimately the extreme sanction can be the exclusion from the community. This informal, but widely accepted, system of social and business rules contributes to creating a very efficient and cooperative system of production, able to satisfy a very diversified and volatile demand.

Wide circulation of information takes also place about products, because component manufacturers are the first to see the novelties and it is quite common for them to offer other firms models similar to those they are already making for one client. The diffusion of information helps smaller firms which do not have the capabilities to produce their own original sample collection to survive. On the other hand, larger firms which may invest a lot of resources in the development of new products try to defend themselves from imitation by other firms in the area through the stability of the relationships with their suppliers, based on trust and long-standing collaboration. Naturally, the component suppliers have their own interests in maintaining stable and good relationships with their best clients and will therefore avoid making exact copies of the same products in the same season for other firms.

Finally, the availability of suppliers of producer services is very high in the two districts analysed: only design, marketing and advertising services are sometimes purchased outside the districts. Nevertheless, it must be stressed that apart from design and accounting, which are carried out completely internally only in five firms, other services are rarely purchased from specialized firms. The limited use of specialized and above all of advanced services is confirmed by a software house working for many local firms, interviewed in Brenta. According to the manager of this firm, 90 per cent of his customers usually ask for very traditional services and he uses computers only for salaries and accounting; besides, only 5 per cent of the local shoe firms have adopted some systems for production planning and cost optimization. He attributes this both to a lack of supply of local firms specialized in advanced services and to a lack of demand from the shoe producers, who in many cases do not have a sufficient managerial background to understand the advantages of these innovations.

Technological linkages

Italy is the world leader in the shoe machinery sector. In 1993 it exported about US$ 360 million, followed by Germany with US$ 100 million. In the same year the footwear machinery sector comprised 315 enterprises, which employed 5000-odd people (ASSOMAC, 1994).

Most of the firms in the machinery sector are located in the area around Vigevano (Lombardy) and therefore shoe enterprises in Marche and Brenta buy their machines from local dealers (56 per cent of the sample firms) or directly from the producers (38 per cent). Only in a very few cases (6 per cent) do they import part of their machines (Table 5.11).

The development of the sector took place together with the growth of the footwear industry and the intense collaboration with the shoe producers favoured its take-off. However, the recent negative trend in the Italian footwear industry also affects results in the machinery sector: in 1991 orders in the domestic market decreased by 11 per cent and in 1992 by 6 per cent. However in 1993, thanks to the devaluation of the Lira, the decrease in orders in the domestic market was more than compensated for by the increase in exports, with the result that total sales increased by 16 per cent.

The difficulties in the domestic footwear sector have a negative impact on collaboration between technological suppliers and shoe manufacturers, and hence a bad effect on the process of technological development. Moreover, the Italian industry has also begun to feel the competition from some new comers from East Asia and particularly Taiwan, where the machinery sector has grown so rapidly as to satisfy almost 80 per cent of the whole Asian market (ASSOMAC, 1994).

The very high rate of entry and exit of firms in the footwear sector also generates a flourishing second-hand machinery market. In the Italian shoe manufacturing districts there are always several traders who buy second-hand machines from firms closing down to sell them on the domestic and the international markets. This trade slows down the adoption of new, technologically advanced machines, because many firms prefer to invest in second-hand machines to reduce their costs. Recently, the flow of second-hand machinery has been directed mainly towards foreign countries, where technology dealers sell machines from Italian firms that have gone out of business.

The relationships among the shoe producers and their suppliers of technology remain quite collaborative. Among the sample firms, 30 per cent declared that they had developed some technological innovations in cooperation with technology suppliers and 66 per cent think their main sources of information about technology are the suppliers (Tables 5.12 and 5.13). A relevant role in the diffusion of technological information is also played by exhibitions and specialized fairs according to 46 per cent of the enterprises interviewed. Finally, 16 per cent of the firms find most of the information they need in the specialized press.

Table 5.12   Sources of technical innovations

Sources of technical innovation	No. of firms
Bought ready-made	33
Adapted internally	2
Adapted in cooperation with the suppliers	15
Other	10

Source: author's survey

Note: Firms can have more than one source for their technology

Table 5.13   Sources of information for process innovation

Sources of information	No. of firms
Exhibitions/Fairs	23
Machinery suppliers	33
Specialized press	8
Other local shoe firms	4
Workers' experience	4

Source: author's survey

Note: Firms can have more than one source of information

Investments in technology are quite limited among the firms interviewed: only 22 per cent of enterprises have introduced many technological innovations over the last 5 years, 34 per cent have adopted
some innovations, 38 per cent very few innovations and 6 per cent
have not innovated at all. Large firms are more innovative than medium and small ones: in fact among large enterprises 36 per cent are
very innovative and 18 per cent have introduced some innovations while
the rates among medium firms are respectively 13 per cent and 47 per
cent and among small firms are 21 per cent and 33 per cent.

Only four large enterprises among the firms interviewed have adopted
a CAD system. In Marche, a small firm which is the only one in Italy
producing a CAD-CAM system specific for the footwear industry told
us that there are only about 100 enterprises using such a system in the
country. This firm, established at the end of 1980s, has produced a
user-friendly, low-priced and highly flexible system also suitable for
small firms and for service firms specialized in the creation and development of models. In the last few years, they sold their systems to all

the main footwear enterprises, including some specialized in the production of tennis shoes. Nevertheless they believe that the diffusion is still very slow because there is little information and some shoe manufacturers have had bad experiences in the past with similar technologies.

The other systems available on the market, which are all produced abroad, are in fact rather complex and expensive and they have been adapted from similar systems used in different sectors like textiles and clothing. Moreover, in Marche some firms were involved in a failed project for the development of a CAD-CAM system for the footwear industry, managed by ISELQUI, the regional service centre[15] and sponsored by the Regional Government of Marche and the National Entrepreneurial Association of the Footwear Industry. The main reasons for the failure of this project can be attributed to the lack of real involvement of firms in a top-down initiative, born at the regional level. According to the CAD producer interviewed and to the entrepreneurial association, the failure of this project has spread a negative impression about the usefulness and advantages of this technology among the local firms.

5.4.2 Forward linkages

In the sample, 74 per cent of the firms belong to the medium-high segment of market, 16 per cent to the medium one and 10 per cent to the top segment.[16] The firms belonging to this last segment of market are all located in Brenta. With regard to exports, 24 per cent of the sample firms export fewer than 30 per cent of their products, 30 per cent of them between 31 per cent and 70 per cent, and the remaining 44 per cent more than 70 per cent of total production. In the sample medium-sized firms are more export-orientated than small and large firms: 73 per cent of them in fact export more than 70 per cent of their production, while in small and large enterprises the proportions are respectively 33 per cent and 36 per cent.

During the last five years exports increased in 30 per cent of the sample firms, remained stable in 40 per cent and decreased in the remaining 30 per cent. 70 per cent of the firms which increased their export volume already exported more than 70 per cent of their production. The increasing penetration of the international market is therefore a strategy mainly reserved to those firms which already have a stable and significant position in it. Moreover, it may be important to observe that 73 per cent of the sample firms which decreased their export share are small enterprises.

Table 5.14   Market channels

Market channel	No. of small firms	No. of medium firms	No. of large firms
Non-exclusive agents	17	11	10
Direct to customers	5	4	2
Exclusive agents	4	3	1
Trading companies and own shops	3	0	1
Consortia with other firms	1	3	0

Source: author's survey

Note: Firms can have more than one market channel

Confirming the data presented in section 5.3, firms in Brenta are more export-orientated than in Marche: among the sample firms 55 per cent of the firms in Brenta export more than 70 per cent of their production, while in Marche only 40 per cent of the enterprises have obtained the same results on the international market.

In our sample, part of the products are sold by non-exclusive agents in 76 per cent of the firms, through direct sales to customers in 22 per cent, by exclusive agents in 16 per cent, through trading companies or in shops owned by the same firms[17] in 8 per cent and in the remaining 8 per cent through consortia with other firms (Table 5.14). The relationship with non-exclusive agents often generates discontent among footwear firms because they believe that it should be hierarchical but in fact they do not control the activity of their agents and receive very little information about the market from them. Many of the enterprises interviewed realize they would need a more active commercial strategy to be successful in an increasingly competitive market.

In the past, until the mid 1980s, the Italian footwear industry led the international market and shoe manufacturers faced a market characterized by excess demand. Many of the entrepreneurs interviewed in Italy emphasized that until a few years ago foreign buyers, mainly from Germany, used to go and visit their firms regularly and all they needed to do was to produce shoes. It was not necessary to make any effort to sell them, the quality reputation of the districts was enough to attract the customers. Therefore, traditionally the Italian shoe manufacturers did not care much about commercialization and marketing. According to the Entrepreneurial Association (ANCI, 1992), most of the entrepreneurs still identify the quality of their product only from a purely manufacturing point of view, according to the quality of processing and raw materials. Rarely are they aware of the importance of other factors like the image of their products or their brand name.

It has been argued that in the Italian footwear districts the efficient way of organizing the production phase is not complemented by an equally efficient system of commercialization (Gaibisso, 1992). In the footwear areas the role of middlemen, who have been so important in other districts, specialized in different sectors, among which we can quote the famous case of Prato and its *impannatori* (page 28), has been very limited. Only recently in Brenta have some wholesalers begun to play an important role in organizing the production of a number of small firms, but they all come from outside the district. They are foreign or Italian wholesalers, who take advantage of the production skills of some local firms unable to sell their own products on the market and therefore obliged to become subcontractors. Among the firms interviewed, the few that sell their products to buyers stressed the risk of the dependence on a few, or more often only one customer. Only one firm, interviewed in Brenta, was satisfied with this way of selling its products because it produces very high quality shoes for two well-known fashion houses and it believes that the quality of its products guarantees a high degree of bargaining power in front of its customers, who have every interest in maintaining successful and stable relationships.

Although most of the firms interviewed realize that they are very weak on the commercial side they also encountered many difficulties in creating a new, more active, attitude towards the market. In fact, in marketing, economies of scale are important and very few among the Italian firms have the financial capability to invest in advertising[18] or in market research, to set up their own shops or to employ exclusive agents. To overcome these problems a collective solution adopted in a few cases is the creation of export consortia, set up for supporting the export activity of firms with an initial public financial contribution. According to the managers of the consortia interviewed, in the first years of their activity, during the 1980s, they did not play a very active commercial role. In most cases they supplied their members with simple services like translation or assistance with export procedures.

Nowadays, some of them are changing their policy: they try to select their members in order to have firms specialized in complementary products. They then choose a few geographical areas of interest in order to concentrate their activities and try to play a more active role of promotion in those areas, in some cases directly selling their members' products. These consortia, which are rather diffused in Marche, seem to have problems taking off in Brenta where there is a great similarity of products in terms of market segment, since the main specialization is women's medium-high priced shoes. Furthermore the opinions of the entrepreneurs interviewed about consortia are quite different: a large part does not believe in the real possibility of selling their products through consortia because they are afraid to share their market and customers with competitors; others believe that consortia may play an important role in entering new markets and, finally, a small number of firms believe that consortia may represent a solution for small firms which have difficulties in creating relationships with the market.

Although it is hard to present an indicator of their real presence on the market, from the information collected it seems possible to conclude that, until now, the role of consortia in the two areas analysed has been rather limited with only a small number of firms involved in their activities. To conclude, in both districts studied there is a wide gap between a very efficient, flexible and specialized production system and a less developed, effective and specialized sales system. However, as a result of increasing international competition in the sector, it is becoming increasingly important to adopt an active commercial strategy. To successfully compete on the international market, the clusters analysed need to become as efficient in the commercial phase as in the production cycle.

5.4.3   Horizontal linkages

Evidence about formal agreements of cooperation is minimal. The only formal agreements among shoe firms found in the sample are agreements for commercial cooperation. Specifically, eight firms have created a trading company with some partners, and in most cases aimed at enter-ing in new markets. In one case, for instance, four firms specialized in complementary products together sell in the Japanese market. The main reasons for cooperating with other shoe firms are access to new markets (mentioned by 70 per cent of the firms involved in cooperation), reduction of costs (50 per cent) and improvement in access to information (30 per cent).

A strategy of growth adopted by two very successful firms interviewed is the creation of a group of firms specialized in the production of complementary products, like shoes of different quality and different market targets (for instance classical shoes for ladies and casual shoes for young ladies) or completely different products like clothes, leather goods or accessories. This strategy, rather uncommon in the Italian footwear industry, follows the example of the clothing industry, trying to supply a line of products that is as complete as possible.

The most common type of linkages among shoe firms are informal relationships: in our sample 42 per cent of the firms have frequent informal contacts with other firms in their area, 28 per cent have some contacts and the remaining 30 per cent very rarely have relationships. In Brenta informal contacts seem to be more frequent than in Marche: 50 per cent of firms have frequent relationships, 35 per cent have some contacts and 15 have rare contacts, while in Marche the rates are respectively 33 per cent, 17 per cent and 37 per cent (13 per cent of firms did not answer the question). Considering size, small (42 per cent of the small firms in the sample) and medium firms (47 per cent) have more frequent informal contacts than large firms (27 per cent) (Table 5.15). Regarding the nature of these informal ties, the most important occasions are the meetings organized by the entrepreneurial associations (42 per cent of the sample). Spatial proximity plays an important role for 24 per cent of the sample firms.

In Brenta 70 per cent of the sample firms believe that informal contacts play a very important role in their performance while in Marche this decreases to 47 per cent. With regard to size, 71 per cent of small firms, 60 per cent of medium and only 18 per cent of large enterprises believe that informal contacts are very important. Section 7.5 shows how this different approach towards informal contacts of the different categories of firms may be interpreted as a tendency of small, low performing firms to rely on informal cooperation as a sort of solidarity network for surviving.

In industrial districts firms cooperate but also compete among each other and in fact in the sample 40 per cent of the firms perceived competition as originating mainly within their local area. The main factors used by the sample firms to out-compete their rivals are price, followed by quality of products, design and speed in delivery. Price is very important, especially in local competition, while in relation to other competitors external to the district and particularly foreign competitors, quality and design become major factors used to out-compete rivals.

Competition appears, therefore, to be based on a whole range of factors, some of them like quality, design and speed are amongst the factors stressed in the literature on industrial districts, but also price

Table 5.15 Informal cooperation between sample firms

Frequency of cooperation exchange	No. of small firms	No. of medium firms	No. of large firms	Total sample firms (%)
Very frequent contacts	11	7	3	42
Some contacts	6	3	5	28
Very rare contacts	7	5	3	30

Source: author's survey

is still important, even in two well developed footwear districts such as Marche and Brenta. According to several sector experts interviewed, fierce price rivalry appears to be a common strategy in facing increased competition among small firms. In the sample 20 out of 24 small firms compete through price. In the two districts analysed competition through innovation and price competition are both present, but, as is shown in section 8.3, there are cases in which price competition is still the dominant strategy, in contradiction with the stylized model of the literature.

5.4.4 Linkages with the labour market

The existence of a reservoir of skilled labour is always assumed to be one of the externalities in highly specialized clusters of firms. The Italian industrial districts are described in the literature as areas where specialized jobs are taught to children by their parents and where skills are accumulated and transmitted from one generation to the other.

This process of collective learning, of accumulation of knowledge among people, and therefore of circulation of know-how among firms through labour force mobility, enhances local innovation capability. In other words, the innovation process, which usually takes place inside the firm, becomes a collective process in the industrial districts, based on common knowledge accumulated in people rather than firms. This mechanism was confirmed by the inquiry: the majority of the firms interviewed employ people who have already been trained in other firms. This strategy is particularly frequent among small firms, which are thus able to save on training costs.

Nevertheless, the local labour market has changed during the last ten years: a majority of the firms interviewed (55 per cent) stated that the availability of skilled labour was good during the period from 1980–

1985, while in the second half of the 1980s, 70 per cent of the firms said it had dropped. According to many entrepreneurs, the increasing lack of skilled labour is due to the tendency of young people to look for alternative jobs in other more attractive sectors, even outside their area of origin. Moreover, a larger share of young people than ever before stays in school after primary education and subsequently they want more qualified, non-manual jobs.

In Brenta in a very successful enterprise that manufacturers for the top of the market, most of the phases of the production cycle still take place by hand because, according to the entrepreneur, this is the only way to maintain the required level of quality. Walking around the plant, it was clear that most of the employees were over 50. This firm will probably close when the entrepreneur, already over 60, retires because he does not have children and in any event it would be very difficult to replace most of the old employees with other similarly skilled people. This case is not unique in the panorama of the two districts analysed.

Another entrepreneur in Brenta, which also produces high quality shoes, told us that in his firm leather cutting is done completely by hand, because he employs some very skilled workers who can do a better job than any machine. Nevertheless, he is aware that it will be very difficult to replace them with similarly skilled workers and therefore in the future it will be necessary to introduce some machines in the cutting phase.

According to the entrepreneurial associations and to a number of firms interviewed, improved welfare and better education, due to the expansion of the footwear sector in the areas, result in an increasing tendency for local young people, who are better educated than their parents, to abandon the sector if they can find alternative, mainly non-manual jobs. The resulting interruption of the accumulation and transmission of skills from parents to children, from one generation to the other could, in the future, undermine the collective learning effect which has been so important in determining the competitiveness of the districts.

Concerning the availability of unskilled labour, it seems to be rather good according to the firms interviewed: 44 per cent of them said that availability is very good, according to another 44 per cent it is rather good and in 10 per cent it is low. There are some differences between the two areas analysed: in Brenta 20 per cent of the firms interviewed believe availability is good, 55 per cent that it is average and 25 per cent that it is low, while in Marche the percentages are respectively: 60 per cent, 37 per cent and 3 cent. Recently, in Brenta, an increasing number of immigrants from African countries are being employed in some of the unskilled jobs for which it is more and more difficult to find Italian workers.

In the literature labour relationships within industrial districts have always been described as very good (see section 3.2). In Brenta where information about labour conflicts was collected, 95 per cent of the firms interviewed declared that social strife in the area has always been very low. In Marche the existence of very friendly and easy relationships with the workforce is one of the main advantages of being located in the area, stressed by a large majority of the entrepreneurs interviewed.

In the two areas labour climate is also characterized by a high flexibility of the labour force, in terms of the willingness to work extra hours and weekends. All but two of the firms interviewed declared that among their workers there is a high availability to work extra hours when needed. This flexibility is crucial in an industry such as footwear where production is almost seasonal and the orders tend increasingly to arrive at the last moment.

5.4.5 Institutional linkages

The importance of institutional support in the growth process of Italian industrial districts has been much emphasized in the literature. This has fueled the myth of an efficient local government able to intervene to support the needs of local industries, creating public or semi-public centres for real services, technological development and commercial promotion (Brusco, 1989, 1992). As seen in section 3.4, from a careful investigation of the available literature on industrial districts in Europe, the picture of institutional intervention coming out is patchy and there are few evaluations of the services supplied from the users' viewpoint.

From the investigation carried out in this study, it was clear that central government intervention was of limited importance. Only 20 per cent of the sample firms said they have received any financial incentives. Moreover, the majority of the firms complained about the enormous bureaucratic difficulties to access the incentive schemes, which mainly consist of easy credit terms for small enterprises with innovative projects. The most important public contribution concerns financial grants supplied for the establishment of some service centres and export consortia described below.

Regarding local governments, they mainly contribute with financial support for some of the initiatives promoted in the two areas by the

Table 5.16   Use of entrepreneurial associations by members

Services available	No. of firms
Advice on management	2
Advice on accounting	10
Advice on marketing	7
Courses and seminars	5
Advice on financial matters	4
Advice on tax matters	26
Organization of trade fairs	21

Source: author's survey

Note: Firms can use more than one service

entrepreneurial associations. Both in Marche and Brenta, in fact, the main institutional actors are the local entrepreneurial associations, which supply a number of services to the members and play an important role in promoting initiatives to support the sector. Among the sample firms the most used services are tax counselling and the organization of trade fairs (Table 5.16).

In Brenta, the local association ACRIB (Associazione Calzaturifici della Riviera del Brenta) was established by some local entrepreneurs more than 30 years ago and since then it has supported several initiatives like a large export consortium and a centre for technological assistance and training. In 1993 the number of members, mainly shoe producers, was 126. The export consortium (named Consorzio Maestri Calzaturieri del Brenta), created in 1967 with an initial public financing, manages collective advertising campaigns, assists firms in their export activities, and runs a databank on 20 000 customers all over the world. Moreover, the consortium organizes a collective exhibition in Dusseldorf twice a year and promotes research and market surveys. In 1986 with public money provided by a law aimed at supporting the crafts, ACRIB promoted a new initiative: the Consorzio Centro Veneto Calzaturiero. The main areas of intervention of this institution are:

(a) technology: the consortium is involved in several projects for the development of CAD-CAM systems and it supplies training courses for CAD users. There is also a project to buy a CAD-CAM system and make it available for the personal use of the members;

(b) quality control: the centre supplies a service for testing raw materials and it is connected with CIMAC in Vigevano, which is the main centre in Italy for quality control testing;

(c) environmental control: the centre supplies assistance to firms dealing with environmental problems. It also manages a service to control environmental quality within the firms;

(d) training: it runs a technical school for modelists, established in 1923. The school provides 28 different specialized programs and is attended by 400-odd students every year. The students are mainly from the area, only about 10 per cent come from other parts of Italy and very few are foreigners. Foreigners are admitted only if introduced by a local entrepreneur, because the school does not want to disseminate those skills which represent the main competitive advantages of the local enterprises to potential competitors abroad.

ACRIB, which traditionally has represented the interests of shoe producers above all else, has recently promoted some initiatives directed towards the whole *filière*, trying to create a relationship with producers of components, local vendors of raw materials and machinery. They believe that, to face the crisis, closer collaboration within the *filière* is needed to create a common strategy and further strengthen the production system. Another recent initiative of ACRIB is the organization of meetings among shoe producers and some groups of representative customers to define fashion trends jointly.

Besides ACRIB, in Brenta there is also a quite active association of artisan firms with more than 500 members in the footwear *filière* which supplies several services like book-keeping, labour and tax assistance, and consultancy for facilitating access to credit. Seven years ago the association created a centre for the promotion of products from Veneto, which includes shoes; the centre supplies assistance on export procedures and promotes market research. The association recently started a relationship with the Mexican entrepreneurial association in Guadalajara for a technological cooperation project in the component industry. The project has not yet started but the availability to cooperate affirms a different attitude from ACRIB, which, as declared by its president, has decided to refuse similar projects for international cooperation, hoping with this strategy to defend local know-how from outside competitors.

In Marche, there are two entrepreneurial associations, in Fermo and in Macerata, which supply services like training, book-keeping and fiscal and financial assistance to their members. In Fermo there are 650 members, and only 140 in Macerata because the footwear area in this province is smaller than in the area around Fermo. The two associations have recently launched a new initiative: a specialized centre (SCAM – Società per la Calzatura Marchigiana) supplying technological assistance, training, fashion information and promotional activities. The services are usually supplied at very low costs because they are partially financed by public grants (for instance the training courses are financed through EC grants). An interesting project of the centre is a monthly trade fair, where local producers exhibit and sell their products, outside the traditional seasonal appointments of the main national and international trade fairs.

During the 1980s thanks to an initial public grant several export consortia were created in Marche, to supply services like translations, fax facilities, assistance with export procedures. Recently, some of them have moved towards a more specialized variety of services like market surveys and promotional activities in new markets, like Japan, Arab countries and Australia. Among the services supplied there is also access to international databanks about customers, inventories of unsold products and subcontracting opportunities. As explained in section 5.4.2, however, the role played by export consortia is rather limited and in fact their importance has been much more stressed at institutional level than by the firms interviewed. In Marche there are also a few consortia to facilitate access to credit. One of them, promoted by the entrepreneurial association in Fermo, has 300-odd members and provides common guarantees, easy credit terms and access to long- and medium-term credit.

Both in Marche and Brenta most of the firms prefer to deal with local banks because they often know the people who work there and usually this helps in obtaining credit. However, it must be said that the easier access to credit in local banks, based on trust, friendship and high circulation of information, as opposed to national credit institutions, may become an important constraint when firms go through periods of crisis. Local banks immediately know about the difficulties and make access to credit even more difficult. This happened recently, according to a large part of the firms interviewed both in Marche and Brenta, when the reaction of local banks to the difficulties in the footwear industry was to drastically reduce credit availability to shoe firms.

To conclude, the activities of Marche and Brenta entrepreneurial associations were, in general, assessed positively by the entrepreneurs interviewed, who also participate in them quite actively. Nonetheless, the tradition of institutional intervention is more firmly established in Brenta than in Marche and this is confirmed by the well organized activities supplied by the specialized centres. In Marche, according to many of the entrepreneurs interviewed, there is little tradition of collaboration and institutional intervention and this is confirmed by

the establishment only recently of a service centre in an area of specialization which is the most important in Italy.[19] The need for greater
institutional intervention is also confirmed by the general opinion among
the entrepreneurs in Marche, who very often quote the Brenta case as
a good example of how institutions can help the sector.

5.5 THE INDUSTRIAL DISTRICT MODEL VS. THE INDUSTRIAL DISTRICT REALITY

The aim of this section is to assess the adequacy of the industrial
district model in representing the two footwear clusters analysed in
this chapter. The main empirical results are reviewed to emphasize the
most important controversies with the essential elements of the model
described in Chapter 3.

The empirical investigation has drawn a picture of two well developed industrial districts, which definitely present some of the features
characterizing the stylized model presented in the literature but also
some important differences. First of all, in the two districts there is a
strong concentration of shoe firms, suppliers, service firms, process
specialized enterprises and institutions. Within the two districts backward linkages are very intense: shoe firms interact and often cooperate
with local suppliers and besides they also have strong ties with process specialized firms to whom they subcontract a large part of the
production cycle.

Considering forward linkages, in the two districts analysed they are
rather weak: footwear enterprises have not developed their commercial
side and small and medium firms are now struggling with investments
in marketing and promotion, too costly for their size. Because of the weakness of linkages with middlemen and the low diffusion of commercial
agreements among firms, footwear enterprises, which on the production
side may count on a wide network of suppliers, process-specialized
firms and technology experts stand alone against the market, facing a
lack of financial and human resources, information and infrastructures.

With regard to horizontal linkages, the importance of informal relationships among economic actors has been strongly emphasized in
the literature on industrial districts. Many stories have been told about
people meeting at the café or the club and exchanging precious information about customers, markets, products and technology. Certainly,
these occasions for meeting and exchanging information exist in the
small towns of Marche and Brenta and the 'industrial atmosphere' is

there too, but only some of the firms tend to rely on it to any extent and attribute importance to informal relationships. Some further elaboration of the data from the sample survey presented in Chapter 7 shows that informal relationships may in fact be interpreted as solidarity networks helping enterprises to survive. They therefore assume a greater importance among poorly performing enterprises than among successful firms. The discussion about the role of informal relationships emphasizes the importance of quality of linkages, an issue which is quite neglected in the literature and which will be taken into consideration later in our work (see 7.2).

Another empirical result contrasting with the stylized facts of the model regards the availability of skilled labour, which is decreasing in the two districts analysed because of the increasing tendency of young well-educated people to search for non-manual jobs outside the footwear sector. From this issue an open question arises, concerning the possible effects of this phenomenon on the collective learning capability of the districts. How does this decrease in the availability of skilled labour affect the process of accumulation of know-how and tacit knowledge in people?

A further point to stress is related to institutional support. The role of institutions, much emphasized in the model, did not appear in the empirical analysis as a crucial element for the development of the two clusters. Above all, very little evidence was found about their importance: apart from the activities of the entrepreneurial associations which were, in general, positively assessed by the majority of the firms interviewed, there is no effective industrial policy at the local, regional or central level. Questions related to the role that institutions can play in enhancing the collective efficiency of the districts therefore remain open and these will be addressed in section 8.4.

A final, more general, issue concerns the need for a more dynamic analysis, taking into account the possibility that some internal characteristics of the districts may change and this may impact the organizational form of the system. The need to move from a static approach to a dynamic perspective will be discussed in greater detail in section 8.3.

Even in the 'land' of districts there are substantial discrepancies between the model and the real world. This point has two important consequences: first, the model has to be taken with a lot of caution, particularly by development economists who have recently begun to see the industrial district as a new alternative form of industrial development, second, there is a strong need for a dynamic approach to capture districts' reality, growth paths and stages of development.

6 The Mexican Clusters of Guadalajara and Leon

6.1 INTRODUCTION

The aim of this chapter is to present the results of the empirical investigation carried out in two clusters of footwear firms in Mexico: Guadalajara and Leon. Through a sample survey, some interviews with key informers and a few network case studies, the goal of the empirical investigation is to assess if and how the core characteristics of the textbook model correspond to the realities of two clusters of firms in an industrializing country.

The areas of investigation are two footwear clusters, which satisfy the first stylized fact of the existence of a large concentration of specialized firms. The presence of the remaining conditions are assessed by the empirical analysis, focusing on the quantity and quality of linkages between the economic actors within the clusters, as was done in the Italian survey.

The chapter is structured as follows:

(a) section 6.2 presents some background information on the Mexican footwear industry;
(b) in 6.3 there is some introductory information about the two areas of investigation;
(c) 6.4 contains the results of the survey on backward, forward, horizontal, labour and institutional linkages;
(d) finally, some preliminary reflections on these findings are presented in 6.6.

6.2 THE MEXICAN FOOTWEAR INDUSTRY

In this section some background information about the Mexican footwear industry is presented, concentrating on performance, structure of the sector and its technological characteristics.

6.2.1 The performance

For a long time Mexico was a protected market, having adopted an import-substitution strategy, which was drastically abandoned in 1988 with the opening up of the economy to foreign competition. For many decades, the Mexican footwear industry produced mainly for the domestic market with a growth rate strictly linked to the increase in domestic demand. The level of domestic per capita consumption of shoes, which sustained the growth of the industry, has traditionally been higher in Mexico than in other developing countries. In 1985–87 the average per capita consumption rate in LDCs was 0.3 pairs per year, while in Mexico it was 3 pairs (ILO, 1992). However, this level has recently dropped to 2.4 pairs per year as a consequence of the decline in real wages[1] (Dominguez-Villalobos & Grossman, 1992).

Together with the fall in domestic demand, the opening up of the Mexican market to international competition through the elimination of import licensing and tariff reduction had a big impact on the footwear industry.[2] The market was flooded with imports which increased from US$ 14 million in 1987 to US$ 148.2 million in 1991 (Table 6.1). Moreover, there was a large amount, difficult to estimate, of illegal imports.[3]

Concerning the composition of imports, 69 per cent of total imports in the period 1988–90 consisted of synthetic and textile shoes. Specifically, fabric is the segment of market most affected by imports, having increased in 1988–89 from US$ 8.5 million (3.4 million pairs) to US$ 42.4 million (16.9 million pairs). Moreover, according to the estimates of the entrepreneurial association about half of illegal imports are textile shoes (CANAICAL,[4] 1991).

In Mexico shoe imports traditionally came from the USA; however, recently countries like China, Korea and Hong Kong have assumed a dominant position (in 1990 US$ 30 million all together); their role in the Mexican market is even more important if imports from these countries which enter through the US are taken into consideration (SECOFI, 1992).

With regard to exports, in 1991 these accounted only for 7 per cent of total production even if since 1985 they have increased continuously from 3.8 million pairs (US$ 13.7 millions) to 16.2 million pairs in 1991 (US$ 104 millions) (Table 6.1) (SECOFI, 1992). About 60 per cent of exports, mainly athletic shoes produced by the *maquilladoras* located along the US border and *botas vaqueras* (cowboy boots), goes to the USA[5] (CANAICAL, 1991).

Table 6.1   The Mexican Footwear Industry, 1970–1991

Years	Manufacturing industry GDP (billion pesos)*	Leather and footwear GDP (billion pesos)*	No. of employees (leather and footwear)	Exports US$ million	Imports US$ million
1970	539.1	16.1	97 555	3.4	15.5
1975	718.9	21.8	118 292	1.1	20.8
1978	847.9	25.5	121 670	25.2	19.0
1979	934.5	28.9	138 155	30.8	17.1
1980	988.9	29.6	138 909	31.0	62.0
1981	1052.7	32.6	152 303	24.5	67.3
1982	1023.8	32.6	155 706	14.9	13.1
1983	943.5	27.7	130 521	12.1	4.6
1984	990.9	29.3	131 478	19.3	11.9
1985	1051.1	30.2	135 390	13.7	15.7
1986	995.8	28.6	135 666	18.4	9.4
1987	1026.1	24.6	128 875	53.5	13.7
1988	1059.0	24.0	119 578	67.1	54.3
1989	1135.1	24.9	117 529	67.4	75.0
1990	1201.2	25.4	114 323	80.6	86.0
1991	1245.3	24.5	n.a.	104.0	148.2

Source: INEGI, 1992

*At 1980 prices

From what has been said so far we can conclude that for many decades the domestic producers took advantage of a market where there was excess demand; making money in the sector was easy because every kind of product was sold, no matter what its quality, design and cost. Nowadays international competition is becoming stronger and the Mexican footwear enterprises are beginning to realize that they must increase their efficiency if they want to survive and grow. Many firms are currently looking for a revitalization strategy to adopt, in order to increase their competitiveness on the international and domestic markets. The 'industrial district' way of organizing production, which has been so successful in the case of the Italian footwear industry, is actually one of the models the Mexican shoe entrepreneurs are now analysing with great attention, considering its potential for application in Mexico.

6.2.2   The structure of the sector

Statistics available on the Mexican footwear industry vary according to the various sources. Official sources particularly tend to underestimate the size of the sector because of the existence of a large number of non-officially registered small enterprises that are not caught by the industrial surveys. The rest of this section therefore presents data that are in most cases estimates made by the entrepreneurial associations or by some research institutes linked to them. All these data must be taken as approximations of the structure of the sector, with a great deal of caution.[6]

According to the last available industrial census (INEGI, 1989), there are 2312 footwear enterprises with a bias towards the small size: 70 per cent of the firms employ fewer than 15 persons (10 per cent of total employment and 9 per cent of total value added), 24 per cent employ between 16 and 100 persons (33 per cent of total employment and 24 per cent of total value added), 4 per cent have between 101 and 250 employees (23 per cent of total employment and 29 per cent of total value added) and finally 2 per cent of the firms have more than 251 employees (34 per cent of total employment and 37 per cent of total value added). The entrepreneurial association of the footwear industry estimates 5373 shoe firms, with a similar size distribution: 96.5 per cent of the firms employing fewer than 100 people, 2.5 per cent between 100 and 250 and only 1 per cent more than 251 (CANAICAL, 1994). Table 6.2 shows that the significant difference between the two sources is due to under-reporting of the smaller firms in the official sources.

The Mexican footwear industry is spatially concentrated in three areas. Table 6.3 shows that 51 per cent of the enterprises are in Leon (Guanajuato), 22 per cent in Guadalajara (Jalisco), 12 per cent in Mexico City and its outskirts (*Distrito Federal* – Federal District) and the remaining 15 per cent are spread out in the rest of the country (CEESP, 1993a).

With regard to product specialization, 73 per cent of the shoes produced are made with leather uppers, 9 per cent are plastic or textile shoes, 4 per cent athletic shoes, 3.5 per cent work boots, 3 per cent cowboy boots, 3 per cent sandals, 3 per cent slippers and 1.5 per cent other types of shoes (CANAICAL, 1991). There is a certain amount of specialization among the three main areas of production: in Leon many shoes for men and children are produced, Guadalajara is specialized in women's shoes and the *Distrito Federal* produces mainly athletic shoes.

Concerning the different market segments: 12 per cent of production is in the top quality segment, 40 per cent in the medium bracket and 48 per cent in the inexpensive segment[7] (CEESP, 1993a).

Table 6.2　Size structure of the Mexican shoe industry

Firms size according to no. of workers	No. of firms (source 1)	No. of firms (source 2)
1–15	1 615	–
16–100	560	5 184*
101–250	101	134
251 +	36	55
Total no. of firms	2 312	5 373
Total no. of workers	69 179	140 000

Source: (1) INEGI, 1989 and (2) CANAICAL, 1994

* 1–100 workers

Table 6.3　Spatial structure of the Mexican shoe industry

State	No. of firms	Total number of firms (%)
Guanajuato	2730	50.8
Jalisco	1176	21.9
Mexico DF	628	11.7
Rest of the country	839	15.6
Total	5373	100.0

Source: CEESP, 1993

It is important to emphasize that the sector is predominantly owned by Mexican entrepreneurs; very few enterprises in the country have a foreign majority share holding. In the footwear industry the phenomenon of *maquilladoras* is more limited than in other sectors, such as the electronics, automotive and clothing industries; in 1990 the number of employees in the leather and footwear *maquilladora* industry was about 7000 which is only 5 per cent of the total employment in the sector (Banco de Mexico, 1991).

Finally, as stated earlier, the vast majority of firms originated as artisan businesses, and many of them are still owned by the same family. In summary, the sector is dominated by small and medium-sized, family firms, spatially concentrated in three different, highly specialized areas. Geographical and sectoral concentration of firms are the two primary features for identifying a cluster of firms.

6.2.3 Technology in the Mexican footwear industry

The different phases of footwear production cycle and their technological characteristics have been described in section 5.2.3, concluding
with the observation that footwear technology is not characterized by
dramatic changes in recent decades. There are no enormous technological gaps between developed and developing countries. Specifically, although among the sample firms the level of innovation is lower
in Mexico than in Italy, it can be added that there are no tremendous
differences between the technological level of the two footwear industries under consideration. Therefore most considerations in section 5.2.3
can be applied to the Mexican industry as well.

According to some estimates of CIATEG[8] in 1991, 46 per cent of
Mexican shoe firms could be defined as artisan from a technological
standpoint, carrying out most of the production process by hand, 44
per cent as partially automated and the remaining 10 per cent as automated. The main differences between the two last categories are in the
assembly phase, which in the most advanced firms is done with a larger
number of specialized machines that carry out operations otherwise
done by hand.

During the 1980s, a progressive process of decapitalization took place
in the Mexican footwear industry and generated a gradual obsoles-
cence of the existing equipment (Banco de Mexico, 1991). Dominguez-
Villalobos and Grossman (1992) also confirm the process of
decapitalization occurring in the footwear industry, with their inquiry
in which most of the firms stated that they did not acquire any new
machines during the last five years.[9]

According to the same study, most acquisitions among the Mexican
firms which introduced new machines belong to the category of semi-
automatic, specialized machinery, sometimes with some rudimentary
electronic controls. The main reasons for adoption stressed by the firms
are: first reduction of turnaround time; second, quality improvement;
and finally labour cost savings. The introduction of new technologies
was mostly devoted to the phases of stitching and embroidering.

Another important aspect to emphasize is the high level of excess
capacity registered in the Mexican footwear industry in the last years.
According to some recent estimates the total production capacity of
the footwear industry stands at 300 million pairs annually, but current
production is approximately 160 million. Moreover, a study on the
footwear industry in Leon reveals that 70 per cent of the firms interviewed[10] do not use their machinery to full capacity (CIATEG, 1992).

A final important point to stress, emphasized by the Boston Consulting Group (1988) and Dominguez-Villalobos and Grossman (1992) studies, is the trend amongst the most innovative firms to introduce organizational innovations, along with technological innovations. The model for reorganizing the production process for most of the firms is the pair-by-pair methodology. This is widely used in the Brazilian footwear industry, and is based on the idea that the production cycle is a *continuum*: when a pair enters the assembly line it has to go through the whole cycle without interruptions; whereas in the traditional way every single phase is considered as a separate entity from the others. The expected advantages are: first a reduction of inventories, second an increase in labour flexibility; third greater uniformity in quality and finally a cut down of 'dead' time (Prochnik, 1992).

'Just-in-time' is another organizational innovation which some of the most progressive firms intend to introduce in the future; however, the reality of the Mexican footwear industry is very far from an ideal environment in which to introduce such an organizational technique. As shown in section 6.3.1, relationships between suppliers and shoe producers are difficult in terms of quality and service. Moreover, the introduction of just-in-time requires efficient inventory control, good knowledge of production scheduling and availability of trained and highly motivated management and staff (Mody *et al.*, 1992). Unfortunately, none of these elements are readily available in the Mexican footwear industry.

Finally, one method adopted in a few cases to reduce the impact of the high rates of labour turnover and absenteeism is the introduction of multifunctional workers, able to undertake several different job functions in the production process and therefore to increase labour flexibility within the firm.

With the adoption of these new organizational models, firms seem to have room for increasing in productivity even without new costly investments in technology and for augmenting flexibility internally and also in their linkages with suppliers and with the market.

6.3   GUADALAJARA AND LEON

The two areas where the survey was conducted are the two most important concentrations of firms in Mexico producing leather street shoes (Figure 6.1). This section presents some background information about their economy and the history of the footwear industry.

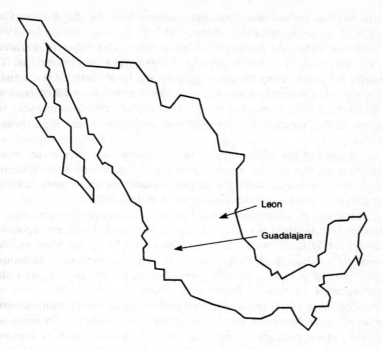

Map 6.1   The Mexican footwear clusters.

Guadalajara

Guadalajara, capital of the state of Jalisco, located at north-west of Mexico City, is the second largest city in the country[11] and the third most important industrial centre after Mexico City and Monterrey. The economy of Guadalajara is traditionally characterized by a high presence of small firms in sectors like food, textiles and shoes (Arias, 1985; Alba Vega & Roberts, 1990). Ever since the last century, in Guadalajara there has been a tradition of shoe production in small workshops to satisfy the local demand. In the second decade of this century, thanks to the continuous growth of the local market and the improvement in communications with the rest of the country, the sector started to expand and was transformed from an artisanal to an industrial activity. In 1927 there were 34 plants producing shoes, one making lasts and one tannery; about 100 small shoe workshops were also located in the town. In that period, the footwear industry was the most important industrial sector in the town (Arias, 1992a).

From the 1930s, the footwear industry began to develop rapidly thanks to the presence of a US enterprise, United Shoe Machinery, which contributed in spreading the know-how among local enterprises. In 1942 the Regional Chamber of the Footwear Industry (Camara Regional de la Industria del Calzado) was established and in 1959 Guadalajara was chosen as the location for the National Footwear Trade Fair (Arias, 1992a).

At the end of the 1950s, the footwear industry was one of the most important sectors in the economy of Guadalajara and with 750-odd firms, was the sector with the largest number of employees (25 000 according to some estimates presented in Arias, 1992a). In the following years, the manufacturing structure of Guadalajara increased its diversification. In 1991 the most important sectors in the manufacturing industry of Jalisco[12] were: the food industry (38 per cent of the regional manufacturing product), the textile-clothing, footwear and leather industries (18 per cent) and the petrochemical industry (11 per cent) (Secretaria de Promocion Economica, 1993).

According to the estimates of the entrepreneurial association, in 1993 the number of footwear firms was about 1100 with 25 000-odd employees, which produce 27 per cent of all footwear made in Mexico. With regard to size distribution, 56 per cent of the footwear enterprises have fewer than 15 employees, 37 per cent fewer than 100, 5 per cent fewer than 250 and only 2 per cent are large firms with more than 250 employees (Table 6.4) (CANAICAL, 1994).

Data about the weight of the industry in terms of employment and value added of the four different size categories are only available from the industrial census and therefore they have to be considered with caution.[13] Moreover, in Guadalajara, the presence of the giant firm Calzado Canadà, with about 10 000 employees in its different activities linked with the footwear industry, generates a bias towards the large sized firms which, in fact, is not representative of the reality of the industry.[14] According to the census, micro enterprises account for 6 per cent of total employment and 2 per cent of value added in the footwear sector of Jalisco, small firms respectively for 25 per cent and 13 per cent, medium enterprises for 14 per cent and 11 per cent and finally large firms for 55 per cent of employees and 74 per cent of value added (INEGI, 1989).

Table 6.4   The footwear industry in Guadalajara and Leon

Firm size according to no. of workers	Guadalajara	Leon
1–15	656	1 263
16–100	434	1 170
101–250	58	216
251 +	25	81
Total no. of firms	1 173	2 730
Total no. of workers	25 000	70 000

Source: CANAICAL, 1994

Leon

Leon is a town with about one million inhabitants, located in the state of Guanajuato (north of Mexico City). Its industrial development has been favoured by its central location, along one of the main routes connecting Mexico City to the North of the country and to the United States. In 1900, footwear was already the second most important industry, after the textile and clothing sector in terms of number of jobs. In 1940, it became the most important industrial sector and some related industries started to develop. During the Second World War, the footwear industry in Leon expanded significantly thanks to a large increase in exports to the USA (Labarthe, 1985).

Since then, the footwear industry has dominated the industrial system of Leon, where 55 per cent of the industrial employees in the state of Guanajuato are concentrated.[15] In 1992, 40 per cent of total employment in the industrial sector in the city of Leon was in the leather (9 per cent) and footwear (31 per cent) industries. Moreover, the footwear *filière* accounts for 15.5 per cent of the GDP of Guanajuato and for 68 per cent of the GDP of the city of Leon (CEESP, 1993a).

According to the estimates of the entrepreneurial association, in 1993 the number of footwear enterprises was about 2700 employing 70 000-odd people. Concerning size distribution, 45 per cent of the enterprises had fewer than 15 employees, 43 per cent fewer than 100 employees, 8 per cent fewer than 250 and 3 per cent more than 250 people (Table 6.4) (CANAICAL, 1994).

According to the industrial census, micro enterprises account for 11 per cent of employment and 13 per cent of the value added in the footwear industry in Guanajuato, small enterprises for 38 per cent and

28 per cent, medium firms for 26 per cent and 33 per cent and, finally, large firms for 25 per cent of employment and 25 per cent of the value added (INEGI, 1989).

From the above information a conclusion can be drawn: both Guadalajara and Leon are characterized by a strong concentration of footwear enterprises and by a long tradition in this field. The existence of a critical mass is the first condition of the industrial district model, which in the empirical survey is, by choice, satisfied *a priori*. A last observation may be useful to point out that Guadalajara, notwithstanding the existence of the critical mass of firms, differs from the typical industrial district model, because it is a large town with a diversified economy, in which the footwear industry is only one of the most important industries. Leon, instead, is closer to the 'model' because is smaller and its economy is dominated by the footwear industry.

6.4 RESULTS OF THE FIELD WORK

The field work in Mexico followed a method similar, in most aspects, to the Italian survey (see Appendix 1): a questionnaire inquiry, a number of open interviews to key informers and some in-depth network case studies. The randomly chosen sample comprises 51 enterprises: 30 of them located in Guadalajara and 21 in Leon. In order to include firms of different sizes in the sample 17 enterprises employ fewer than 50 people, 14 between 51 and 100 and 20 more than 100 (Table 6.5).

Following the same framework adopted for the presentation of the results of the Italian field work, this section assesses the existence and the quality of backward, forward and horizontal linkages among firms, of linkages with the labour market and finally of institutional linkages.

Before presenting the study of linkages, here are some general features of the sample firms:

1. with regard to product specialization, not every firm is specialized in just one type of shoe, 14 of them produce a mix of products;
2. almost 70 per cent of the firms were established after 1970; however, some of the new firms are in fact transformations of old firms into new companies for fiscal reasons, and others were recently created by second generation entrepreneurs, who decided to diversify the family business by entering a new segment of the market;
3. the vast majority of the sample firms are family firms. However, there are a few cases of firms established by people who had for

Table 6.5 The sample

No. of firms	<50 employees	51–100 employees	>100 employees	Total firms
Guadalajara	12	9	9	30
Leon	5	5	11	21
Total firms	17	14	20	51

Source: author's survey

long been working in other local firms, often as supervisors. Frequently, their former employers helped them to start up their new business, and then they often work as subcontractors for them;
4. all the entrepreneurs interviewed have local origins. Only in very few cases did the father of the entrepreneur come from another part of the country to establish a shoe firm in Guadalajara or Leon.

6.4.1 Backward linkages

As in 5.4.1, this section distinguishes between subcontractors, suppliers of raw materials, components, services and technology.

Subcontracting

In Mexico, according to several recent surveys (Boston Consulting Group, 1988; Concalzado, 1991; Dominguez-Villalobos & Grossman 1992) and to the results of this survey, the degree of division of labour is generally low (Table 6.6) and certainly much lower than in Italy (see Table 5.11) in all the various phases of the production cycle. Mexican shoe firms generally decentralize some phases of the production cycle only when they receive orders too large for their internal capacity. About 50 per cent of the sample firms does not externalize any stage of the production process.

This low level of the division of labour can be explained by two factors:

1. backward-linked industries have remained at a low level of development with regard to design, fashion content, quality of components and service because protection of the domestic market has limited competition and, therefore, the incentive to innovate. We know from Adam Smith that the division of labour is limited by the extent of the market and this seems to apply to the Mexican case;

Table 6.6   The extent of externalizing production tasks (% of sample firms)

% of pairs externalized	0%	<50%	51–90%	>90%
Cutting	94%	6%	–	–
Sewing	80%	20%	–	–
Bottoms	59%	4%	4%	33%
Finishing	100%	–	–	–

Source: author's survey

2. the sector lacks a standard technical language and a common, universally accepted, system of measurement and this strongly increases transaction costs.[16]

The poor level of development and the difficulties in communicating with backward-linked industries induce many shoe firms to internalize as many phases of the production cycle as possible in order to reduce their dependency on an unstable, low quality supply. Vertical integration means that the whole production cycle is carried out inside the firm, with a lot of organizational problems, because, as seen in section 5.2.3, the different phases are characterized by very different economies of scale, different skills, different degrees of labour intensity and different processing times. This production structure is even common among very small enterprises. For instance, in a very recently established firm interviewed, with about 25 employees, every phase of production, from leather cutting to sole production, to finishing, was internalized. The manager of this firm was very proud of its ability to producing everything internally, without depending on outside suppliers.

Among the sample firms decentralization, even if it is not widely practised, shows a positive relation with profits: 47 per cent of the decentralizing firms have attained an average profit, 21 per cent a very good profit, while only 24 per cent earned no profit or incurred a loss (the remaining 8 per cent did not answer the question). For firms which do not decentralize the percentages are respectively: 33 per cent, 17 per cent, 50 per cent.

Among Mexican shoe firms, decentralization seems, therefore, to have a positive effect on performance, flexibility and specialization. These positive results together with the diffused knowledge about the highly decentralized Italian production system have recently induced a greater use of subcontracting among Mexican firms. This was confirmed by several sector experts interviewed in Guadalajara and Leon. There is an increasing number of firms which, after having interrupted their activity as shoe producers because they were hit by fierce competition, began to work as subcontractors specialized in the production of uppers. However, the subcontracting firms interviewed during the network case studies stated that they strongly depend upon and suffer from the still very unstable flow of work from the shoe producers. According to them, this instability limits possibilities for the development of a well-organized and efficient system of process specialized enterprises, such as occurs in the Italian districts.

In two of the enterprises interviewed for the network case studies, an alternative strategy to overcome some of the quality control and reliability problems of subcontracting firms, without having to tackle the difficulties of vertical integration, is the creation or the participation in firms specialized in some specific phases of the production cycle. Several interviews with sector experts confirmed that this strategy is increasingly adopted by firms that want to diversify their activities and grow externally, as an alternative to the traditional strategy of vertical integration.

The main reasons for decentralization stressed by the sample firms are: the lack of a specialized labour force (by 25 per cent of the firms), the search for high flexibility (23 per cent) and the need to reduce labour costs (23 per cent). Concerning labour costs, a strategy recently adopted by some firms in Leon is the subcontracting of labour-intensive phases, such as sewing and *teijido* (puckered seam), to artisan firms or homeworkers located in small villages around the countryside.

These first attempts were supported by the local Camara del Calzado which helped reach an agreement with the local authorities for obtaining a space to start the manufacturing activity at favourable conditions. Local authorities have also sponsored training courses to facilitate the introduction of the rural local labour force in the footwear industry. Entrepreneurs involved in this decentralization experiment are satisfied with the initial results: first, because the cost of rural labour is lower than in the urban cities; secondly, because in rural areas there is a large underemployed labour force and in Leon the labour force has recently begun to be a scarce resource (see section 6.4.3); finally, in small rural villages absenteeism among workers is very low and flexibility (willingness to work extra hours or during the weekends) is extremely high. Anyway, it is important to emphasize that if many of the entrepreneurs interviewed have stated a willingness to move the most labour-intensive phases of the production cycle away from Leon, none of them would like to move the whole firm outside the urban area, because they do not want to lose the clustering advantages of being located in a specialized centre. Almost all the entrepreneurs interviewed are, in fact, very conscious of the advantages deriving from being located close to suppliers, in a town where circulation of information is very high and, being well known for shoe production, it attracts many customers.

From what we have seen so far, we can conclude that in the Mexican footwear industry the decentralization of some phases of production has some positive impact on performance and efficiency and it is, therefore, a strategy several firms in Guadalajara and Leon are trying to pursue. However, to increase the degree of division of labour, the Mexican footwear industry needs to become a well-organized system where shoe producers may rely on quality and prompt deliveries and where on the other hand subcontracting firms may count on a more stable demand. From this point of view the Italian footwear districts may actually provide some interesting lessons.

Supplier relations

It is not an easy task to draw a picture of the different sectors of suppliers in Mexico due to a lack of statistical information: in Leon and in Guadalajara the exact number of firms which produce components and raw materials for the footwear sector is not known and there are only specific studies about the tanning industry. This section presents the information collected through interviews with suppliers, with shoe firms and with sector experts.

According to a study from the Boston Consulting Group (1988), in Mexico there are 700-odd tanneries, 95 per cent of which are in Leon. Moreover, the entrepreneurial association of tanneries (ANACU – Asociación Nacional de Curtidores) estimates that in Leon there are also about 200 unregistered tanneries. The leather industry is dominated by small-sized enterprises: 68 per cent of tanneries employ fewer than 10 people, 20 per cent employ fewer than 30 people and 12 per cent more than 30 people. Medium and large tanneries account for about 80 per cent of total production.

The Mexican leather industry is highly vertically integrated: according to the entrepreneurial association about 85 per cent of the firms internalize the entire production cycle. Vertical integration has a negative impact on product quality because it permits a very low level of specialization, it reduces flexibility and increases processing times. In Italy, where the inter-firm division of labour is very high, the average delivery time is between 15 to 25 days, while in Mexico it runs from 30 to 45 days.

When considering the component industry, like soles, insoles, heels, lasts and accessories, there are no data available in the official statistics and the only source of information to obtain a general picture about these backward-linked industries is the directory of the members of the National Association of Suppliers of the Footwear Industry (ANPIC – Asociación Nacional de Proveedores de la Industria del Calzado).[17] In the ANPIC directory there are a total of 126 enterprises, including trading companies, and particularly there are about four enterprises producing lasts, six plastic heels, five synthetic soles and three small metal accessories. The majority of component and accessory producers are located in Leon. In Guadalajara, apart from a few important sole and heel manufacturers, there are mainly retailers, or sometimes the plants of Leon's producers. Notwithstanding the small concentration of component producers, when compared with the two Italian districts analysed in Chapter 5, sample firms buy the majority of their inputs locally. The most relevant exceptions are lasts, which 80 per cent of the firms in Guadalajara buy in Leon and accessories, which half of the firms, both in Guadalajara and in Leon, buy elsewhere in the country or abroad.

According to some estimates by sector experts, only about 30 per cent of suppliers produce a competitive product in terms of quality, fashion, design and service. The producers of lasts and leather soles are generally indicated as good suppliers offering a good quality product; on the other hand, apart from a few exceptions, the producers of synthetic soles have problems with quality and fashion content; finally, the accessory sector is almost absent.

Many of the sample firms complain about the low quality of components and raw materials, the scarce attention to fashion changes and the bad service provided by their input suppliers. Shoe producers are usually very dissatisfied about their relationships with raw material and component suppliers because they can only buy what is offered on the market, without much possibility of obtaining products suited to their needs. The entrepreneurs interviewed in the network case studies generally defined their relationships with suppliers as market relations and in a few cases as dependency relationships. The entrepreneurs, who believe they depend on their suppliers, complain about the limited supply of products and the imposition of payment and delivery terms, which they have to accept due the lack of alternatives on the domestic market.

In turn, the suppliers interviewed do not accept complete responsibility for their low development and accuse the shoe entrepreneurs of having always adopted a strategy focused more on price than quality. Suppliers complain of unstable demand, small orders, continuously changing products and payment delays. Both the suppliers of components and the manufacturers blame each other and the main shortcomings are in communication and collaboration between the two linked sectors.

However, with the opening of the domestic market and the increase in shoe and component imports, the relationships between shoe producers and suppliers are improving and becoming more collaborative. The majority of the suppliers interviewed agree that they now try to work close to their customers in developing products and they are also available to adapt products to the needs of the shoe producers. On the other hand, some of the footwear firms interviewed in the network case studies are now more satisfied about their relationships with suppliers and they are trying to set up stable linkages, building up an ability to cooperate in defining fashion trends and product characteristics.

One of the interviews for the network case studies in Guadalajara took place in the plant of a sole producer where the shoe entrepreneur was spending the day so that they could work on a new model of sole together. Both shoe producers and input suppliers agree that a different attitude towards difficulties is also spreading: instead of changing suppliers, the shoe producers now try to collaborate with them to solve the problems. Moreover as in the Italian districts, when a supplier does not respect the agreements or is unable to supply the requested quality, its bad reputation affects its image among a large number of firms, because information circulates rapidly within the district.

To increase the stability of demand, some groups of shoe producers have tried to organize common purchases. Some wholesalers are also working in this direction, organizing the purchases of components and raw materials for all their clients and therefore guaranteeing large and stable orders for the suppliers. Moreover, both in Leon and Guadalajara, the local Credit Unions of shoe entrepreneurs have recently launched a programme for pool purchasing; their objective for the near future is to import components from abroad jointly. The import of components is not seen as a real alternative to the development of a competitive domestic supply because shoe entrepreneurs realize that day-to-day collaboration with local suppliers would be the best strategy both in terms of cost and product quality. Nevertheless, they see imports as a temporary solution to overcome the current limitations of the domestic supply, hoping that this could also represent an incentive for local suppliers to bring their products up to international standards.

Some efforts towards a more cooperative attitude between shoe producers and suppliers have also been undertaken by the Camara del Calzado and ANPIC in Leon, which have begun to organize meetings to discuss and jointly elaborate fashion trends. Together with the Camara del Calzado in Guadalajara, the two associations in Leon have also begun to work on the standardization of the measurement system. The lack of a standard, commonly accepted measurement system is a major obstacle for the development of an efficient system of specialized firms. The case of lasts is well representative of the situation: in Mexico every footwear firm requires its own models, based on a measurement system which is different for every firm. The entrepreneurial associations' programme, managed by a German consulting firm, has not yet achieved substantial results. Some more effective results have instead been attained through an informal agreement between the two largest producers of lasts and the largest manufacturers of heels and soles to sell compatible components, made according to a common measurement system. Through this agreement they hope to gradually be able to impose their measurement system on the market, convincing an increasing number of smaller firms to harmonize their systems.

An important incentive to improve the quality of products and services in the component and raw materials industries can also come from foreign investments, which can take the form of joint ventures, technological cooperation, licensing or equity agreements. Technological cooperation with Italian, Spanish or Brazilian firms has recently increased and a few successful cases have been found among our sample firms. The Camara del Calzado of Guadalajara has developed a project for the creation of an industrial park where some producers of components, established in joint ventures with foreign partners, could be located. The feasibility study of the park will be financed by the EU, which will also make available easy credit terms to firms interested in investing in the initiative. For the realization of the project there are already some informal contacts between the Camara del Calzado and the association of artisan firms in Brenta (see 5.4.5).

Finally, considering services, local availability seems rather good in the two areas analysed. The only type of services which is sometimes bought outside the clusters is design (13 enterprises), while the other services, accounting, machinery repair, software, advertising are all bought from local firms or internalized. As already emphasized in the Italian districts, in Mexican firms too the demand of services is very traditional and in general in this respect there are no particular complaints from the sample firms, which seem to satisfy most of their needs on the local market.

To conclude, in the Mexican clusters notwithstanding the local concentration of suppliers, the lack of competition has often reduced the advantages in terms of price and service deriving from the good local availability. Nevertheless, with the opening of the market the quality of linkages between suppliers and manufacturers have begun to improve. There are in fact some recent examples of initiatives undertaken to foster the systematic approach in the two clusters analysed, showing a real effort towards building up a system of production that is in some way inspired by the industrial district model.

Technology suppliers

In Mexico most of the machines for the footwear industry are imported: about 80 per cent from Italy and the rest from Brazil, Spain and Taiwan. Only about 20 per cent of the machines in use in the Mexican footwear industry are produced locally, mainly by very small mechanical firms, which build very simple machines at a competitive cost in comparison with the more sophisticated imported machine tools.[18]

According to the survey, Mexican footwear firms in Guadalajara and Leon mainly buy new machines from local dealers. There are, however, cases in which machines are imported directly through a middleman usually at lower cost, but with a problem for after-sales service, which is not guaranteed by the local agents. According to the sector experts, there is also a large second-hand market with machines coming mainly from the US, Italy and Brazil.

Only a few of the technology suppliers guarantee complete service, which includes training, maintenance, adaptation of the machines to the specific needs of the firm and consultancy about technological innovations coming up on the market. Only 20 per cent of the sample firms have cooperated with suppliers of technology to develop some process innovations, while 66 per cent of them have simply bought innovations ready made in the market and 12 per cent have made some adaptations to this technology (Table 6.7). We must add that the overall picture is clearly one of little technical progress, lower than in the two Italian districts: only 18 per cent of the sample firms say they have introduced many innovations over the last 5 years and 20 per cent have not innovated at all. Besides, small firms are definitely less innovative than medium and large ones: 82 per cent of them, in fact, did not innovate at all or introduced only very few innovations, while the rates among medium and large firms are respectively 32 and 25 per cent.

Table 6.7   Sources of technical innovation

Sources of technical innovation	No. of firms
Bought ready-made	32
Adapted internally	6
Adapted in cooperation with the suppliers	10
Other	5

Source: author's survey

Note: Firms can have more than one source for their technology

Only 20 per cent of the sample firms gives technology suppliers as an important source of information about technology. More important sources are: the specialized trade fairs, according to 58 per cent of the sample firms, and other shoe firms, according to 28 per cent (Table 6.8). With regard to the circulation of information among shoe firms, this takes place usually among groups of firms which are linked by family or friendship ties and within the *agrupamientos industriales*,[19] which organize regular visits to their members' workshops. It is important to note that otherwise the shoe entrepreneurs interviewed in the network case studies said that they do not usually allow other entrepreneurs to visit their plants.

In a few cases among the enterprises interviewed, there are some foreign experts who supply technological consultancy. Foreign experts, who often come from Brazil[20] and sometimes Italy, are provided to the shoe firms in most of the cases by foreign subcontractors or wholesalers[21] and they have the duty to control quality and assist shoe producers in improving their production process from a technological and organizational standpoint. Visits by foreign technological experts are a service which is also provided by the two entrepreneurial associations in Leon and in Guadalajara.

To conclude, technological cooperation is not very intense in the two clusters analysed, the innovation level is generally low and most of the machines are bought ready-made on the market. The lack of a domestic industry specialized in the production of machinery for the shoe sector is probably the main drawback to increasing technological cooperation and introducing innovation.

Table 6.8   Sources of information for process innovation

Source of information	No. of firms
Exhibitions/Fairs	29
Machinery suppliers	10
Specialized press	9
Other local shoe firms	14
Workers' experience	6

Source: author's survey

Note: Firms can have more than one source of information

6.4.2   Forward linkages

The firms in the sample manufacture for different segments of the market:[22] 23 per cent of them are specialized in the high-priced segment, 59 per cent in the medium-priced range, 18 per cent in the low segment. With regard to exports, 10 per cent of the sample firms export less than 10 per cent of their products, 15 per cent between 10 per cent and 40 per cent and only 8 per cent more than 40 per cent. The most export-orientated firms are large, located in Leon and they mainly export 'cow-boy' boots.

Considering marketing channels, 74 per cent of the sample firms sell part of their production through non-exclusive agents, 51 per cent through wholesalers and finally 16 per cent through trading companies or shops owned by the same firms and another 16 per cent directly to retailers (Table 6.9). According to some estimates reported in a study by Boston Consulting Group (1988), the structure of distribution is the following: independent retailers have around 40 per cent of the market, chains have 20 per cent, supermarkets have 20 per cent and the remaining 20 per cent is distributed by wholesalers.

The Mexican footwear industry traditionally neglected commercialization and marketing because, as shown above (6.2.1), the domestic market was closed to international competition for a long time and this allowed the domestic producers to produce shoes which were easily sold in the closed market, no matter what the quality, design, fashion content were. Generally speaking, therefore, the Mexican footwear firms suffer from problems similar to those of the Italian enterprises: they have limited control over their market and little knowledge of it; they depend on non-exclusive agents and they are not used to adopting an

Table 6.9   Marketing channels of products

Market channels	No. of small firms	No. of medium firms	No. of large firms	% of total sample firms
Non-exclusive agents	13	8	16	74%
Buyers	8	8	10	51%
Trading companies and own shops	1	3	4	16%
Direct to retailers	2	3	3	16%

Source: author's survey

Note: Firms can have more than one channel for marketing

active commercial strategy to sell their products on a competitive market. Among 63 per cent of the sample firms the main factor of competition is price; only 24 per cent of the firms interviewed believes that design is an important factor and 12 per cent that quality is important.

One of the main consequences of a very fragmented distribution system dominated by independent retailers is the small size of orders: according to the Boston Consulting Group study the most frequent size of orders in the domestic market is around 300 pairs, but sometimes shoe producers receive orders for very few pairs. The possibility of working on the basis of larger orders and therefore to be able to plan production process on a longer term basis and to exploit the economies of scale deriving from specialization in a few products, is the main reason that has pushed an increasing number of firms to sell to retail chains and supermarkets. Another important reason stressed by some of the firms interviewed is related to better payment terms, guaranteed by retail chains and supermarkets as compared with small family shops.

According to the firms interviewed which sell to retail chains, the relationships are definitely of dependency because these chains generally adopt a strategy based on the search for the lowest possible price on the market. Many stories are told about some of these chains contacting some firms to buy their models and then commissioning other firms, on the illegal market, to manufacture the same products at a lower price. Some of these chains are also believed to be responsible for most of the illegal imports of very cheap synthetic or fabric shoes, which have invaded the low-price market during the last few years.[23]

However, one of the firms interviewed in the network case studies told us that, although most of the retail chains still maintain a very traditional strategy of commercialization based on price, some of them, and particularly supermarkets, are progressively increasing their attention to quality and therefore some of the shoe producers try to limit their dependency on them, increasing the stability of their relationship by supplying good service and a stable quality of product.

Recently, an interesting experiment was started aimed at developing a stable and constructive relationship thanks to a few wholesalers.[24] They have adopted a new strategy aimed at selling a quality product and have therefore selected a group of shoe firms with which to collaborate. Technical staff employed by the wholesalers regularly call on the shoe enterprises, controlling quality and giving advice on technological and organizational matters; moreover the wholesalers organize a system of pool purchases of some key components or raw materials like leather, in order to guarantee a stable quality level, better prices and good service. Among the firms interviewed, the ones linked to wholesalers through such a relationship were generally very satisfied, not only with the sales, but mainly with the complementary services, like technological and organizational assistance, they receive. Many of them have been able to introduce important improvements in the organization of the production process and in the quality of their products thanks to the collaboration with these wholesalers.

Naturally, the firms involved realize that depending on one main customer, who can always find another enterprise able to make the same product at a lower price, is very risky; but most of the firms also realize that they do not have enough marketing and commercialization skills to compete on the market on their own. Therefore they try to build up a linkage with the wholesalers where both parties have an interest in collaborating, at least partially offsetting dependency.

Also in the export market Mexican shoe firms depend on foreign buyers, who often provide the characteristics of the products, the raw materials, technological assistance and sometimes credit to their suppliers, selected on the basis of product quality and price. In most of the cases the relationships with foreign buyers are very unstable; only very few sample firms have stable linkages with the foreign market.

An alternative strategy to the dependency on wholesalers and buyers is the creation of trading companies owned by the shoe firms. This has been attempted by two groups of firms interviewed during the survey: one of them has set up a network for mail order sales throughout the country and the other has created a trading company to sell in Mexico

City. Both are very recent initiatives and it is therefore difficult to evaluate their results at this stage. However, with regard to the direct entry of shoe producers in the commercialization phase, it may be appropriate to point out that many entrepreneurs said that they are afraid to make this choice because wholesalers and retail chains will not buy their products anymore.

From what we have seen so far, we can conclude that commercialization is one of the weakest points in the Mexican footwear industry. Nevertheless, investments in marketing and commercialization are generally too costly for most of the small and medium footwear firms and require different skills than the production phase: therefore, a more active strategy of commercialization may require collaboration among firms and much emphasis on the role of middlemen and wholesalers.

6.4.3 Horizontal linkages

Cooperation among sample firms is more common in the two Mexican footwear clusters than in the Italian districts (see section 5.4.3). The reasons for interacting are the exchange of technological information and sometimes of machines in 12 firms, subcontracting and farming out part of the production when they have excess orders in 9 firms and the establishment of commercial agreements in 6 cases. In the majority of the firms interviewed the interactions take place among small groups of firms linked by family ties or long-standing friendship. So for instance among the sample firms in Guadalajara, there is a group of firms which includes three enterprises managed by three brothers who jointly run the purchases of raw materials and components and together sell part of the production.

Another group interviewed was created by a successful young entrepreneur, who in a decade created seven enterprises managed by himself and some of his cousins. The group includes four shoe firms specialized in complementary segments of the market, a firm specialized in the production of uppers, another firm which produces insoles and rubber soles and finally a firm which produces packaging materials and cardboard boxes. Within the group they jointly buy inputs, deal with customers, bureaucratic matters and banks and each cousin, aside from managing his own firm, is also specialized in a particular activity for the group. So, for instance one deals with marketing, another with technology or credit. They have a project for moving to a new site together, where they could have all the enterprises close to each other and therefore further integrate their activities and for example have a single warehouse for the group.

Finally, in Leon, an informal group of four firms that export complementary products to the same German buyer, organizes several joint activities like importing raw materials and components needed to manufacture a product of international standard quality, participation in international trade fairs, exchange of information about markets and technology.

In Guadalajara, linkages among firms outside family groups have been favoured by an initiative promoted by the local Camara del Calzado, inspired by a UNIDO methodology initially aimed at favouring the growth of small rural enterprises to reduce emigration towards urban centres.[25] The project consists of promoting the creation of *agrupamientos industriales*, initially based on a course for entrepreneurs who had to agree to organize a visit to their own firms by the other entrepreneurs in the group and to allow an outside expert (a business student in her/his final year) to make diagnoses of their firms. In seven years, seven groups, involving about 120 enterprises, began in this way and afterwards some of these groups have carried on with regular meetings to discuss problems related to technology, marketing, suppliers and to exchange information about clients, machines, workers and orders.

Another interesting initiative has very recently been promoted at national level for the creation of *empresas integradoras*. The programme, which was inspired by the Ministry of Trade after a visit to the Italian industrial districts, aims at creating companies established by groups of firms for jointly selling products or buying inputs or any other common objective. The new companies enjoy financial and tax incentives and facilitated bureaucratic procedures. In the survey we found three projects for the creation of *empresas integradoras*: one is the group described above for the creation of the new site, another is a group of 15 very small firms in Leon (with fewer than seven employees in each firm), which after a successful experience of joint participation in the local trade fair, would like to create a trading company with a single brand name for all their products and finally there is a group of five tanneries in Leon, which would like to create a company for joint buying and selling, and supplying common services like book-keeping and training.

Apart from these initiatives aimed at favouring interactions among firms, informal relationships are frequent among 80 per cent of the enterprises interviewed and they are considered an important asset by almost all (Table 6.10). The role of the entrepreneurial associations seems to be very important in inducing informal contacts among firms because, according to 37 firms, events organized by the Camara are the most important opportunities for informal exchange with their colleagues.

Table 6.10   Informal cooperation between sample firms

Frequency of cooperation exchange	No. of small firms	No. of medium firms	No. of large firms	% of total sample firms
Frequent contacts	14	11	16	80%
Rare contacts	3	3	4	20%

Source: author's survey

Family ties also play an important role in 17 firms and, finally, social events are important for 11 firms.

Several forms of cooperation in many different aspects of a firm's life arise from these informal contacts. These include exchanges of technological and market information, exchanges of machinery and workers, subcontracting of orders in case of excess demand, joint commercialization, joint purchases of inputs and joint recovery of credits.

Notwithstanding this, a lot of informal linkages are going on within the two districts analysed; significantly, 65 per cent of the interviewed firms expressed a desire for more formal agreements, in the sense of more stable relationships with other firms, organized and focused on specific objectives. This need to transform informal and sometimes involuntary linkages into explicit cooperation with selected groups of firms will be analysed in greater detail in section 7.5.

6.4.4   Linkages with the labour market

Analysing the characteristics of the labour market, the main problems emphasized by the sample firms, were in order of importance: the low availability of skilled workforce, the high turnover of the labour force and the low availability of unskilled workforce.

According to 65 per cent of the sample firms, skilled labour is a scarce resource and qualified workers demand relatively high salaries and good working conditions. This explains why small and medium firms, which usually can only afford to pay lower salaries and offer more unstable working conditions, because of the irregularity of orders, have more difficulty in hiring skilled workers. Unskilled labour represents a less important problem (only four firms believe that locally there is a low availability), because there is a large reservoir of young people, mainly women, available to work. The footwear industry has traditionally employed only a relatively small proportion of women, mainly in sewing operations. During recent years, however, women's recruitment has increased for two main reasons: first of all women perform many production tasks better than men and secondly women, particularly young women, are paid less than men because, even if there is no direct discrimination, there is discrimination on the basis of skills definitions and evaluations of particular skills (Baud, 1992).

So, as the network case studies clearly showed, an increasing number of firms prefer to employ unskilled young women to train on the job, instead of depending on the conditions imposed by the scarce skilled workers. Women are also frequently recruited as homeworkers, mainly for stitching. Shoe enterprises usually deliver partially made shoes needing further processing and pay on a piece-work basis.

According to most of the sample firms, the main problem with unskilled labour is the high turnover, because workers move away from the footwear sector as soon as they find a job in other, more remunerative sectors or, in the case of women, when they get married. Some employers are attempting to halt the high turnover of unskilled labour in the industry by paying better wages: the average remuneration of leather and footwear workers is now about 2.5 times the minimum wage (ILO, 1992). However, the average salary in 1990 in the textile, clothing and footwear industry was still lower than the average for the manufacturing sector (Nacional Financiera, 1991).

Competition from other sectors to recruit people is higher in Guadalajara than in Leon, where the footwear and leather sectors are the main manufacturing activities. As reported in some recent studies (Alba Vega, 1986; Baud, 1992), the labour market in Guadalajara, where the economic structure is dominated by a strong concentration of small enterprises, is very dynamic and characterized by great mobility of workers from one job to the other.

According to many entrepreneurs, in the near future even in Leon the labour force may become scarce if the Free Trade Agreement attracts a lot of foreign investments in sectors other than the traditional footwear and leather industries. The attractiveness of the region in which Leon is located is explained by its strategic geographical position, just north of Mexico City, along the highway to the USA. The eventual establishment of other more remunerative sectors in the area will oblige Leon's shoe entrepreneurs to look for alternative locations for their firms outside the town in the countryside, where there is still a great availability of unskilled, cheap labour. As seen in section 6.4.1, a few enterprises have already started an experiment in decentralizing some phases of production outside Leon, to overcome the rising difficulties in the labour market.

Concerning the question of labour availability, it may be opportune to conclude that the scarcity which footwear firms encounter both in Guadalajara and in Leon may be interpreted as a positive sign from a collective viewpoint. In other words, the footwear industry, together with other sectors in Guadalajara, has created a large number of jobs in the two towns and in Leon it has also recently started to create jobs in the surrounding countryside.

Training was also investigated. In most of the sample firms training takes place inside the same firm. External training is generally reserved for supervisors, technicians or designers; less skilled workers like edgers are very rarely trained outside the firms. A problem emphasized by many firms is the risk of losing their workers sent to be trained outside, because they find better paying jobs. Skilled workers are heavily sought after and frequently 'pirated' from one firm to the other. This is a very common problem among small-scale enterprises, which usually pay lower salaries than larger firms: a typical case of market failure which justifies some kind of extra-market intervention to make up for the firms' negative attitude about external training for their workers.

Finally, the rate of unionization is very low both in Guadalajara and in Leon, because the sector grew up in a family environment with entrepreneurs who, in most cases, started as manual workers in other firms and therefore establish relationships based on friendship and solidarity with their employers. In Leon, 95 per cent of workers do not belong to trade unions (Bazan *et al.*, 1988). According to a field survey carried out by Morris and Lowder (1992), many firms in Leon provide services to workers, like factory canteens with low-priced meals, free medical care, incentives of various kinds for punctuality and productivity, and other social facilities such as football teams and excursions, aimed at creating a favourable social climate.

Moreover, the usually good relationships between workers and entrepreneurs, in many cases strengthened by family ties, allow a high flexibility of the labour force, which is usually available, when needed, to work extra hours or weekends.

From what we have said so far, the following conclusions can be drawn:

1. the footwear industry has generated a large number of jobs both in Guadalajara and in Leon and labour has recently become a scarce

resource, which is an unusual situation in a developing country and therefore a very positive result;

2. the labour market is characterized by features similar to the Italian industrial districts: high flexibility of the labour force, high mobility among firms, low rate of unionization and good social climate between workers and entrepreneurs, while the low availability of skilled labour contrasts with the Italian reality.

6.4.5 Institutional linkages

At the national level there are no specific policies addressing the footwear sector; nevertheless some of the sample firms which export part of their production have access to the scheme of financial incentives for exporting enterprises. Other firms have obtained easy credit terms from National Financiera, the Mexican bank for industrial development.[26] A recent policy initiative which seems to have some potentialities for supporting the footwear industry is the programme to favour the creation of *empresas integradoras*, described in section 6.4.3.

At local level, a number of important institutions have been identified both in Guadalajara and in Leon; some are associations of firms, while others provide special services to the footwear industries. Entrepreneurial associations (Camara del Calzado) are the most important institutions supporting the footwear industry in Mexico; there are three local associations, in Guadalajara, Leon and Mexico City, and a national one aimed at coordinating the activities of the three local Camaras. The role of these associations, financed through the membership fees[27] and the profits from the organization of trade fairs, is to supply services like fiscal, legal and labour advice, managerial training, organization of trade fairs[28] and lobbying activities at a political level (Table 6.11).

In Guadalajara the Camara has 500-odd members. According to some estimates of the Camara, in 1990 about half of its members used at least one of the services supplied and about 25 per cent actively participated in several activities. In our survey we found a rather positive evaluation of the activities of the Camara in Guadalajara: 83 per cent of the firms interviewed judged the organization of trade fairs, 63 per cent the lobbying activity, 56 per cent the diffusion of information and 34 per cent the training activity as very good. Finally, the Camara is very much involved in the promotion and support of the credit union and of the Instituto Tecnologico del Calzado, whose activities are described in greater detail below.

Table 6.11 Use of entrepreneurial associations by members

Services available	No. of firms
Advice in labour issues	2
Information service	27
Courses and seminars	14
Advice in legal matters	11
Advice in fiscal matters	5
Organization of trade fairs	33
Lobbying	28

Source: author's survey

Note: Firms can use more than one service

In Leon the Camara has 800-odd members. The opinions about its services are less enthusiastic than in Guadalajara: 34 per cent of the firms interviewed said that none of the services are useful, while the most appreciated activities include the diffusion of information (mentioned by 48 per cent of the firms), lobbying (43 per cent) and the organization of trade fairs (38 per cent). Small firms often complained about the little attention paid to some of the issues more relevant for them. In the interviews we were informed about an informal group comprising several of the most important firms in town; this lobby seems to influence the activities of the Camara quite a lot and this may explain why small firms feel quite neglected.

However, it must be added that in 1993 the Camara's management changed and there is now more attention to the needs of small firms. This change was confirmed by some of the small entrepreneurs interviewed in the second phase of the field work. Moreover, some projects for initiatives specifically addressed towards small enterprises were also being prepared when we visited the entrepreneurial association. It is interesting to observe that in Guadalajara, the two largest firms interviewed complained because they feel neglected by the entrepreneurial association, which in their opinion is too much involved in initiatives for small and medium enterprises.

Entrepreneurial associations also exist for the tanning (Camara de la Curtiduria) and component sectors – in Leon there is ANPIC (Asociación Nacional de Proveedores para la Industria del Calzado) and in Guadalajara APICEJ (Asociación de Proveedores para la Industria del Calzado de Jalisco).

ANPIC has 126 members and, besides providing some general services to the firms, organizes an annual trade fair which is the most important one in this field in Latin America. As seen in section 6.4.1, they recently began to collaborate with the Camara del Calzado to improve the relationships among shoe producers and component enterprises.

In Leon there is also a centre for research and technological assistance (CIATEG – Centro de Investigacion y Asistencia Tecnologica del Estado de Guanauajato), created as an agency of the central government, and which can be considered an arm of the Mexican National Science and Technology Council. The centre was created with the objective of supplying technical and quality control services and specialized training to the footwear industry at national level; in fact, it is mainly used by Leon's enterprises, leaving shoe firms in the rest of Mexico almost without any technological support.

A similar institution in Guadalajara is the Instituto Tecnologico del Calzado, established in 1984 with support of the local Camara and a grant from the World Bank and devoted to training and technological research. Its activities include a diversified programme for training designers, skilled manual workers like edgers, and also managers and entrepreneurs. The training programme, addressed to two crucial positions within the firm – the entrepreneur and the supervisor – is rather innovative. With entrepreneurs a lot of work is done to create a business and managerial culture, to favour a more collaborative attitude among them and to guarantee better access to information. One of the most successful projects is the *Jornadas Empresariales*, which are a yearly series of seminars presenting new issues relevant for the sector, like quality control techniques, production planning systems and other organizational and managerial innovations. Mexican and foreign experts are also usually invited to the seminars in which a large number of local entrepreneurs actively participate.

Concerning supervisors, the idea is to focus on the training of key figures, crucial for an efficient firm's operation, so they will be able to plan and control the production process and provide on-the-job training for the unskilled labour force. The advantages of this approach are twofold: first it reduces the dependency on the skilled labour force which, as seen above, is a rather scarce resource and second it amplifies the impact of training because supervisors learn how to train other workers.

Finally, in the technological area there is a project for establishing a testing laboratory for materials and components in collaboration with the University of Guadalajara, a project for an international databank on technological information and a project for the creation of a CAD-CAM station.

Both in Guadalajara and Leon there is a credit union aimed at obtaining credit for its members at more favourable conditions than the market rates because it can borrow directly from National Financiera. In Guadalajara the credit union is linked with the Camara and it was promoted by an initiative of some entrepreneurs taking part in the *agrupamientos industriales*. Its activity has recently increased thanks to the active participation of a number of small entrepreneurs who got involved in 1991 when the union was suffering a bad crisis due to the decrease in credit availability in the country. According to its president, the owner of a small enterprise (40 employees), some entrepreneurs close to the Camara, realizing the importance of the credit union for improving access to credit for small firms, decided that it was worthwhile to participate actively in its management and in relaunching its activity.

From 1991 to 1993 the number of members increased from 188 to 235[29] (60 per cent of them have fewer than 15 employees) and the employees of the union from one to seven. According to its director, the amount of credit supplied showed an increase of 200 per cent in 1993. The union supplies different types of credit, basically working capital credit (about 80 per cent of the total credit supplied) and long-term credit (from three to five years, for the remaining 20 per cent) for investment in technology. The interest rate is the same as the market but the union guarantees easier access for small firms, which otherwise are usually discriminated against by commercial banks. The access to credit is decided by a committee elected by the members of the union, which takes its decision on the basis of the financial situation, a diagnosis of the economic structure and the real guarantees supplied by the applicant firm. The advantage of the credit union in comparison with the commercial banks is the easier access to information about small firms, which reduces the transaction costs of supplying credit.

In Leon, the credit union is fairly recent (established in 1992) and it does not have any linkage with the local Camara. The union has only 46 members due to an explicit choice of selecting the enterprises which could take part in it, reducing the risks of potential insolvency. In 1993 the union organized a joint sale of products made by some of its members; this was a rather successful initiative and they would therefore like to repeat the experience by trying to joint export. Finally as seen in section 6.4.1, both the unions also supply a service of group purchases of several components.

In general access to credit is identified by the majority of the sample firms as the main constraint to their growth which obliges them to rely mainly on self-financing. This is confirmed by the results of a survey carried out on a sample of 200 enterprises in Leon, according to which 45 per cent of the sample firms believe that the main constraint to growth is the lack of access to credit and its high cost (CEESP, 1993b).

The existence of a relatively well developed institutional support network for the footwear *filière* is a very important condition in the case of adoption of a growth strategy based on an approach at system level. Institutions like the Camara del Calzado can have a very relevant role in diffusing among entrepreneurs a systemic vision of their business, in other words the idea that the survival and growth of their own firms strongly depends on the development of the whole system of shoe firms, suppliers, buyers, market agents, service firms and supporting institutions. Nevertheless, as in the Italian case, it is very difficult to evaluate the real role played by the existing institutions in the development process of the two clusters analysed.

6.5 INDUSTRIAL CLUSTERS IN MEXICO: SOME REFLECTIONS

The brief overview of the literature available on industrial clusters in LDCs presented in Chapter 4 stresses the need for more studies specifically focused at analysing the clustering phenomenon in developing countries. From the results of the empirical investigation in two footwear clusters in Mexico presented in this chapter, some initial interesting considerations can be made with regard to the effects generated by clustering. Clustering *per se* does not necessarily imply the existence of linkages and above all it does not tell much about the quality and depth of these relationships. The investigation in Mexico, aimed at assessing the usefulness of the industrial district model, has allowed us to obtain some original information about these aspects, traditionally neglected in studies on SMEs in developing countries.

There follows a brief summary of the main results, which will be investigated further in the next chapter where they are compared with the results obtained in the two Italian districts (Chapter 5) and with the stylized facts of the 'model' (Chapter 3).

Concerning backward linkages, clustering has induced the concentration of a critical mass of suppliers of inputs. This means that the Mexican shoe firms can buy their inputs locally and this applies to small and medium firms, too. Therefore, in the two analysed cases clustering has made it possible to overcome one of the constraints on

SME's growth traditionally stressed in the literature (Schmitz, 1982): the difficulty of access to inputs. However, the lack of competition in the domestic market has favoured the development of producers of low quality inputs. Notwithstanding the intensity of linkages existing between shoe firms and input producers, their quality is therefore low. Most of the relationships are market links, based on a pure price mechanism, and little cooperation can be found. Technological cooperation is also limited within the two clusters, due to the little development of the domestic capital goods sector. This is a typical constraint found in developing countries, and it contrasts with the stylized facts of the industrial district model.

Also the low division of labour among process specialized enterprises contrasts with the 'model' as well as with the results of the Italian field work. In the two Mexican clusters shoe firms, even of small size, are highly vertically integrated and this can be explained by two main facts, external to the clusters: the Smithian argument of the limited dimension of the market and the lack of standardization in the measurement system. This brought to our attention the importance of considering the impact of external events on the development of the organizational structure of clusters, an issue neglected in the discussion about industrial districts in developed countries.

The weakness of forward linkages is another point which contrasts with the 'model'. This discrepancy also characterizes the two Italian districts, as stressed in section 5.5. Some recent attempts to develop cooperative relationships have also been emphasized as a reaction to the increasing competition following the opening up of the market. Different forms of horizontal linkages have also been detected in the two clusters. Many of these relationships are informal and in the next chapter their quality and their contribution to the efficiency of the local production system are discussed extensively.

Clustering has a positive effect on employment. In Leon, some recent signs of decreased availability of labour may be taken as an indicator of a positive job creation effect of the local shoe sector and its related industries. Skilled labour is a scarce resource in the two clusters and this contrasts with the 'model' and possibly reduces the collective learning effect.

Finally, there are some local institutions aimed at supporting the shoe industry. Their impact on the system's growth cannot be quantified, but their existence is an important factor in a developing country. As seen in section 4.4, sectoral and business associations usually play little role in supporting SMEs in LDCs clusters, while one of the lessons of the experience of districts in developed countries is the important role played by institutional intervention at the local level, with a high involvement of firms.

To conclude, in Guadalajara and Leon, clustering has generated some of the expected effects, matching the stylized facts of the 'model'. Nevertheless the empirical investigation has also identified some discrepancies. The next chapter, which is a systematic comparison of the results of the Italian and Mexican cases and the ideal-type of industrial districts, suggests some new keys of analysis to understand these differences and to overcome some shortcomings of the 'model' in representing reality.

Part III
The Comparison

7 External Economies and Cooperation in Italy and Mexico

7.1 INTRODUCTION

In the last two chapters the results of the field work carried out in Italy and Mexico have been presented, analysing the presence and the features of the relationships linking the economic actors in both cases. The next step is therefore to compare these results and to analyse their similarities and differences. Although they do not fully match the ideal–typical model described in the literature (see section 5.5), the Italian districts nevertheless represent examples of highly developed, complex and long-standing systems, characterized by intense and qualified linkages. The comparison is aimed at investigating the likeness between the Mexican clusters and the Italian industrial districts, specialized in the same sector.

On the basis of a classification of the collective effects which derive from the linkages detected, some important differences in their intensity and quality are stressed. In order to explore beyond these discrepancies, a statistical analysis is undertaken on the data sets of the two sample surveys.

The structure of this chapter takes the following form:

1. section 7.2 extensively discusses similarities and differences of the collective effects which derive from the linkages detected in the Italian footwear districts and in the Mexican clusters, as described in some detail in Chapters 5 and 6. These collective effects are classified according to a typology, based on the distinction between static and dynamic external economies and cooperation effects, presented in section 3.2;
2. section 7.3 summarizes the findings of the statistical analysis on the data sets of the two sample surveys. The section presents the results of the application of different statistical techniques:
   (a) in 7.3.1 with factor analysis, a concise representation of the systems analysed is achieved through the identification of a few main underlying factors;

(b) in 7.3.2 with cluster analysis, some groups of sample firms, homogeneous in terms of these factors, are defined;

(c) in 7.3.3 the results of correspondence analysis are presented. This technique is used to classify the sample firms according to their performance, identifying different types of structure and of internal and external conduct;

3. the concluding section (7.4) provides some considerations about the threefold comparison of the Italian and Mexican clusters and the 'model' to discuss some of the discrepancies between the stylized facts indicated in the literature and the empirical realities of the field work. Some further reflections, stimulated by the results of the comparison, about the districts' development trajectories and the policy lessons for enhancing collective efficiency are dealt with in the concluding chapter.

7.2   A CLASSIFICATION OF COLLECTIVE EFFECTS

In Chapters 5 and 6 we described the linkages among economic actors detected in the case studies in Italy and Mexico. The aim of this section is to classify the collective effects deriving from these linkages in terms of the concepts introduced in section 3.2: external economies and cooperation effects. The main distinction between these two categories of collective effects is that external economies are the by-products of some activities undertaken within the districts, freely available to every economic actor, while cooperation effects are the result of explicit and conscious cooperative behaviours among limited groups of self-interested economic actors. Furthermore, external economies and cooperation effects can be static, when they impact the level of productivity of the system, or dynamic, when they impact the system's capability to grow and innovate. Static and dynamic external economies and cooperative effects bring about collective efficiency and hence those efficiency gains which individual producers can rarely attain (Schmitz, 1995b).

In order to classify the collective effects that emerged from the linkages identified in the empirical investigation, a two-dimensional typology may be therefore usefully introduced. In Table 7.1 the collective effects are mapped out on one side according to their being incidental and excludable and on the other side according to their static or dynamic objective.

Table 7.1 Collective efficiency: a classification of effects

		External economies	*Cooperative effects*
Static	*Marche and Brenta*	High availability of free information; High availability of inputs at competitive prices, at great speed, at low-transaction costs; High division of labour; Collective reputation;	Cooperation with process specialized firms; Cooperation in export and credit consortia, entrepreneurial associations;
	Guadalajara and Leon	High availability of free information; Good availability of inputs at market conditions; Low division of labour; Collective reputation;	Cooperation in export and credit consortia, entrepreneurial associations; Cooperation in *agrupamientos industriales* and *empresas integradoras*; Cooperation with buyers;
Dynamic	*Marche and Brenta*	Demonstration effects on attitudes and motivation; High collective learning;	Strong cooperation with suppliers of raw materials, components, machinery; Cooperation with process specialized firms; Rare cooperation in export and credit consortia, entrepreneurial associations;
	Guadalajara and Leon	Demonstration effects on attitudes and motivation; Some collective learning.	Very little cooperation with suppliers of raw materials, components, machinery; Rare cooperation in export and credit consortia, entrepreneurial associations; Rare cooperation in *agrupamientos industriales* and *empresas integradoras* Cooperation with buyers.

Let us begin with external economies which derive from unplanned, incidental relationships among the economic actors who interact within the system. The most typical incidental relationships usually going on in every agglomeration of specialized firms and therefore also in the Italian and Mexican footwear clusters are the frequent social occasions, like casual meetings in the streets, cafés, clubs, and business occasions, like meetings at entrepreneurial associations or at suppliers' facilities. A flow of information about products, markets, fashion trends, technology, bad and good customers, suppliers and process specialized firms is generated from these continuous interactions and freely circulates within the districts. This circulation of information generates both static and dynamic external economies.

With regard to static external economies, the free circulation of information may allow firms to survive or even to grow, because they get access to information which otherwise they could not afford. This type of external economy is particularly relevant for small firms, which can rarely afford activities like market studies, participation in foreign exhibitions or subscriptions to databanks. The free availability of information also contributes to the birth and survival of small firms; this allows a continuous renewal of firms and recycling of the human and capital resources available in the districts. Nevertheless, it also permits the survival of some inefficient firms, which only have a very superficial market knowledge and which base their competitive edge on their ability to make shoes and take advantage of low entry barriers.

This category of firms can be defined as followers, or, even free-riders of the district, because they usually tend to exploit resources created by other more innovative firms, for instance they imitate successful products at lower costs and lower quality. It can be said that these firms 'use' the district to compensate their structural and strategical internal shortcomings. Furthermore, it should be added that, although during the period of excess demand they could easily find a market for their products both in Italy and in Mexico, nowadays facing increasing competition they are usually the first to suffer. So, for instance, in Italy many small firms unable to develop an independent product and marketing strategy become subcontractors for other enterprises, or even close down.

In Mexico, the same phenomenon occurs, with an increasing number of firms closing down in the formal market to become informal activities, non-officially registered and therefore able to survive without paying taxes. Although the impacts of increasing competition on the clusters analysed is dealt with in greater detail in Chapter 8, we can conclude that these external economies contribute to the collective efficiency of the systems analysed, but firms which rely too much on such incidental effects have shown low performances. The profiles of low performing firms identified below in the correspondence analysis (section 7.3.3) confirm this result.

The free circulation of information can also have dynamic effects, generating a sort of demonstration effect on attitudes and motivations which may induce economic actors to introduce innovations in processes, products or forms of organization and contributes to the growth of the system. This positive spontaneous effect of clustering is common in Brenta, Marche, Guadalajara and Leon, as well as in many other agglomerations of firms in industrialized and developing countries.

The local concentration of firms which produce or sell inputs, machinery and services and firms specialized in some phases of the production process at competitive prices and at a high level of specialization generates some important static external economies. Every firm located within the district can in fact save on costs for its production factors because of the high competition, because transaction and transport costs are lower due to the spatial and cultural proximity and because firms can maintain very little inventories, being able to buy what they need rapidly. Moreover, shoe firms can easily put out some phases of the production process to highly specialized firms, able to exploit the different economies of scale which characterize the phases of the production cycle (see section 5.5.1). These external economies definitely characterize the two Italian footwear districts and, as seen in section 5.2.1, they represent one of the main competitive advantages that prompted the growth of the Italian footwear industry during the 1970s.

With regard to the Mexican clusters, the situation is different because the long closure of the domestic market has not encouraged the growth of a competitive industry of suppliers and process specialized firms. Mexican shoe producers in Guadalajara and Leon can therefore locally buy most of the inputs they need and they may save on transportation costs, but the lack of competition has greatly reduced advantages in terms of price, quality and service. Moreover, Mexican shoe firms are usually more vertically integrated and they tend to put out some phases of the production process only when they have excess orders, without any important gains in terms of specialization. The low degree of division of labour is also partly due to the high transaction costs generated by the lack of a standardized measurement system. From the empirical investigation it appears that the advantages in terms of face-to-face contacts, typical of clustering, are partially offset by the high transaction costs deriving from the lack of standardization. This makes the relationships of shoe producers with suppliers of components and process specialized firms particularly difficult and costly and limits the gains from clustering in Mexico.

Another type of static external economies, typical of industrial districts, is the effect of collective reputation, in other words the attraction of customers achieved by a large concentration of specialized producers. So for instance, German buyers know very well that they can find high quality women's shoes in Brenta and they go there to buy. The same is true in Mexico: Guadalajara is the largest market in the country for women's shoes and Leon for men's and children's shoes. This enormously facilitates access to distant markets.

There is a negative side of these external economies, too. The collective reputation of the district is in fact usually rather homogeneous and therefore, for instance, shoe makers from Marche are known for producing a medium-low quality product. This reputation may have a negative effect on firms trying to differentiate their production towards different segments of market. An example is the case of a local enterprise which has recently invested a lot of resources in creating a well-known brand in the fashion world and does not like to be imitated by other local producers selling similar products and creating confusion on the market.

Finally, the high local availability of skilled labour is a dynamic external economy from which the firms located in Marche and Brenta and to some extent the firms in Leon and Guadalajara take advantage. As seen in section 5.4.4, the accumulation of know-how in people moving from one firm to the other generates a process of collective learning which enhances the system's innovation capability. This typical characteristic of Italian industrial districts is less evident in the Mexican clusters, where the availability of skilled labour is more limited. This lack of skilled labour mainly characterizes Guadalajara, where the existence of a diversified economic structure gives workers different employment opportunities. It must be added that some changes may soon occur also in the Italian districts with respect to collective learning as a consequence of the increasing tendency of well-educated young people to seek non-manual jobs, mainly in sectors other than the footwear industry.

Moving to cooperative effects, in Italy explicit cooperative linkages between the shoe producers and their suppliers of raw materials, components and technology have been frequently found in the empirical investigation. As seen in section 5.4.1, shoe firms and their suppliers often work together to develop new products and the cooperation is based on the self-interest of both parties in maintaining a stable relationship. Above, we stressed that the existence of a very efficient network of suppliers represents one of the main advantages of the Italian shoe system, furthermore the cooperative linkages frequently set up by the shoe enterprises represent an important contribution to the system's capability of innovation and growth and their effects can be therefore defined as dynamic. Thanks to those linkages, shoe firms are able to supply a very diversified, quality product in a time-to-market which is shorter when compared with the shoe industry in many other countries.

The links between shoe producers and process specialized firms are quite frequently characterized by a clear dependence of subcontractors on shoe enterprises, which define the payment conditions and can choose another firm if they are not satisfied with the quality or the service. Nevertheless, in some cases there is also some sort of cooperation, when shoe firms choose to have stable relationships with their subcontractors and therefore they try to solve incidental problems and supply the needed training and sometimes even financial or technical help. Moreover, these linkages are facilitated by the low transaction costs within the districts due to the easy face-to-face contacts. The cooperative effects deriving from these linkages can be either static or dynamic.

In Mexico, similar cooperative linkages with process specialized firms are very rare because shoe firms, as seen above, tend to be highly vertically integrated and to put out work only in cases of excess orders. Section 6.4.1 shows that a few firms have been recently pushed by increasing competition to move towards a higher division of labour and more cooperative linkages. But generally in the Mexican clusters this is still a tendency to come.

Also the linkages with suppliers are less cooperative than in Italy and they can be defined as market relationships, based on a price factor. This means that thanks to clustering the Mexican shoe producers can locally buy raw materials, components and machinery but, as opposed to the Italian districts, they rarely cooperate developing these inputs and they must buy what is available on the market, at the market terms. The weakness of backward cooperative linkages can be explained by the long closure of the domestic market, which has not favoured competition based on product quality, fashion contents and design, either in the shoe market or in the component and accessory market. Only with the recent change in trade policy, namely with the opening up of the market, have some of the shoe firms and some of their suppliers begun to realize that they belong to a system in which the success of one firm strongly depends on its interactions with other firms. Therefore, relationships are becoming more cooperative and firms are trying to build stable linkages based on a mutual self-interest in improving quality and service.

In Italy, some cooperative linkages have been found among firms which belong to export consortia and to other commercial agreements. Linkages in export consortia may be defined as dynamic if they are aimed at discovering new markets; they are otherwise static. In Mexico, these types of consortia have not been found. Relationships within credit consortia, entrepreneurial associations and other service centres aimed at supporting the footwear industry can be also defined as cooperative linkages, and they can be found both in the Italian districts and in the Mexican clusters. All these relationships are characterized by an explicit decision of a selected group of firms to cooperate for several aims like jointly selling their products, dealing with banks or utilizing joint services supplied by entrepreneurial associations. Their effects are therefore static, apart from when they involve cooperation for carrying out some joint innovative projects.

In Mexico, other forms of cooperative agreements are the *agrupamientos industriales* and the *empresas integradoras*. These are two experiences, described in some detail in section 6.4.3, promoted precisely with the aim of favouring the development of cooperation among selected groups of firms. Their effect is more frequently static, when they regard cooperation among firms which exchange machinery, labour force and orders or jointly buy inputs. They became dynamic when, more rarely, they involve cooperation on innovative projects. Besides, we may add that these forms of cooperation can also be found among groups of firms linked by family ties.

Finally in Mexico, a few cases of linkages have been reported between shoe producers and buyers, based on cooperation to produce good quality products and sometimes to introduce innovations on products, processes and organizational forms (6.4.2). However, relationships based on a strong dependence on buyers are also common, because there are shoe producers often selling most of their production to only one customer. In Italy aside from a few exceptions, buyers do not play a really significant role in commercialization and they tend to have a market relationship with their customers, without intervening in the phase of product development and production.

The linkages with non-exclusive agents can be also defined as pure market relationships both in Italy and in Mexico. From the empirical investigation it appears in fact that the relationships with non-exclusive agents very rarely involve an exchange of information; in most cases they are instead pure market linkages in which agents sell the products of different firms, without a real contribution to the development of new products based on market needs. This represents an important limitation both for the Italian and the Mexican footwear industries, which have developed very weak forward linkages with the market and it represents one of their biggest weak points in terms of commercial function.

In the Mexican case the reason for this weakness may be found again in the lack of competition, which has made it unnecessary to develop the marketing and commercial function for selling products in the closed market. The source of the weakness of forward linkages in the Italian districts is more complicated. In this case the reason can be found in the capability of the Italian footwear firms, during the 1970s and the first half of the 1980s, to impose their products on the international market without the need to develop a commercial and marketing function. As seen in section 5.2.1, before the advent of international competitors like Brazil, Spain or Portugal, Italian shoes were in fact bought for their quality and fashion content and for the service supplied in terms of speed, variety of products and flexibility. Most of the entrepreneurs interviewed admitted that it was not necessary to make any marketing effort to sell their products.

This characteristic of the market has favoured the development of districts that are highly developed on the production side but weak in commercial and marketing functions. Since the mid 1980s, the increasing competition in the international market, due to the 'arrival' of new producers, mainly from newly industrializing countries, has generated some difficulties in the two footwear industrial districts analysed, as well as in many other Italian areas specialized in footwear. The number of firms has begun to decrease, the exports have slowed their continuous growth and the domestic market has been invaded by imported shoes competing with the Italian products.[1] As a result of these changes, the need to develop a marketing function has become clear to an increasing number of firms, which react to these changes with diverse strategies, influencing the original organizational structure of the industrial districts. Some examples of these strategies are presented in the section on the dynamics of industrial districts (8.2).

To conclude, some general considerations about the degree of collective efficiency in the four cases analysed can be drawn from Table 7.1. These are useful for the objective of comparing districts in Italy and clusters in Mexico to assess the adherence of the realities analysed to the textbook model, which is the focus of the final section of this chapter. Therefore on the basis of the classification presented, the main conclusions are the following:

1. external economies emerge both in Italy and Mexico. However, there are some main differences concerning the availability of inputs, the degree of labour division and the availability of skilled labour. In all these cases the production of external economies is higher in the Italian districts than in the Mexican clusters;
2. cooperative effects are definitely more common among the Italian firms than the Mexican ones. The main differences are in the relationships with suppliers and process specialized firms, which are often based on cooperation in Italy and mostly on market rules in Mexico.

From what has been said so far, we may conclude that the degree of collective efficiency to which external economies and cooperative effects contribute is higher in the Italian districts than in the Mexican clusters, where firms can exploit fewer clustering advantages. The reason put forward to explain some of the contrasts between Italian and Mexican clusters is related to differences in the trade policies in the two countries. In Mexico the long closure of the domestic market has not favoured the development of efficient backward-related industries as in the open Italian market, generating a lower production of external economies and very little cooperation. This argument brings out an important question, which is not considered in the European industrial district debate: the impact of external conditions on the structure of clusters. The results of the empirical investigation suggest that differences in external conditions represent an important dimension in explaining discrepancies between the two realities analysed and the 'model'. The important lesson which can be drawn concerns the opportunity to carefully take into consideration these differences when the 'model' is used as a reference point for analysis in different contexts.

7.3   A STATISTICAL ANALYSIS OF THE SAMPLE SURVEYS

With the objective of investigating further the likeness between the Italian districts and the Mexican clusters, the two data sets of the sample surveys are analysed with the support of several statistical techniques. Accordingly, two sub-sets of variables are selected to represent the Italian and Mexican footwear clusters, including the main aspects of the economic systems analysed: firm size, performance, degree of technological innovativeness, market segment, marketing strategy, frequency of relationships with other firms, linkages with entrepreneurial associations and investment strategies (Tables 7.2 and 7.3).[2]

The statistical analysis consists of three different exploratory multivariate techniques, aimed at obtaining a comprehensive and composite representation of the sample variability, namely factor, cluster and correspondence analyses. Factor analysis has a primary objective of simplifying the description of the economic systems analysed in Italy and Mexico. It identifies a relatively small number of underlying principal elements or 'factors', which parsimoniously represent a set of many interrelated variables, selected to describe the Italian and Mexican footwear clusters. The comparison of the principal factors extracted from the two samples allows some interesting considerations and these are presented in section 7.3.1.

Furthermore, factor analysis is needed to run a multivariate cluster analysis, based on the factors identified instead of the original variables. Cluster analysis groups firms according to their degree of vicinity in respect to the main underlying factors, characterizing the economic structures of the samples. If such clusters emerge, with significant differences between the groups, the hypothesis of heterogeneous behaviour of firms within the districts is supported (7.3.2).

This hypothesis is further supported by the results of correspondence analysis, which classifies the sample firms according to their performance (7.3.3). Correspondence analysis, like factor analysis, is a multivariate technique, therefore permitting simultaneous analysis of the correlations of many qualitative variables.[3]

7.3.1   A comparison of the underlying principal factors

Many variables can be used to describe the economic systems analysed in Italy and Mexico; however, the description might be greatly simplified if it were possible to identify a few underlying dimensions or factors. The fundamental assumption behind factor analysis[4] is that the underlying factors, which are fewer than the observed variables, are responsible for the overall variation in the variables. In essence, factors are synthetic variables, embodying all the original variables, explaining the sample variability as much as possible. At the same time, within factors, variables are classified according to their importance in the overall variation.

From a statistical point of view, the results obtained with the factor analyses on the Italian and Mexican samples are very satisfying because

Table 7.2   Variables selected: Italy

Variables	Factor and cluster analyses	Variables	Correspondence analysis
B1	Number of employees	*B1N1*	Small size (< 50 employees)
		B1N2	Medium size (between 50 and 100)
		B1N3	Large size (> 100 employees)
B1012	High availability of skilled labour	*B1012*	High availability of skilled labour
		B1013	Low availability of skilled labour
B25	% of exported sales	*B25N1*	> than 50% of exported sales
B612	Increasing trend of employment over the last five years		
		COL1	Increasing production
		COL2	Stable production
		COL3	Decreasing production
D3	% of sewing put out to other enterprises	*D31*	< than 50% of sewing put out
		D32	> than 50% of sewing put out
F112	Good or very good technological level	*F111*	Very good technological level
		F112	Good technological level
		F113	Low technological level
G142	Forms of commercialization other than agents	*G142*	Commercial strategy based on direct sales to customers
		G144	Commercial strategy based on agents
G31	High or medium high segment of market	*G31*	High or medium high segment of market
H21	Equity shares in local firms	*H41*	Non-equity agreements with local firms
H41	Non-equity agreements with local firms		
H612	Frequent informal relationships within the cluster	*H612*	Frequent informal relationships within the cluster
		H613	Rare informal relationships within the cluster
L21	Use of more than one service of the entrepreneurial association	*L21*	Use of more than one service of the entrepreneurial association
M11	Investments in technology	*M11*	Investments in technology
M15	Investments in commercialization	*M15*	Investments in commercialization
M18	Investments in other sectors		

Table 7.3   Variables selected: Mexico

Variables	Factor and cluster analyses	Variables	Correspondence analysis
B1	Number of employees	B1N1	Small size (< 50 employees)
		B1N2	Medium size (between 50 and 100)
		B1N3	Large size (> 100 employees)
		B1212	Difficulty in hiring skilled labour
		COL1	Increasing profits
		COL2	Stable profits
		COL3	Decreasing profits
		C222	Putting out of one or more phases of production
C3512	Good or very good technological level	C3512	Good or very good technological level
D16	% of products sold by agents	D1550	> than 50% of products sold by wholesalers
		D1650	> than 50% of products sold by agents
D7812	Original design	D7812	Original design
DIII1	High segment of market	DIII1	High segment of market
		DIII2	Medium-high segment of market
F1	Equity shares in local firms	F1	Equity shares in local firms
G1	Frequent informal relationships within the cluster	G1	Frequent informal relationships within the cluster
G131	Use of more than one service of the entrepreneurial association	G131	Use of more than one service of the entrepreneurial association
H55	Investments in commercialization	H55	Investments in commercialization
H56	Investments in technical training	H56	Investments in technical training
H57	Investments in managerial training	H57	Investments in managerial training
H76	Access to information as as a competitive advantage of the firm	H73	Availability of skilled labour as a competitive advantage of the firm
H78	Institutional assistance as a competitive advantage of the firm	H76	Access to information as a competitive advantage of the firm
H7A	Product quality as a competitive advantage of the firm	H78	Institutional assistance as a competitive advantage of the firm
		H7A	Product quality as a competitive advantage of the firm

continued on page 146

Table 7.3   Continued

Variables	Factor and cluster analyses	Variables	Correspondence analysis
		NH81	Difficulty of hiring skilled labour as a weakness of the firm
		NH84	Low availability of components as a weakness of the firm
		NH8B	Commercial strategy as a weakness of the firm

the extracted factors represent the relationships among the sets of variables parsimoniously (the explained variability is 87 per cent in Italy and 76 per cent in Mexico with only three factors) and they are also interpretable. A good factor solution is in fact both simple and interpretable. The ideal situation is when factors can be identified as summarizing sets of closely related variables, in other words when they are strongly correlated with a set of variables which express similar economic content. In this case, it is possible to give a concise description of a complex system of variables, based on a small number of interpretable factors.

In the rest of this section, first of all we present the principal factors extracted from the Italian and the Mexican samples[5] and their interpretation, then some considerations concerning the comparisons of the two sets of factors are suggested.

In Tables 7.4[6] and 7.5 the three principal factors extracted from the Italian sample are presented; for their interpretation, the variables appearing in each factor with the highest factor loadings are taken into account. The first factor, explaining 33 per cent of the total sample variance, characterizes expanding firms and it is composed of variables like increasing employment, investments in technology, a mixed strategy of commercialization and a tendency to own equity shares in other local firms. These firms have some difficulties in finding skilled labour.

The second factor (30 per cent of sample variance) can be interpreted as a size factor: firms of large size, exporting a product of low quality and producing with advanced technological processes. These firms seem to be rather removed from the district and indifferent to its collective effects, as indicated by the diversification of their investments towards other sectors and the scarce use of the services supplied by the entrepreneurial association.

Table 7.4 Rotated factor matrix*: Italy

Variables	Factor 1	Factor 2	Factor 3
B612	0.57	0.06	−0.23
M11	0.41	0.40	0.03
G142	0.38	0.06	0.17
B1012	−0.30	−0.20	−0.15
H21	0.30	0.11	−0.05
B1	0.11	0.45	−0.26
L21	0.28	−0.44	−0.07
B25	0.06	0.42	0.05
F112	0.33	0.42	0.28
M18	−0.25	0.39	−0.12
G31	0.32	−0.38	0.15
H41	0.02	0.08	0.47
H612	−0.14	−0.02	0.46
D3	−0.34	0.02	0.39
M15	0.24	−0.26	−0.31
Explained variability (%)	33.10	29.75	23.75

Source: statistical processing of the author's survey

* The matrix provides the correlation between variables and factors (see Appendix 4 for further details)

Table 7.5 The principal factors: Italy

Factor 1	Factor 2	Factor 3
B612 increasing employment	B1 number of employees	H41 non-equity agreements with other local firms
M11 investments in technology	L21(−) use of more than one service of the entrepreneurial association	H612 frequent informal relationships within the cluster
G142 forms of commercialization other than agents	B25 % of exported sales	D3 % of sewing put out
B1012(−)* high availability of skilled labour	F112 good or very good technological level	M15(−) investments in commercialization
H21 equity shares in local firms	M18 investments in other sectors	
	G31(−) high or medium-high segment of market	

Source: statistical processing of the author's survey

* The minus sign means that the correlation with the other variables is negative

Finally, the third factor (24 per cent of sample variance) stresses the importance of the collective dimension of the system: high decentralization of the production process and frequent cooperation based both on formal and informal contacts with other economic actors within the district.

Going on to analyse the results of factor analysis on the Mexican sample, three factors can be identified, explaining 76 per cent of the total sample variance (Tables 7.6 and 7.7). The first factor (39 per cent of the total sample variance) is dominated by the size of firms. Other variables, representing the strategies of investments, the technological level, the quality of product and the frequency of informal relationship together with the limited importance attributed to institutional assistance, are correlated with size. This factor can be interpreted as a confirmation of the importance of size and the indifference of large firms to institutionalized cooperation, as in the Italian sample. Nevertheless, in Mexico, large firms have frequent informal contacts with other firms within the cluster.

The second factor explains 22 per cent of the total sample variance and is characterized by variables representing the quality of products, the design originality and the commercialization through agents, negatively correlated with external investments.

Finally, the third factor accounts for 15 per cent of the total sample variance. In this last factor, two variables related to the spatial environment are identified together with a good technological level. The factor can therefore be interpreted as the collective dimension of the analysed systems, emphasizing the role of supporting institutions and information access.

Concisely, the three main dimensions of the production systems, identified with factor analysis, are in order of importance: expansion, size and collective efficiency in Italy and size, product quality and collective efficiency in Mexico. Moving then into the comparison of the findings, the first important issue to emphasize is the relevance of size that emerges as the most important element in the first factor in Mexico, while in Italy it appears in the second factor. In Mexico, investments and technological innovations are strongly related to size and this implies that there is some heterogeneity among enterprises within the clusters. In the Italian districts, size appears to be related to a good technological level and to production for a low segment of market, with a high share of exports.

In addition, it can be stressed that in the first factor extracted from the Italian sample, investments in technology and the adoption of an active strategy of commercial diversification, are not related to size.

Table 7.6   Rotated factor matrix (*): Mexico

Variables	Factor 1	Factor 2	Factor 3
B1	0.64	−0.33	0.09
H57	0.63	0.11	0.13
H7A	0.57	0.06	−0.19
H78	−0.51	0.29	0.19
H55	0.47	0.27	0.14
H56	0.46	0.31	0.02
G1	0.32	0.24	0.03
F1	0.38	−0.57	0.21
D7812	0.18	0.54	−0.04
DIII1	0.33	0.39	0.06
D16	−0.01	0.31	−0.30
G131	0.01	0.15	0.49
C3512	0.46	−0.05	0.46
H76	−0.22	0.24	0.37
Explained variability (%)	38.75	21.55	15.50

Source: statistical processing of the author's survey

(*) The matrix provides the correlation between variables and factors (see Appendix 4 for further details)

Furthermore, both in Italy and Mexico, large firms appear quite indifferent to institutional support. Two elements deserving further analysis can be advanced: first of all, size is a determinant of differentiation among firms within districts and secondly, the higher degree of collective efficiency of the Italian districts can be considered as somewhat responsible for the more limited role played by size in carrying out investments and commercial diversification.

Considering the second factor, both in Italy and in Mexico, product quality has been emphasized as one of the main dimensions of the economic system. In the footwear industry, quality differentiates the structure of firms: in the high segment of the market, the production process is highly labour intensive, labour force skills play an essential role and scale economies can be insignificant.

Finally, the third principal dimension is the collective one, stressing institutional support and information access in Mexico; formal and informal relationships and division of labour among specialized firms in Italy. This is a very relevant finding because it confirms the importance of the local environment, of the enterprises' embeddedness in

Table 7.7　The principal factors: Mexico

Factor 1	Factor 2	Factor 3
B1 number of employees	F1(−) equity shares in local firms	G131 use of more than one service of the entrepreneurial association
H57 investments in managerial training	D7812 original design	C3512 good or very good technological level
H7A product quality as a competitive advantage of the firm	D1111 high segment of market	H76 access to information as a competitive advantage of the firm
H78(−) institutional assistance as a competitive advantage of the firm	D16 % of products sold by agents	
H55 investments in commercialization		
H56 investments in technical training		
C3512 good or very good technological level		
G1 frequent informal relationships within the cluster		

Source: statistical processing of the author's survey

Note: the minus sign indicates that the correlation with the other variables is negative

their local area and of collective efficiency in both the Italian and the Mexican clusters under investigation.

With cluster and correspondence analyses, presented in the next two sections, some of the main findings of factor analysis, like heterogeneity among firms within clusters and the importance of collective efficiency, will find further empirical support.

7.3.2　Identifying homogeneous groups of firms

The next logical step after factor analysis from a statistical standpoint is cluster analysis, which aims at constructing homogeneous groups of firms in terms of the variables considered.[7] Clusters of firms are formed on the basis of the principal factors identified in section 7.3.1,[8] with the aim of identifying the structural characteristics shared by each group. The identification of clusters of enterprises, characterized by significant differences relative to the principal factors and their structural features is a confirmation of the hypothesis of heterogeneity among firms within the districts. The rest of this section presents the identified clusters, characterizing them both according to the factors and to their structural characteristics.

From the Italian sample 6 clusters were identified in terms of the first and the second factor[9] (Figure 7.1). The first factor can be identified as an indicator of growth, characterizing firms with increasing employment, investment in technology, commercialization and equity shares of other firms. The second factor can be identified as an indicator of size.

Using these indicators, the 6 Italian clusters are characterized as follows:

1. Cluster A is an outlier: a large expanding firm, very heterogeneous in comparison with the rest of the sample;

2. Cluster B is composed of 10 expanding medium size firms (71 employees is the average size of the group), presenting the following similarities:
   (a) investments in technology;
   (b) high or medium-high market segment and diversified strategy of commercialization;
   (c) rare informal relationships within the district but intense use of the services supplied by the entrepreneurial association.

3. Cluster C is composed of 10 large, non-expanding firms (97 employees is the average size of the group), characterized by:
   (a) investments in technology;
   (b) low market segment and a traditional strategy of commercialization through non-exclusive agents;
   (c) rare informal relationships within the district and little use of the services supplied by the entrepreneurial association.

4. Cluster D is composed of two outliers which are large firms, clearly non-expanding and investing only in other sectors;

5. Cluster E is the largest group, composed of 24 non-expanding medium to small enterprises (the average size is 48). Their similarities are:
   (a) low technological level;
   (b) high or medium-high market segment;
   (c) use of the services supplied by the entrepreneurial association.

6. Cluster F is composed of three non-expanding very small firms (average size is 26 employees), which have in common:
   (a) low technological level;

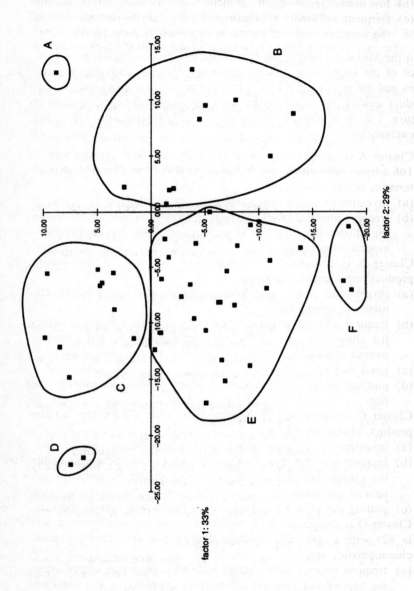

Figure 7.1 The Italian clusters.

(b) low market segment and production only for the domestic market;

(c) frequent informal relationships within the district and use of the services supplied by the entrepreneurial association.

In the Mexican sample, the first factor can be interpreted as an indicator of the importance of size, correlated with the investment strategies and the technological level and the second one as an indicator of product quality. As can be seen from the graphical representation in Figure 7.2, 6 clusters were also identified with the following characteristics:

1. Cluster A is composed of 5 large enterprises (the average size is 166 employees) with a good quality product. The common characteristics of the cluster are:

   (a) investments in commercialization and training;

   (b) frequent informal relationships with other economic agents within the cluster but rare use of services supplied by the entrepreneurial association.

2. Cluster B is composed of 7 very large firms with a low quality product and characterized by:

   (a) investments in commercialization, training and external investments in other firms;

   (b) frequent informal relationships with other economic agents within the cluster but rare use of services supplied by the entrepreneurial association;

   (c) good technological level;

   (d) putting-out of at least one phase of production outside the firm.

3. Cluster C is composed of 5 large firms with a very low quality product, characterized by:

   (a) investments in equity shares of other local firms;

   (b) frequent informal relationships with other economic agents within the cluster but rare use of services supplied by the entrepreneurial association;

   (c) putting-out of at least one phase of production outside the firm.

4. Cluster D is composed of 18 medium-sized enterprises (average size is 82) with a generally medium quality product. Their common characteristics are:

   (a) frequent informal relationships with other economic agents within the cluster but rare use of services supplied by the entrepreneurial association;

   (b) putting-out of at least one phase of production outside the firm.

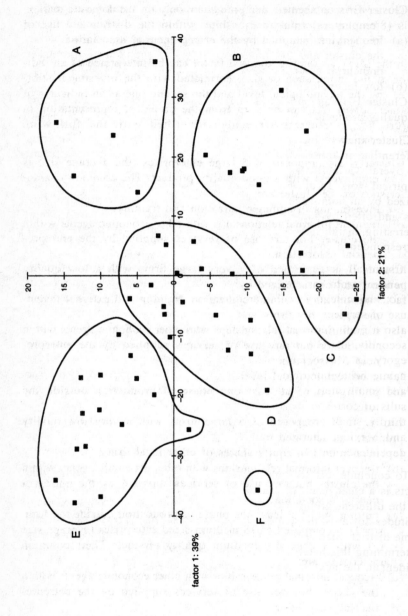

Figure 7.2 The Mexican clusters.

5. Cluster E is composed of 15 small to medium firms (average size is 48 employees) with a good quality product and characterized by:
   (a) frequent informal relationships with other economic agents within the cluster and frequent use of services supplied by the entrepreneurial association;
   (b) low technological level.
6. Cluster F is an outlier: a small firm (18 employees) with a low quality product.

Cluster analysis has made it possible to define how the sample firms differentiate in terms of the main underlying factors, which represent the overall variability of a large number of variables selected from our empirical work. In other words, a cluster is composed by firms characterized by an homogeneous behaviour concerning to the principal factors and often by some common structural features. Ultimately, some interesting insights, confirmed in the next section by the results of correspondence analysis, can be underlined:

1. first of all, large firms, both in Italy and Mexico, are rather independent from institutionalized cooperation within the districts. In fact, this category of firm is always characterized by an occasional use of services supplied by the entrepreneurial association. This is also a finding stressed by factor analysis;
2. secondly, in Italy medium-sized firms are the most dynamic category. In Mexico, the results are less clear-cut, but the more dynamic behaviour of medium-sized firms, in comparison with large and small ones, will be more evident from the analysis of the results of correspondence analysis;
3. thirdly, small firms form a large homogeneous group, both in Italy and Mexico, characterized by low technological level and large dependence on the collective effects of the districts.

To conclude this section, the heterogeneity among firms within districts is a clear result of cluster analysis: the structural characteristics of the different groups of enterprises, their behavioural patterns, their attitudes towards the collective effects can differ greatly within the same district. Size seems to be a very important discriminant factor in determining this heterogeneity among firms. This result becomes very evident in the next section on correspondence analysis.

7.3.3   The profiles of the sample firms

The objective of this section is to classify the sample firms according to their performance, identifying different profiles of structural characteristics and of internal and external conduct. This is done with correspondence analysis, a multivariate exploratory statistical technique that graphically represents the rows and columns of a contingency table (Greenacre, 1984).[10] In the Italian and Mexican analyses the contingency table is a data matrix where along the columns the sample firms are classified according to an index of performance (the trend of production over the last 5 years in Italy and the trend of profits in Mexico) and along the rows according to a sub-set of qualitative variables, selected as indicators of size, localization, segments of market, technological level, type of relationships within the districts (Tables 7.2 and 7.3). The main output of correspondence analysis is a graphical display that can be interpreted to identify the profiles of firms characterized by similar performance.[11]

Both in Italy and Mexico, the first significant result is the localization of the three performance profiles in three separate sub-areas of the graphical displays, identifying three different sets of characteristics for each profile (Figures 7.3 and 7.4).

In Italy, the indicator of performance is the production trend over the last 5 years: increasing (*COL1*), stable (*COL2*) and decreasing (*COL3*). Based on Figure 7.3 we can characterize the profile of firms increasing their production over the last 5 years (*COL1*) as follows:

(a) medium size, between 50 and 100 employees (*B1N2*);
(b) a very good or good technological level (*F111* and *F112*) and investments in technology (*M11*);
(c) a commercial strategy based both on direct sales to customers and on agents (*G142* and *G144*) and investments in commercialization (*M15*);
(d) rare informal relationships within the district (*H613*);
(e) use of more than one service supplied by the entrepreneurial association (*L21*).

The profile of firms with stable production (*COL2*) is characterized by:

(a) large size, more than 100 employees (*B1N3*);
(b) more than 50 per cent of production exported (*B25N1*);
(c) decentralization of less than 50 per cent of the sewing phase (*D31*);
(d) low availability of skilled labour force (*B1013*).

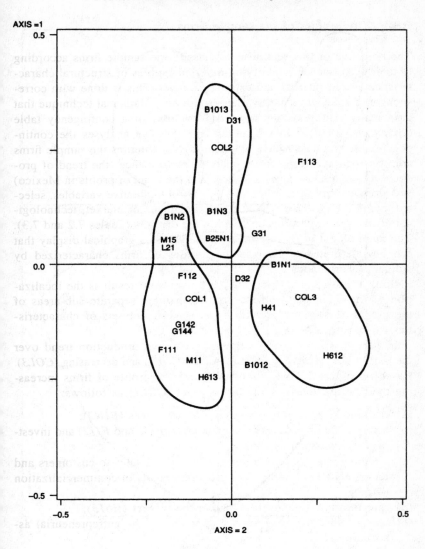

Figure 7.3 The profiles of the Italian sample firms.

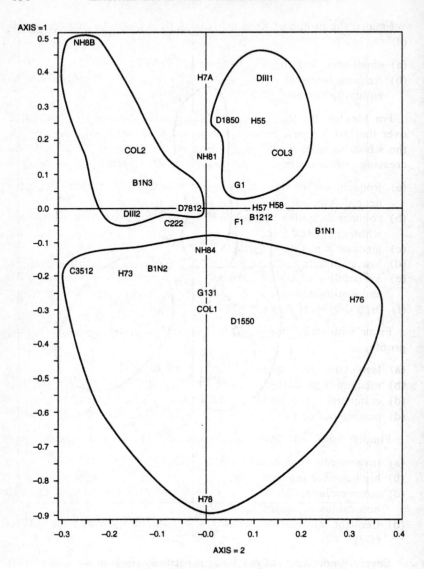

Figure 7.4 The profiles of the Mexican sample firms.

Finally, the profile of firms decreasing their production is composed of:

(a) small size, less than 50 employees (*B1N1*);
(b) frequent informal relationships within the district (*H612*) and non-equity agreements with other local firms (*H41*).

For Mexico, the indicator of performance is the trend of net profits over the last 5 years, because production data were not available for the whole sample. Based on Figure 7.4, the profile of firms with increasing profits over the last 5 years (*COL1*) is characterized by:

(a) frequent use of more than one service supplied by the Entrepreneurial Association (*G131*);
(b) commercialization of more than 50 per cent of the products through wholesalers (*D1550*);
(c) medium size (50–100 employees) (*B1N2*);
(d) low availability of components as a weakness of the firm (*NH84*);
(e) availability of skilled labour (*H73*), access to information (*H76*) and institutional support (*H78*) as competitive advantages of firms;
(f) high degree of technological innovation (*C3512*).

Firms with stable profits (*COL2*) are characterized by the following profile:

(a) large size (more than 100 employees) (*B1N3*);
(b) medium-high market segment (*DIII2*) and original design (*D7812*);
(d) commercial strategy as a weakness of the firm (*NH8B*);
(d) putting out of one or more phases of production (*C222*).

Finally, firms with decreasing profits (*COL3*) are characterized by:

(a) investments in commercialization (*H55*);
(b) high market segment (*DIII1*);
(c) commercialization of more than 50 per cent of products through non-exclusive agents (*D1650*);
(d) frequent informal cooperation with other firms within the district (*G1*).

Several interesting insights can be highlighted from the comparison of the different profiles identified through the correspondence analysis. First of all, institutional support in Italy (*L21*) and in Mexico (*H78* and *G131*) and external economies like access to information (*H76*) and availability of skilled labour (*H73*) in Mexico appear to be significant elements that characterize the successful performance of firms.

Accordingly, this is a further confirmation that collective efficiency is important and has a positive impact on firms' performance, both in the Italian and in the Mexican clusters. Nevertheless, in Mexico the degree of collective efficiency is lower than in Italy, as shown by the absence of a very important collective dimension of clustering: the easy availability of components. This negative characteristic of the clusters has been stressed by successful enterprises as one of the main constraints for their growth.

The second important consideration is related to firm size: both in Italy and in Mexico medium size (*B1N2*) characterizes successful enterprises, large size (*B1N1*) stable ones and small size (*B1N3*) low performing firms.[12] Medium-sized firms, with very similar profiles both in Italy and in Mexico, are capable of benefiting from the collective effects available in the clusters and, at the same time, they reach a scale large enough to invest in technology (*C3512* in the Mexican sample and *F111*, *F112* and *M11* in Italy). Moreover, in Italy and Mexico alternative commercialization strategies, other than the traditional one, are also attempted: in Mexico medium-sized firms sell through wholesalers (*D1550*) and in Italy they sell directly to their clients, increasing their knowledge of the market (*G142*) and investing in market promotion (*M15*).

In Mexico, the profile of stable firms is characterized by large firms making original-design products (*D7812*) for the medium-high segment of the market (*DIII2*), finding difficulties in marketing their products (*NH8B*), notwithstanding their size, and confirming therefore the structural commercial weakness of the footwear industry. In Italy, stable firms are large too and tend to be quite vertically integrated (*D1*) and export-orientated (*B25N1*); in addition they encounter some difficulties in employing skilled labour.

Finally, the profile of low performing firms is characterized by small size and by frequent informal cooperation within the district (*G1* in Mexico and *H612* in Italy) both in Italy and in Mexico. Informal relationships in both countries therefore assume an important role mainly among enterprises in crisis, unlike relationships with supporting institutions which are important for successful firms. Informal cooperation may therefore be interpreted as a kind of solidarity network, helping small enterprises to survive in the market.

In Italy, during the long period of growth when the market was characterized by excess demand, a myriad of enterprises flourished under the protective umbrella of the district. This result confirms what we said in 7.2 about firms that rely heavily on the exploitation of information about products, new fashion trends and technology, freely available in the district, selling a product which benefits from the collective reputation of the district.

In Mexico, small, low performing firms are characterized by the manufacture of high quality products (*DIII3*) and investments in promotion (*H55*), even though most of their products are sold through non-exclusive agents (*D1650*). The conclusion which can be drawn is that small firms, strongly orientated towards high quality, do not reach the scale needed to create a commercial capability to distribute their products.

Ultimately, some interesting conclusions can be drawn from correspondence analysis:

1. first, collective efficiency matters. The results of correspondence analysis confirm the important role played by external economies and cooperation effects among the enterprises located in the clusters analysed. Moreover, correspondence analysis also confirms the existence of a lower degree of collective efficiency in the Mexican clusters than in the Italian districts;

2. second, correspondence analysis stresses an important difference between the 'ideal-type' of industrial districts and the case studies analysed: the heterogeneity of structural features and conduct among different groups of firms within the same cluster. In the samples, heterogeneity depends on size: both in Italy and in Mexico there are, in fact, separate profiles for small, medium and large enterprises. This issue, already raised in the discussion of the results of cluster analysis (section 7.3.2), represents an important shortcoming of the 'model' for interpreting the situations analysed;

3. third, this heterogeneity is reflected in the different attitudes of firms towards the various types of collective effects of the district. In Italy and in Mexico, large firms are rather indifferent to the collective advantages supplied by the entrepreneurial associations, they tend to be self-sufficient and less embedded in the socio-territorial space than medium and small enterprises. Small firms are embedded in the territory and depend highly on the network of informal relationships within the district, but most of them seem unable to really exploit district advantages in order to grow. In this case, the district seems to play the role of a solidarity network, allowing firms to survive beyond market rules. Finally, medium-sized enterprises seem to be able to exploit the advantages deriving from collective effects for their growth.

7.4   ITALIAN AND MEXICAN REALITIES VS. THE 'MODEL'

The preceding sections of this chapter compared the results of the empirical investigations in the two Italian footwear districts and in the two Mexican clusters under analysis. The next step is to go back to the threefold comparison to identify similarities and differences of the empirical cases with the industrial district model. In sections 5.6 and 6.6 some differences between the Italian districts, the Mexican clusters and the 'model' have already been introduced, now with all the information collected to answer the initial question about the adherence of the situations studied to the list of stylized facts indicated by the literature and summarized in Chapter 3 of this work, we may attempt a summary of the results.

An initial consideration of method is appropriate. The comparison is based on two original empirical investigations in which a combination of methods in the collection and analysis of the information are adopted. The collection of information is based on a sample survey, on in-depth network case studies, on interviews to key informers, and on secondary sources. The analysis of the results of the sample survey is also based on different statistical techniques that complement and cross-reference a qualitative comparison of the collective effects deriving from the linkages identified in the case studies.

With regard to the comparison between the 'model' and the real situations analysed, the first important result is the confirmation of the importance of collective efficiency. Both in Italy and in Mexico, clustering opens up possibilities for efficiency gains (7.2), also recognized by collective efficiency appearing as one of the main underlying factors in the two samples in factor analysis (7.3.1) and as one of the driving forces of successful enterprises in correspondence analysis (7.3.3).

Nonetheless, although collective efficiency matters both in Italy and Mexico, the empirical investigation has clearly highlighted some important differences concerning the intensity and quality of collective effects between the realities studied and the ideal–type of district.

The first important difference is the scarcity both in Italy and Mexico of forward linkages as well developed as the backward linkages in the Italian districts. Moreover, in the Mexican clusters the intensity and the quality of the linkages with suppliers and with process specialized firms is definitely lower than in Italy. Concerning external economies, their production in the Italian districts and in the Mexican clusters is quite high but some of them do not only contribute to the level of efficiency and the growth rate of the systems, rather they allow the survival of some low performing firms on the market. In Mexico, the low availability of skilled labour generates a weaker effect of collective learning than in Italy. The general conclusion that can be drawn is the existence of different degrees of collective efficiency in the cases analysed. In Italy, collective efficiency is high but not as high as in the ideal–type and in Mexico it is even lower than in Italy.

The differences in the degree of collective efficiency between the Italian districts and the Mexican clusters may be explained in part by the existence of differences in external conditions. The most evident difference is trade policy: in Italy the existence of a competitive market has favoured the development of a highly efficient system of production, based on a high degree of division of labour among specialized enterprises and intense cooperative linkages with suppliers, while in Mexico the long closure of the domestic market to international competition has induced the development of vertically integrated firms linked to their suppliers through pure market linkages.

It must also be stressed that Mexican firms have recently tried to change and to invest increasingly in their relationships with suppliers on a more collaborative basis in response to expanding competition. The same is true for forward linkages both in Italy and in Mexico: a few firms try to develop new marketing strategy and new links with the market to face their commercial weakness. A similar process of change in the quality of relationships was stressed in a study on the footwear industry in the Sinos Valley in Brazil (Schmitz, 1995a). This issue introduces the question of how the systems react to changes in external conditions and the possibility that differences between districts can be explained by the existence of different stages and paths of development of clusters. This important issue is addressed in the next chapter (section 8.2).

Another important result of the comparison is the existence of heterogeneity within clusters: even if a certain degree of collective efficiency has emerged both in Italy and Mexico, it is important not to expect an island of unity and uniformity among enterprises belonging to the same cluster. From factor (7.3.1), cluster (7.3.2) and correspondence (7.3.3) analyses, the heterogeneity of structures and behaviour among firms composing the same area of geographical concentration and sectoral specialization comes out as one of the main results, expressing an important shortcoming of the 'model' versus the two real situations analysed. This aspect, which appears clearly from the empirical investigation both in Italy and Mexico, has usually been neglected by the literature on the industrial district model, in which the emphasis on adopting the whole system as a unit of analysis has probably induced most of the studies to neglect the analysis of the different sub-systems comprising it.

Humphrey (1995) recently wrote: '. . . the industrial district model focuses almost exclusively on relations between firms and the characteristics of the district as a whole. In the Italian industrial districts many of the firms are sophisticated producers, and to some extent their technical competence can be taken for granted, but in developing countries this cannot be assumed.' (p. 159)

The results of the empirical analysis show that even in Italy the focus on the economic actors composing the district, above and beyond the study of the system as a whole, is an important element for understanding this model of organizing production.

Specifically, the empirical analysis stresses the importance of the differentiation by size, ignored by the 'model'. Both in cluster and correspondence analysis, size is the characteristic around which firms homogeneous in structure and conduct agglomerate. This implies that belonging to a peculiar system of organization, characterized by a certain degree of collective efficiency, does not entirely offset the importance of size. Within the areas investigated, firms are not all equal, but there are small, medium and large firms, which are different and behave heterogeneously. Besides, it is important to stress that both in Italy and in Mexico firms of similar size show similar characteristics and behaviour:

(a) large firms appear to be little embedded in their area, not particularly innovative in technology or marketing. According to the results of correspondence analysis they have registered a stable performance;

(b) medium-sized firms are well-embedded in the territory and attribute more relevance to explicit cooperation, like institutional support or formal linkages with other firms, than to the generic external economies freely available in the districts. They invest in technology, marketing and commercial strategies, registering positive performance;

(c) small sample firms have performed less well. Like medium-sized firms they are also well-embedded in the territory, but they seem to rely much more on external economies, without really pursuing an explicit strategy of cooperation with other economic agents in the districts.

Two main conclusions can be drawn from these results:

1. first of all, in the empirical cases investigated, medium-sized firms have been more successful than large and small enterprises and they were also the group of firms that have invested more in inter-firm relationships and best exploited the opportunity of explicit cooperative behaviour given by the district situation;

2. secondly, heterogeneity, an element of the districts often neglected in the literature, characterizes the behaviour of firms in relation of collective effects. Firms are not all equal in relation to collective efficiency. With regard to this point, Schmitz said: 'Even where a collective capacity to compete, adapt and innovate has emerged, it is important not to expect an island of unity and solidarity. Collective efficiency is the outcome of an internal process in which some enterprises grow and others decline.' (1995b: 534)

The empirical investigation clearly shows that different categories of firms identified in the statistical analysis 'use' the district in a different way. The different attitude with regard to collective effects can be explained by referring to the evolutionary approach (Nelson & Winter, 1982; Dosi *et al.*, 1988), as seen in section 3.3.2. The firms' capability to exploit the collective effects and to invest in inter-firm relationships differs according to their past history and to their previously accumulated know-how.

To conclude, the comparison between the ideal–type of industrial districts and the case studies in Italy and in Mexico has allowed to identify two important shortcomings of the 'model' presented in Chapter 3:

1. differences in external conditions can explain differences between the districts. This is an important lesson to take into account when industrial districts are adopted as a blueprint for analysis and policy on small scale industry in diverse circumstances;

2. within districts, economic actors can be highly heterogeneous. This stresses the need for examining differentiation, particularly by size and by the capacity to invest in cooperative relationships.

The impact of external conditions on districts and the existence of heterogeneous behaviours within districts suggest that one needs to go beyond the 'model' to understand the real situations analysed in Italy and Mexico. These limitations, brought out very clearly from the empirical investigation, have some relevant implications for the need to move from a static to a dynamic approach and for policy; these implications are discussed in the next chapter.

8 Implications for Policy and Further Research

8.1 INTRODUCTION

In the preceding chapter some important results were reached comparing the findings of the empirical investigations carried out in two Italian footwear districts and two Mexican clusters with the stylized facts of the ideal–type of industrial districts described in Chapter 3. First of all, clustering brings gains in both cases. Secondly, the Italian districts and the Mexican clusters are characterized by different degrees of collective efficiency: in Italy both external economies and cooperative effects are higher than in Mexico. Thirdly, to some extent the differences between the Italian districts and the Mexican clusters are explained by introducing into the 'model' the impact that different external conditions may have on the structure of clusters. Finally, districts are not an island of unity but there is heterogeneity among economic actors within them.

In this concluding chapter, a crucial issue for further research is addressed: the need to move from a static to a dynamic approach. This emerged clearly from the empirical research as an important step in further understanding how clusters and heterogenous economic actors within them react to radical changes and how these reactions influence clusters' trajectories of development. Some questions about change are therefore highlighted in section 8.2.

The purpose of section 8.3 is to present some policy implications. Based on the experience of the clusters analysed in Italy and Mexico, some considerations on whether and how collective efficiency can be fostered through public and private institutions are presented.

The final section draws together the major findings of the research, reiterating its objectives. It presents a summary of the empirical results and stresses the limitations of the 'model' and the implications for further research.

8.2 SOME DYNAMIC CONCERNS

The industrial district model described in Chapter 3 is strictly a static model. As Humphrey said (1995): 'Models tend to take the form of snap-shots of a production system at a given point in time. They freeze development at this point, and as a result it becomes out-dated and abstracted from the process of change. In fact, the experiences upon which models are constructed continue to change. As a result, models often suffer from being out-of-date and failing to capture the forces which lead to change.' (p. 152)

Industrial districts in the literature have, in fact, been traditionally outlined as characterized by a number of stylized facts, without really considering the possibility that these facts can change over time. To the extent that change in industrial districts was considered at all, it was incremental change: creation of new firms, increase in outputs or exports, improvement in quality and in the local per capita income. Discontinuous change did not attract the attention of most of the scholars dealing with industrial districts, apart from Garofoli (1983), who was probably the first to stress the possibility that a modification in external conditions and/or internal conditions can generate radical changes in the structure of industrial districts (see section 2.3), and a few other scholars who, following his lead, put some emphasis on this important aspect (Bellandi & Trigilia, 1991; Nuti, 1992; Storper, 1990). More recently the crisis of some Italian industrial districts, stressed by Bianchi (1994) in his article 'Requiem of the Third Italy', has made the importance of moving from a purely static model to a dynamic approach more evident (Ferrucci & Varaldo, 1993), but there is still a great lack of empirical studies addressing the question.

Although the dynamic approach did not guide our empirical investigation, nevertheless some interesting insights came out during the research and are drawn together in the rest of this section. First of all, the different trade policy regimes adopted in Italy and Mexico have a significant impact on the districts' structures and on their development processes; they also have an effect on the quality and intensity of linkages and on the degree of collective efficiency of the clusters analysed, as has been stressed already several times in this work (see particularly section 7.2).

Besides, the empirical investigation in the Italian districts has made evident that some internal features of the systems can also change. The appropriate example is the decreased availability of skilled labour due to the increasing number of young people who prefer to look for non-manual jobs outside the footwear industry, mainly in the tertiary sector. This change in one of the main internal characteristics of the districts can have an important impact on the collective learning process within the local industrial systems. Socio-cultural conditions, which as seen in section 3.2 play an important role in the districts, may change along the growth path of the production system, influencing the evolution of its organizational structure. An important question for further research concerns therefore how the change in the attitude towards work will influence the trajectory of growth of the districts.

Given that an important empirical finding of our work is the existence of heterogeneity within clusters, in a dynamic perspective this implies that we can expect economic actors to have different reactions to change. Some evidence of heterogeneous dynamic behaviour can be found in the Italian districts, where some leading firms have shown an ability to react while others try to resist changes. The reaction to increased competition on the market of the more dynamic firms consists of developing active marketing strategies, inducing some important changes in the structure of the districts analysed.[1]

To present some significant examples, one of these leading firms has acquired some well-known brand names to enter new market segments to diversify its product mix. Another firm has adopted a very aggressive marketing strategy, building up a commercial reputation for its products through advertising and the creation of a network of exclusive franchising shops. To consolidate its reputation and extend its presence to related niches of products, a number of licences have also been acquired to sell products like leather accessories and clothes. With regard to the production phase, this firm counts on a network of 15 exclusive local sub-contractors, often established by its former employees and assisted on technical and financial matters.

Another interesting case is a firm which produces top-quality shoes and invests a lot of resources in advertising and marketing. The crucial role assumed by the marketing phase in the firm's strategy has recently induced it to transfer its headquarters to Milan, leaving only the production, which for a large part is decentralized, to a network of exclusive sub-contractors, in Marche.

What is common among all the experiences presented is the replacement of generic, incidental relationships by strategic collaboration with selected partners, aimed at providing specific complementary resources. These partners may be located in the districts but are not necessarily so if the resources are not available locally, as in the case of commercial and marketing functions.

Facing these progressive firms there are some conservative enterprises, united by a common interest to resist change. According to
Bianchi (1989), the resistance to change in industrial districts may be
particularly high because there are very strong barriers to exit from
the system. The same elements, creating what has been defined in
the literature as 'industrial atmosphere', could become barriers to
exit, locking the local system in a trajectory of conservatism and atro-
phy. In an area completely specialized in one sector it is difficult to
find alternative ways to utilize the human and capital resources left
free by the closing of firms in the main sector of specialization and
therefore the resistance to be pushed out from the production system
can be strong.

In the districts analysed the conservative firms try to resist change
with strenuous price competition, trying to reduce costs when possible,
and with a policy of excessive product diversification. Some resistance
to change may also come from the local institutions, as seen in Brenta
(5.4.5) where the entrepreneurial association systematically refuses any
request for cooperation from new manufacturing countries. They hope
that the refusal to transfer local know-how to potential competitors
will be enough to defend, at least for some time, their comparative
local advantages from international competition.

Moving to the Mexican clusters, a few firms leading the reaction of
the system to the new market situation can be identified. In Chapter 6
we emphasized that the opening up of the market favours an improvement in the quality of the relationships among some shoe producers
and their suppliers, more cooperative behaviour among firms (see for
instance the experiences of *agrupamientos industriales* and *empresas
integradoras*) and a new form of relationship among shoe producers
and wholesalers. All these initiatives go in the direction of an increase
in the degree of collective efficiency of the systems and particularly
towards more explicit cooperative relationships. Schmitz (1995a) documents a similar process of change in the quality of the relationships
among footwear firms in the Sinos Valley in Brazil.

Nevertheless, it is appropriate to specify that increasing competition
may not necessarily force the Mexican clusters to cooperate in the
way seen in the Italian districts. In other words they may follow a
different development trajectory. For instance, in the Mexican clusters
external actors, domestic or foreign, providing complementary resources,
may well assume a significant role in the development process, push-
ing the clusters towards a hierarchical structure dominated by a few
leaders; without necessarily going through a phase characterized by a

high degree of cooperation among economic actors within the clusters.

Contrasting these innovative firms, there is a group of conservative firms which resist change with fierce price competition and little attention to quality. Some of these firms have officially closed their activity to open again in the illegal market, saving on taxes and labour costs. Both in Leon and in Guadalajara, many of the firms interviewed complained about the increasing importance of the informal market and the unfair competition from the illegal firms. According to the entrepreneurial association, in a city like Guadalajara, there are more than 150 street stalls in which the shoes made by informal enterprises are sold at very low prices.

Nevertheless, it must be added that although conservative firms do not participate directly in the process of upgrading linkages induced in the clusters, they may receive some advantages from the changes occurring in the local production systems. They may benefit from the increasing competition among the suppliers and from the improved quality and fashion content of raw materials and components, things which come about from the collaboration between the most innovative shoe producers and suppliers. In other words, even if they do not take part in cooperative linkages they may reap the external economies deriving from the joint action of other more dynamic firms.

The characteristics which the structures of the local systems will assume are questions for future research in the footwear districts and clusters analysed. Here, notwithstanding that they will likely follow different paths of growth, some common patterns in the processes of change described in Italy and Mexico can be stressed:

1. change brings about differentiation within the districts because some firms react to the new situation and others do not. The response to change depends on their ability to build cooperative inter-firm linkages within and outside the districts. This differentiation further stresses the need for studying the behaviour of firms: the mechanisms of decision and bargaining, the reasons for cooperation, the sanctions for enforcing agreements and the foundations of trust within the clusters.

    Besides, it is necessary to understand how these mechanisms change when new firms enter the system or when some local firms assume a leading role within the district. The stability of the system, which as seen in section 3.2.2 guarantees the creation of mechanisms of self-enforcement, reputation and trust, that facilitate cooperative

behaviour among the economic actors, may be hit by some changes in external and/or internal conditions;
2. change in the international market brings about upgrading of linkages. Both in Italy and Mexico, increased market competition has pushed some enterprises to build up strategical cooperation linkages with other economic actors, supplying complementary resources. 'Shifting gear' from passive to active collective efficiency emerges as the crucial requirement for clusters' development; the clusters' capacity to respond to new market opportunities depends on it (Schmitz, 1995b).

These common patterns of change identified in the clusters under analysis emerge as important hypotheses for further research: are external economies important for growth but not sufficient for riding out major changes? Is cooperation linked with the capacity of clusters to respond to major challenges? Will the response of the enterprises within the clusters be differentiated: some will increase cooperation, others will not? Ultimately, a more general indication for future research can be derived: the comparison of different clusters at a given point in time is an exercise which has severe limitations. A more fruitful exercise should appropriately compare trajectories of development, searching for common patterns in these trajectories. Are the trajectories of development of LDCs clusters characterized by some common patterns? And do these patterns differ from those which characterize districts in developed countries? These are all open questions for future research.

8.3   IMPLICATIONS FOR POLICY

The objective of this section is to reveal some policy implications from the empirical investigation in the Italian districts and in the Mexican clusters. This includes whether and how public and private institutions can enhance collective efficiency.

The first important aspect to stress is that both in Italy and in Mexico there is a network of institutions aimed at supporting the clusters analysed, as documented in sections 5.5.5 and 6.5.5; this could represent an important basis for a strategy aimed at enhancing collective efficiency. However, we must also emphasize that none of the clusters analysed was the result of planned action of a local, regional or national industrial strategy. This confirms an important point made by Schmitz (1995b), that public and private institutions can play a role in the growth process of clusters but they cannot build up a district from scratch. The general point to be made here is that the industrial district experience is of greater relevance to those institutions which seek to foster industrialization in areas which already have a minimal density of local small industry.

Once there is a minimum concentration of industrial activity, the assessment of the role actually played by institutions in the growth process however is not an easy task. The little knowledge about the effectiveness of the institutions' role is emphasized in section 3.1.4 on the policy lessons from the European experience. The empirical investigation in the Italian and Mexican footwear clusters confirms the difficulty in making a clear assessment of the results of institutional interventions and in drawing clear policy lessons. Only a rough indication of a positive role played by the institutional support from entrepreneurial associations can be found in the result of correspondence analysis. The use of the services supplied by the associations is, in fact, one of the features of the profile of successful enterprises both in Italy and in Mexico (7.3.4).

Nevertheless, given the lack of systematic assessment of the institutional supports in the case studies, what lesson can be learned? At the macro level, an issue arising from the empirical investigation is the role of trade policy. In Mexico, the protection of the market from international competition has on one side permitted the creation of a critical mass of economic actors but on the other it has not stimulated innovations in products, processes and organizational systems and it has induced little collective efficiency (7.2). Besides, the recent opening of the market has prompted a process of upgrading the linkages and increasing cooperation among some economic actors (8.2). The question, particularly crucial for developing countries, concerns the need for some initial protection of the market to allow the creation of a critical mass of economic actors which is the initial, necessary condition for clustering. This issue is not developed further in this book, but its relevance is connected with the vast and unsolved debate about the 'infant industry' argument.

The Mexican experience draws the attention to an important aspect of regulation: the need to establish common standards of measures and norms of qualities. This is a crucial obstacle to a higher degree of division of labour in the case of the Mexican footwear industry and a very common constraint in developing countries. The lack of a standardized measurement system is in fact responsible for the high transaction costs in the two Mexican clusters, which make it easier and cheaper for shoe firms to carry out internally as many phases of the production process as possible, instead of putting out to some specialized enterprises as in the Italian districts (6.5.1).

In both areas studied, the majority of firms, sector experts and institution managers interviewed agree that some form of harmonization is crucial for the future growth of the clusters. At the time in which the field work took place, two contrasting initiatives existed: in one the two footwear entrepreneurial associations of Guadalajara and Leon and the association of the component producers were involved with the technical assistance of German consultants; while the other was a spontaneous initiative of a small group of large component producers. In the opinion of some of the entrepreneurs interviewed, the initiative supported by the associations was a top-down intervention, with little involvement of the enterprises. The fact that the most important producers of components are in fact involved in the other initiative throws some doubts on its possibility of succeeding in establishing a measurement system commonly accepted by the majority of Mexican producers. On the other hand, it is difficult to judge the strength of the group of component producers to impose their agreement to the rest of the market. While nobody doubts the need for the harmonization of norms and measurement systems, it is a huge task, which requires participation from the institutions and the industry itself and in which foreign technical assistance can probably help a great deal.

Moving to policy at the micro level, the aim here should be to enhance the firms' capability to cooperate and invest in external linkages. The empirical investigation has shown that firms differ in their capacity to interact with other economic agents: some firms mainly rely on external economies while others invest in cooperative relationships, particularly with their suppliers.

The Italian and Mexican experiences show that entrepreneurial associations can play a very important role in increasing the entrepreneurs' sensitivity to the advantages that can be derived from investing in cooperation and improving the quality of inter-firm linkages. Both in Italy and in Mexico, a number of initiatives have been promoted focused at increasing the cohesion within the system, at creating occasions for meetings, for exchanges of information and for developing common strategies. The promotion of the *agrupamientos industriales* by the Camara del Calzado in Guadalajara is particularly noteworthy. Through this initiative, described in some detail in section 6.5.3, the entrepreneurial association promotes among a number of firms the setting up of stable cooperative linkages. Initially the groups are led by a leader appointed by the entrepreneurial association who organizes the activity of the *agrupamiento*, sees that the group respects the commonly settled objectives, and launches initiatives of cooperation. Then, after three or four years, the groups are left alone to organize their activities autonomously.

A first positive assessment of the success of this initiative can be derived from the fact that among the seven original *agrupamientos*, involving about 120 enterprises, promoted by the Camara in seven years, there are three of them which continue to cooperate spontaneously, even after the end of the experience coordinated by the association. As seen in 6.5.3, the forms of cooperation involve exchanges of machines, workers, orders, information about technology, customers and suppliers and some initiatives of common purchasing of inputs. Meetings organized in the framework of *agrupamientos industriales* have also been the origin of an initiative undertaken by a group of entrepreneurs to relaunch the activity of the local credit union (see section 6.5.5).

To conclude, a point that it may be opportune to stress further concerns the heterogeneous behaviour of firms with respect to collective efficiency. The empirical investigation has shown that small, medium and large firms benefit from being in the clusters in rather different ways, implying therefore that they can need different policy initiatives targeted at their specific needs. A confirmation comes from the assessment of the activity of the entrepreneurial association in Leon by the firms interviewed. In the first phase of the field work, many small and medium sized firms complained that the association was dominated by a group of large firms, using the association mainly as a lobby to sustain their interest. During the second phase, a more positive assessment of the association was registered among small and medium firms, following a change of strategy with the appointment of a new management, more keen to consider also the interests and needs of small entrepreneurs, getting them more actively involved in the association's life.

8.4 CONCLUSIONS

This final section draws together the major findings of the research, reiterating its objectives, summarizing the main empirical results and stressing their implications for further research. The success story of industrial districts in Europe during the 1970s and 1980s attracted the interest of some development economists, searching for new models of industrial development legitimizing the economic viability of small enterprises. The initial objective of this research was, therefore, to compare two footwear industrial districts in Italy – which we expected to match the 'model' – with two clusters of footwear enterprises in Mexico in order to understand the potentiality of the industrial district 'model' in capturing reality in a less developed country. The empirical research, however, immediately brought to our attention some important discrepancies between the Italian reality and the 'model'. The comparison was therefore extended to a third level and became a threefold comparison between the 'model', the Italian districts and the Mexican clusters.

Reiterating from Chapter 3, the industrial district model can be characterized by the following four key stylized facts:

1. a cluster of mainly small and medium spatially concentrated and sectorally specialized enterprises;
2. a strong, relatively homogeneous, cultural and social background linking the economic agents and creating a common and widely accepted behavioural code, sometimes explicit but often implicit;
3. an intense set of backward, forward, horizontal and labour market linkages, based both on market and non-market exchanges of goods, services, information and people;
4. a network of public and private local institutions supporting the economic agents in the clusters.

The focus of this work is on the analysis of the collective effects stemming from the above features and particularly from the last two key stylized facts. Two main categories may be distinguished among the collective effects:

1. external economies, which are the spontaneous by-product of economic activities undertaken within the districts;
2. cooperation effects, which are the results of explicit and deliberate cooperative behaviours of the economic actors within the districts.

External economies and cooperation effects define the degree of collective efficiency of the systems and therefore the gains made by firms which cluster together.

In the empirical investigation, these collective effects were analysed in the four clusters of footwear firms selected in Italy and Mexico and classified according to the typology suggested above, comparing the results with the 'model'. A combination of methods in both the collection and the analysis of data were used in the empirical work. As has been said, the collection of information is based on a sample survey with a closed questionnaire, on in-depth network case studies, on open interviews with key informers and on secondary sources. The analysis of information brings together the results of a statistical analysis of the questionnaire survey with a qualitative analysis based on case studies and open interviews.

The first relevant result of the empirical investigation is the confirmation of the importance of collective efficiency: most of the firms located in the areas analysed derive some gains from clustering. However, and this is the first shortcoming of the 'model', there are some considerable differences concerning the intensity and quality of collective effects between the real situations studied and the ideal–type of district. Among these disparities, both in Italy and in Mexico forward linkages are not as strong as the backward linkages in the Italian districts. In the Mexican clusters backward linkages generate less external economies and cooperation effects than in the Italian districts, specifically the degree of division of labour is generally very low and the relationships with suppliers rarely involve cooperation. Furthermore, in Mexico the low availability of skilled labour also generates a weaker effect of collective learning than in Italy.

Exploring further the differences in the degree of collective efficiency three shortcomings of the 'model' become apparent:

1. the impact of disparities in the outside environment on the core characteristics of distinct districts generates differences between districts;
2. the heterogeneity of economic actors originates differences within districts;
3. districts change over time and thus there is a need to move from a static to a dynamic approach for explaining differences between their stages of development and trajectories of growth.

At first glance, these are different points, but in fact they are very much interrelated and should be considered together in analysing industrial districts. This point emerges most clearly from the recent changes in the Italian districts, hit by increasing competition on the international market. The reaction to this radical change in the external environment has not been homogeneous within the systems, but, as seen above in section 8.3, some leading firms have begun to face competition by developing aggressive marketing strategies, for which they have set up cooperative relationships with other enterprises, sometimes located outside the districts.

The impact of these new strategies on the structure of the districts is a tendency towards hierarchization with the leading firms, which on one side organize the activities of a number of subcontracting firms within the districts and on the other interact strategically with other economic actors on the outside. To capture the realities of the Italian footwear districts it would be worthwhile to study how the structures of the systems evolve from one stage to the other, along their trajectory of development, as a reaction to external events and this involves explaining the different ways the economic actors face change within the districts.

Similarly, in Mexico with the opening up of the market to international competition, a few leading firms have begun to change their relationships with suppliers and buyers, trying to set up cooperation linkages, aimed at improving the product quality, fashion content, design and service. Some attempts to increase the division of labour among process specialized firms have been also registered in the two clusters studied. Therefore, in the Mexican clusters too it is necessary to understand the evolution of the system, generated by a change in the trade policy, and led by the actions of some economic actors.

Overall, we can conclude that the industrial district model is a helpful guide for identifying clustering advantages. The empirical analysis has confirmed the existence of a certain degree of collective efficiency within the agglomerations of sectorally specialized firms, from which enterprises can derive some efficiency gains. Given a critical mass of economic actors, the degree of collective efficiency may also become the objective of policy interventions at the macro and micro level. Nevertheless, the comparison of the 'model' with the Italian and Mexican realities has made apparent some shortcomings, which warn against using industrial districts as a blueprint for analysis and policy in different contexts. Going beyond these shortcomings means moving from a static to a dynamic approach, comparing trajectories and stages of development instead of snap-shots at a given point in time and analysing the rationale of behaviour of the economic actors within the systems, in addition to the rationale of the organizational structure of the systems as a whole. Indeed, these are the priorities for further research.

Appendix 1:
The Methodology

The field work for this study was carried out in Marche and Brenta in Italy and in Guadalajara and Leon in Mexico. In every cluster investigated there is a critical mass of spatially concentrated and sectorally specialized shoe enterprises, backward- and forward-linked firms and institutions (see Chapters 5 and 6, sections 5.3 and 6.3). The inquiry was organized in two steps: a first phase in which the investigation was based on a questionnaire distributed to a sampling of shoe producers and on a number of open interviews to key informers and a second step in which some network case studies were undertaken.[1]

In Italy, the sample of 50 firms was randomly taken from the registry of members of the local entrepreneurial associations. The decision to include only members of the associations was justified by the focus of the inquiry on the different forms of explicit and implicit cooperation among firms. It was assumed that firms belonging to the associations were more likely to entertain relationships with other firms; joining the associations may in fact be interpreted as a sign of interest in getting in touch with other firms. The sample was also stratified by size: 24 enterprises employ fewer than 50 employees, 15 between 51 and 100 employees and 11 more than 100 people.

In Mexico as in the Italian inquiry, the sample was randomly chosen from the register of the entrepreneurial associations. According to the associations and some sector experts interviewed, the register is well representative of the formal enterprises because when firms decide to register officially to pay taxes and social benefits they usually become members of the entrepreneurial association, which takes care of all the bureaucratic procedures. The sample comprises 51 enterprises: 30 of them located in Guadalajara and 21 in Leon. Also in this case, the sample was selected in order to include firms of different sizes: 17 enterprises employed fewer than 50 people, 14 between 51 and 100 and 20 more than 100.

The questionnaire used to interview the sample firms is included in Appendix 2.[2] In several cases we also visited the workshop/factory. The results of the questionnaire were analysed with different statistical instruments:

(a) frequency tables to identify the existence of relationships among variables;
(b) factor analysis to summarize the main structures characterizing the universe analysed;
(c) cluster analysis to identify groups of firms characterized by homogeneous characteristics;
(d) correspondence analysis to identify the profiles of sample firms according to their performance.

As with any survey of this kind there are potential problems surrounding the accuracy of the results. The reliability of the answers varies with the questions and in fact some findings were left out of the analysis because there were problems of inconsistency, misunderstanding or lack of trustworthiness. To overcome some of the problems related to the accuracy of the data collected with the questionnaire, they were complemented and cross-referenced with secondary data as well as with interviews to entrepreneurial associations, sector experts, suppliers, buyers and representatives of institutions supporting the sector.

In the second phase of the field work, three firms in Brenta[3] and six in Mexico (three in Guadalajara and three in Leon), within the random sampling of the questionnaire, were arbitrarily selected to carry out in-depth network case studies[4] about their relationships with other economic agents within and outside the district. These include: backward linkages with suppliers of components, raw materials and services, process specialized firms, machinery dealers and repair shops, forward linkages with buyers and sales agents, horizontal linkages with other shoe firms, financial linkages with credit institutions and linkages with private and public institutions.

To conclude this section we must emphasize the enthusiastic reaction to the inquiry on the part of the Mexican entrepreneurs and the entrepreneurial associations in general. Our work was supported in many ways and there was a clear interest in the results of the comparison with the two Italian districts, from which entrepreneurs and associations hope to derive some interesting lessons for the future growth strategy of the Mexican industry. During the field work we encountered firms, not included in the sample, that asked to be interviewed and almost every entrepreneur interviewed insisted on making us visit her/his workshop. During the second phase, when a meeting was organized by the entrepreneurial association in Guadalajara to present the results of the first phase, a good number of the entrepreneurs interviewed participated actively. The Mexican entrepreneurs' interest in being involved in the research contrasted with the more reserved attitude of most of the Italian entrepreneurs, the majority of whom saw the interview as a necessary burden to tolerate for their public reputation.

Appendix 2: Questionnaire

This is an edited version of the questionnaire which was used for the surveys of shoe firms in Brenta and Marche (Italy) and in Guadalajara and Leon (Mexico).

1 GENERAL INFORMATION
1.1 Name of enterprise
1.2 Address
1.3 Name of respondent
1.4 Age
1.5 Position in the enterprise
    (a) Owner
    (b) Manager
1.6 Main Products (as % of total output)
    –Ladies' Shoes   –Leather
    –Men's Shoes   –Synthetic
    –Children's Shoes   –Textile

2 HISTORY OF THE ENTERPRISE
2.1 When was the firm established?
2.2 By whom?
2.3 What is your relationship to the founder(s)?

3 LABOUR FORCE
3.1 Number of workers:
    (a) Non-family
    (b) Family
3.2 Change in number of workers over the last 5 years:
    (a) increased   (b) remained the same   (c) decreased
3.3 Labour turnover in the last 5 years:
    (a) increased   (b) remained the same   (c) decreased
3.4 Do you have any difficulty in finding
    (a) skilled workers?   Yes   No
    (b) unskilled workers?   Yes   No
3.5 Where do your workers receive their training?
    (a) in some training institutions financed by this firm
    (b) in some training institutions financed by the previous employee
    (c) on the job in this firm
    (d) on the job in previous employment
    (e) other (specify)
3.6 Which are the most important problems you have to face in relation with local labour market?
    (a) labour turnover
    (b) lack of unskilled labour force
    (c) lack of skilled labour force
    (d) absenteeism

4 PERFORMANCE
4.1 Sales turnover (in value)
4.2 Trend over the last 5 years
     (+)   (=)   (−)
4.3 Last year net profit was:
    (a) very good
    (b) good
    (c) reasonable
    (d) nil
    (e) loss
4.4 Trend of net profit over the last 5 years
     (+)   (=)   (−)
4.5 % of production exported
4.6 Trend over the last 5 years
     (+)   (=)   (−)
4.7 Number of pairs of shoes produced per year
4.8 Trend over the last 5 years
     (+)   (=)   (−)

5 RELATIONSHIPS WITH SUPPLIERS
5.1 What percentage of inputs do you buy from the following sources?

	local	national	abroad
raw materials			
new machines			
second-hand machines			
components (specify)			

5.2 What kind of problems do you have to face in the relationships with your suppliers?

	availability	price	quality
raw materials			
new machines			
second-hand machines			
components (specify)			

6 SUBCONTRACTING

6.1 Indicate to what extent each stage of production is put out to other enterprises (%):
  (a) leather cutting
  (b) edging and sewing
  (c) lasting
  (d) finishing
  (e) upper production
  (f) sole production
  (g) insole production
  (h) heel production
  (i) other (specify)

6.2 Why do you decentralize some of the production phases to external enterprises?
  (a) lack of specialized machinery
  (b) lack of specialized labour force
  (c) lack of space
  (d) need for greater specialization
  (e) need for greater flexibility
  (f) need for quality improvement
  (g) reduction of costs
  (h) certitude of costs
  (i) lack of investment capability

6.3 Where are the firms to which you have put out some production phases (%)?
  (a) local
  (b) national
  (c) abroad

7 WORKING AS A SUBCONTRACTOR

7.1 In the last 5 years, have you worked as a subcontractor for other enterprises?
    Yes   No

7.2. What do you produce as subcontractor (%)?
  (a) shoes
  (b) uppers
  (c) other (specify)

8 MARKET

8.1 Which is your segment of market (%):
  (a) low
  (b) medium
  (c) medium-high
  (d) high

8.2 Specify to whom you sell your products as a percentage of total sales:
  (a) directly to the consumer
  (b) direct to the retailer
  (c) direct to the wholesaler
  (d) through a non-exclusive agent
  (e) through an exclusive agent

    (f) through a consortium with other manufacturers
    (g) other (specify)
8.3 Which countries did you export to in the past year? Give your answer as a percentage of total export sales.
    (a) EU
    (b) Rest of Europe
    (c) USA
    (d) South America
    (e) Japan
    (f) Rest of the world

9 PROCESS INNOVATION
9.1 Over the past 5 years, has the standard of your equipment improved:
    a) a lot?   b) a little?   c) not at all?
9.2 Generally, where do technical innovations come from?
    (a) developed internally
    (b) adapted internally
    (c) in cooperation with other local manufacturers
    (d) bought ready-made in the national market
    (e) bought ready-made in the international market
    (f) other (specify)
9.3 What are your sources of information for process innovation?
    (a) visits to other enterprises in the local area
    (b) visits to other enterprises in other regions
    (c) machinery suppliers
    (d) exhibitions/fairs
    (e) specialized publications
    (f) workers previously employed in other firms
    (g) other (specify)

10 PRODUCT INNOVATION AND SALES STRATEGY
10.1 In the last 5 years, has the quality of your products:
    (a) increased?
    (b) remained the same?
    (c) decreased?
10.2 Are your sample sets based on:
    (a) design developed internally
    (b) design developed by an outside designer
    (c) imitation
10.3 With which brand name do you sell your products (%)?
    (a) with your own brand name
    (b) with the retailer's brand
    (c) with the wholesaler's brand
    (d) other (specify)
10.4 Do your agents provide you with information about markets and products?
    (a) very frequently
    (b) rarely
    (c) never

11 INTER-FIRM COMPETITION

11.1 Where are your main competitors located?
 (a) in the local area
 (b) in other parts of the country
 (c) abroad

11.2 Are your main competitors:
 (a) large enterprises?
 (b) medium enterprises?
 (c) small enterprises?

11.3 In order to out-compete your rivals, what are the main factors?
 (a) price
 (b) quality
 (c) new designs
 (d) speed and punctual delivery
 (e) other (specify)

12 INTER-FIRM COOPERATION

12.1 Do you have any equity share in other firms? If yes, please indicate the type of firm:
 (a) shoe firm
 (b) backward linked firm (heels, uppers, soles, etc.)
 (c) forward linked firm (trading companies, shops, etc.)
 (d) firm in an unrelated sector

12.2 Do other shoe firms own any equity share in your firm?
 Yes   No

12.3 Do you have any formal agreements with other firms?
 Yes   No

12.4 Do you cooperate with local producers in your industry in the following ways:
 (a) technology development
 (b) lending machinery
 (c) marketing
 (d) other (specify)

12.5 What are the main reasons for cooperating with other firms?
 (a) increase in specialization
 (b) improvement in quality
 (c) reduction of costs
 (d) reduction of risks
 (e) increase in the availability of information
 (f) access to new markets
 (g) other (specify)

12.6 Do you exchange ideas or discuss problems or strategies with other local shoe producers?
 (a) often   (b) occasionally   (c) never

12.7 Do you believe that the possibility of having easy and friendly contacts with other local shoe firms is an important asset for your firm?
 Yes   No

12.8 How do your informal relationships usually come about?
 (a) family ties

(b) neighbours or spatial proximity
(c) social occasions
(d) meetings organized by the local entrepreneurial association
(e) other (specify)

13 INSTITUTIONS

13.1 Does your firm belong to the entrepreneurial association?
                    Yes   No

13.2 Do you use the association for?
(a) information
(b) advice in legal matters
(c) advice on technological issues
(d) book-keeping
(e) advice on labour issues
(f) advice on fiscal questions
(g) courses and seminars
(h) trade fairs
(i) other (specify)

13.3 Do you belong to:
(a) export consortium?
(b) credit consortium?

13.4 Do you have any contacts with the following institutions?
          Never   Occasionally   Frequently
(a) training centre
(b) technology centre
(c) other (specify)

14 GOVERNMENT POLICY

14.1 Have you got access to some form of incentive supplied by government policy?
(a) financial incentives
(b) real incentives:
    –for process innovation
    –for product innovation
    –for training
    –for exporting
    –other (specify)

14.2 Have you encountered any problems in the provision of:
(a) difficulties related to bureaucratic procedures:
    –for obtaining building licences
    –tax procedures
    –for obtaining incentives
    –other (specify)
(b) lack in communication services:
    –telephone and fax
    –mail service
    –other (specify)
(c) shortcomings in the educational system
(d) shortcomings in the training system

(e) shortcomings in the transport services
(f) other (specify)

15 INVESTMENTS
15.1 In which of the following areas have you invested recently?
(a) technological development
(b) product development
(c) backward linked industries (heels, soles, etc.)
(d) forward linked industries (trading companies, shops, showrooms)
(e) marketing (advertising, trade fairs, etc.)
(f) training
(g) managerial training
(h) plant maintenance
(i) other activities not related to footwear

16 STRENGTHS AND WEAKNESSES
16.1 Indicate the two most important strengths and the two main weaknesses
of your firm:

	Strength	Weakness
(a) availability of labour		
(b) labour cost		
(c) labour force skills		
(d) degree of specialization in the different production phases		
(e) availability of components and services		
(f) access to information on technology, products, markets		
(g) cooperation with other local firms		
(h) institutional support (Entrepreneurial Association, consortia, etc.)		
(i) technological level		
(j) quality of products (design, components, etc.)		
(k) marketing strategy (advertising, sale network, etc.)		
(l) access to credit		
(m) other (specify)		

17 VIEWS ON CLUSTERING
17.1 Could you obtain the same results as you now get if you were not
located in this area?
                              Yes   No
17.2 What are the advantages of being located in this area?
17.3 What are the disadvantages of being located in this area?

Appendix 3: Network Case Studies

The objective of network case studies is to probe the character of inter-firm linkages.[1] These include: backward linkages with suppliers of components, raw materials and services, process specialized firms, machine dealers and repair shops, forward linkages with buyers and sale agents, horizontal linkages with other shoe firms, financial linkages with credit institutions and linkages with private and public institutions.

Network case studies have to be detailed and open-ended. The following are the main questions used in evaluating the linkages in Italy and Mexico.

1. What where the reasons for choosing this firm/agent (price, quality, service credit, location, no choice but imposition)?
2. What is the history behind this relationship? How long has it been going?
3. Are there any social/family ties that exist with this firm/agent? How does this influence the relationship?
4. Do you provide your supplying firm (particularly phase enterprises) with: raw materials, credit, technical assistance?
5. Are agreements with the firm/agent of a formal or informal nature?
6. What sanctions do you apply if the firm/agent breaks the agreement (for instance in terms of quality, late delivery)? Will the same sanctions be applied to this firm/agent by other producer firms as well?
7. If you are dissatisfied with the quality of the products/services you obtain from this firm/agent, do you look for an alternative source, or do you collaborate with the existing one to improve quality?
8. Do you know if this firm/agent undertakes tasks for other customers (producers/firms)?
9. Do you receive information about your competitors from this firm/agent?
10. Are you afraid that this firm/agent spreads information about you and your production activities to your competitors?
11. Is the relationship between you and this firm/agent best described as hierarchical, collaborative or competitive?
12. How are the terms of the transactions (price, quality, timing) fixed? By whom? What are the payment conditions?
13. What benefits (for example technical, commercial or financial) do you obtain from this relationships?
14. How has this relationship changed over time?

Appendix 4: Factor Analysis

Factor analysis is a statistical technique used to identify a relatively small number of factors that can be used to represent relationships among sets of many interrelated variables (Kim & Mueller, 1978; Norusis, 1985). The basic assumption of factor analysis is that underlying dimensions or factors can be used to explain complex phenomena. Observed correlations between variables result from their sharing these factors. The goal of factor analysis is therefore to identify the not-directly-observable factors based on a set of observable variables, reducing their number without losing too much of their explanatory power.

The mathematical model for factor analysis appears somewhat similar to a multiple regression equation. In general, the model for the i_{th} standardized variable is written as:

$$X_i = A_{i1} F_1 + A_{i2} F_2 + \cdots\cdots\cdots\cdots + A_{ik} F_k + U_i$$

where

(a) X_i is the observed variable;
(b) The F's are the common factors, which are not-directly-observable variables, common to the X's;
(c) the U is the unique factor, which represents that part of X_i that cannot be explained by the common factors;
(d) the A's are the constants used to combine the k factors.

The factors are inferred from the observed variables and can be estimated as linear combinations of them. While it is possible that all of the variables contribute to a generic j_{th} factor F_j, we hope that only a subset of variables characterizes that factor, as indicated by their large coefficients. The general expression for the estimate of F_j is

$$F_j = \sum W_{ij} X_i = W_{j1} X_1 + W_{j2} X_2 + \cdots\cdots\cdots\cdots + W_{jp} X_p.$$

The W_j's are known as factor score coefficients and p is the number of variables.

For each set of variables more factors can be derived, under the constraints that factors are not correlated between each other. In other words, factors are orthogonal and therefore there is not overlapping information among them: each factor explains a specific amount of the sample variability.

Before examining the mechanics of a factor analysis solution, let us consider the characteristics of a successful factor analysis. It has two main goals:

1. One goal is to represent relationships among sets of variables parsimoniously. That is, we would like to explain the observed correlations using as few factors as possible;
2. We would also like the factors to be meaningful. A good factor solution is both simple and interpretable. When factors can be interpreted, new insights are possible. The ideal situation is when factors can be identified as summarizing sets of closely related variables, in other words when they are strongly correlated with a set of variables which express similar econ-

omic content. For example, if only variables related to size are correlated with a principal factor, then that factor can be interpreted as a size indicator.

With these objectives in mind, the results of the factor analysis presented in section 7.3.1 are very satisfying:

(a) in both samples the explained variability with only three factors is very high (87 per cent in Italy and 76 per cent in Mexico). The objective of parsimony is therefore well satisfied: it was possible to reduce the number of explanatory variables, without losing much of the explanatory power of the original variables considered;
(b) all the factors identified are interpretable and make it possible to present a concise and meaningful picture of the structure of the two samples of firms.

Factor analysis usually proceeds in four steps:

1. the correlation matrix for all variables is computed. Since one of the goals of factor analysis is to obtain factors that help explain these correlations, the variables must be related to each other for the factor model to be useful;
2. the number of factors necessary to represent the data and the methods of calculating them must be determined. The method adopted for obtaining the results presented in 7.3.1 is based on the creation of linear combinations of the observed variables, so that factors can be ranked in decreasing order, according to the amount of variance explained. To help us to decide how many factors we need to represent the data, it is helpful to examine the percentage of total variance explained by each. The larger the number of factors, the larger the amount of variance explained but the less concise is the information given by the analysis. Given the number of factors, the matrix of factor loadings, also called factor pattern matrix, can be calculated. The factor loadings are coefficients which indicate how much weight is assigned to each factor. Factors with large coefficients (in absolute value) for a variable are closely related to that variable;
3. a rotation phase of principal factors attempts to transform – by rotating factors' axes – the initial factor pattern matrix into one that is easier to interpret. Rotation does not affect the goodness of fit of a factor solution. Rotation redistributes the explained variance for the individual factors. The method for rotation adopted here is the *varimax* method, which attempts to minimize the number of variables that have high loadings on a factor. This should enhance the interpretability of the factors;
4. scores can be computed for each observation. The factor scores can then be used in a variety of other analyses. In this case, as shown in Appendix 5, factor scores are used for running a cluster analysis on the two samples of firms.

Two important issues must finally be stressed. The first one is related with the number of factors taken into consideration. The choice is arbitrary, based on a compromise between the amount of variance explained and the aim to extract the lowest possible number of interpretable factors. The second bias is in the choice of the variables composing the principal factors: as said above the criterion is the factor loading; however, some discretionality can intervene in the decision to include a variable in a certain factor for the sake of its interpretability.

Appendix 5: Cluster Analysis

The aim of cluster analysis is to determine whether the objects (in our case the firms) fall into distinct groups or clusters, and, if so, to determine the number of groups or clusters and their membership (Everitt, 1983; Norusis, 1985).

This statistical procedure follows some basic steps:

1. the first decision refers to the variables to utilize in forming clusters, the choice being between the original variables or the three principal factors identified in Section 7.3.1. We opted for the second alternative because experience suggests that differences in results are negligible and moreover a smaller number of included variables improves clusters' interpretability;
2. the second choice regards which algorithm to use for combining objects into clusters. This study opts for an agglomerative hierarchical method, according to which clusters are formed by grouping cases into bigger and bigger clusters. There are many criteria for deciding which cases should be combined at each step. In the cluster analysis on the Italian sample, the average linkage between groups method is adopted. This method defines the distance between two clusters as the average of the distances between all pairs of cases in which the two members of the pair are from each of the clusters. In the analysis on the Mexican sample, the median linkage method is instead adopted to avoid some 'chain effects' (in other words progressive agglomerations of objects which are not homogeneous with regard to one principal factor) detected in a first phase with the average linkage method. In the median method, the two combined clusters are weighted equally in the computation of the centroid (which is the distance between two clusters, calculated as the distance between their means for all the variables), regardless of the number of cases in each;
3. the problem is then to decide how many clusters it is worthwhile to choose. This can be done by cutting the dendrogram (the 'tree' which describes the grouping dynamics) above the low aggregations (which bring together the elements that are very close to each other) and under the high aggregations (which lump together all the groups in the population).

To conclude, it may be worth stressing a potential pitfall in the use of cluster analysis: some discretionality can intervene in the choice of the algorithm for combining objects into clusters and in the number of clusters to choose.

Appendix 6: Correspondence Analysis

Correspondence analysis is an exploratory data analysis technique for the graphical display of contingency tables and multivariate categorical data (Greenacre, 1984; Hoffman & Franke, 1986). Correspondence analysis scales the rows and columns of a rectangular data matrix in corresponding units so that each can be displayed graphically in the same low-dimensional space. This representation can then be used to reveal the structure and patterns inherent in the data; correspondence analysis can reveal relationships that would not be detected in a series of pairwise comparisons of variables and furthermore it helps to show how variables are related, not just that a relationship exists.

In the Italian and Mexican analyses the contingency table is a data matrix where along the columns the sample firms are classified according to an index of performance (the trend of production over the last 5 years in Italy and the trend of profits in Mexico) and along the rows according to a sub-set of qualitative variables (20 in Italy and 24 in Mexico), selected as indicators of size, localization, segments of market, technological level, type of relationships within the districts.

Each row of the contingency table represents a point 'profile' in a p-dimensional space (in Italy there are therefore 20 point profiles belonging to a three-dimensional space and in Mexico there are 24 point profiles); while each column represents a point profile in an m-dimensional space (in Italy there are three profiles in a space with 20 dimensions and in Mexico again three profiles in a space with 24 dimensions).

The correspondence analysis problem is to find a low-rank approximation to the original data matrix that optimally represents both the column and row profiles in k-dimensional subspaces, were k is generally much smaller than either p and m. These two k-dimensional subspaces (one for the row profiles and one for the column profiles) have a geometric correspondence, which enables us to represent both in one joint graphical display. The geometric display of each set of points reveals the nature of similarities and variation within the set, and the joint display shows the correspondence between sets. Distances between points in the same set are expressed in terms of the chi-square distances, given by

$$d_{ii'}^2 = \sum 1/c_j(p_{ij} / r_i - p_{i'j} / r_{i'})^2$$

for row points i and i' and

$$d_{jj'}^2 = \sum 1/r_i(p_{ij} / c_j - p_{ij'} / c_{j'})^2$$

for column points j and j'. These are similar to ordinary Euclidean distances, except that each squared term is weighted by the inverse of the relative frequency corresponding to them. The weighted sum of squared distances from the points to their respective centroids is defined as the total inertia.

Correspondence analysis then proceeds to measure the total inertia of a contingency table, decomposing it along the principal axes to identify the groups of profiles with a high correspondence level, which means very close to each other in the graphical display. In our analysis two axes recover exactly the original data matrix because with three levels of performance – increasing, stable and decreasing production/profits – there are at most two mutually exclusive dimensions.

Practically, the interpretation of the results involves:

(a) the analysis of the total inertia explained by each profile;
(b) the analysis of the total inertia explained by each axis;
(c) the analysis of the partial contribution to inertia of each profile to define the axes;
(d) the graphical analysis of the display, in which each point represents a row or a column profile.

To conclude, it must be recognized that correspondence analysis is a subjective technique. Many different portrayals of a data set are often possible, leading to different categories of analysis and solutions. Subjectivity is also an important limitation in the graphical analysis of the results.

Notes

1 INTRODUCTION

1. Among the first studies in which the phenomenon was identified are: Bagnasco (1977), Becattini (1979, 1987), Brusco (1982), Fuà (1983), Garofoli (1981) and Goglio (1982).
2. The term 'Third Italy' (*Terza Italia*) was first coined by the Italian sociologist Arnaldo Bagnasco (1977) to define and distinguish the industrializing areas of north-central and north-east Italy from the underdeveloped south of the country and from the traditionally industrialized north-western region. It consists of the regions of Friuli-Venezia Giulia, Veneto, Trentino-Alto Adige, Emilia-Romagna, Tuscany, Marche and Umbria.
3. The book which first brought the success of the districts to the attention of English-speaking audiences was the *Second Industrial Divide* by Piore and Sabel (1984). Later a number of articles, some of which had previously appeared in Italian, were translated into English and published in Goodman and Bamford (1989), Pyke, Becattini and Sengenberger (1990) and Pyke and Sengenberger (1992).
4. In what follows, the terms 'industrial district' and 'cluster' are sometimes interchangeable, but it is important to remember that the term 'cluster' only implies geographical concentration and sectoral specialization of firms, while since Marshall, 'industrial district' implies at least inter-firm division of labour as well.
5. In this thesis the term 'linkage' is used in the sense proposed by Stewart and Ghani (1991): "Linkages describe all transactions between economic agents, whether through the market or outside it, fully or partially priced." This concept was originally introduced in development economics by Hirschman (1958), who, in connection with the process of industrialization, identified backward and forward linkages as two important stimuli towards further investment flows.

2 THE ORIGIN OF THE DEBATE

1. For a more detailed discussion about the concept of external economies in industrial districts see section 3.2.1.
2. A *filière* is a particular sector together with all its backward- and forward-linked activities. So, for instance, the footwear *filière* includes the production of shoes, the producers of machinery and equipment, the tannery industry, the producers of components, the product designers, the export specialists and the marketing firms.
3. A further recent attempt to identify industrial districts on the base of more qualitative criteria was proposed by *Il Sole 24 Ore*, an Italian financial

newspaper, which in 1992 published a series of articles on 65 areas characterized by spatial concentration of small firms and sectoral specialization (Moussanet & Paolazzi, 1992). This provided useful examples and brought industrial districts to the attention of a wider audience but it was not useful for analytical purposes.

3 THE INDUSTRIAL DISTRICT MODEL

1. Most recently, in the Northeast a newly established political force – the Northern League – has strongly increased its popularity, campaigning in favour of federalism and increasing autonomy of the northern regions from the south of the country.
2. From Marshall's early economic writings edited by Whitaker (1975, pp. 196–7).
3. Marshall also suggested some examples of dynamic externalities, as discussed in section 3.3.1.
4. Artisan firms are defined as individual firms with only one single plant, where the owner takes care of all the managerial functions and also contributes continuously to the production process and to the training of the workforce. The legal limit for artisans is 20 employees.
5. The role played by districts in reducing uncertainty is also stressed by Dei Ottati (1987), who relates this to an effect of reducing transaction costs.
6. A different way to explain the notion of cooperation in industrial districts based on the transaction cost approach is proposed by Knorringa (1995) in a case study about the footwear industry in Agra, India.
7. Club goods were first introduced to the economic theory in a seminal paper by James Buchanan (1965) to bridge the gap between private and pure public goods. A club good is an impure public good, characterized by partial non-rivalry and excludibility.
8. A number of aspects of the club definition deserve highlighting. First, clubs must be voluntary, in other words members choose to belong because they anticipate a benefit from membership. Second, clubs involve sharing the use of an impure public good or the enjoyment of the benefits of membership. Sharing often leads to a partial rivalry of benefits as larger memberships crowd one another, causing a detraction in the quality of the services received. Third, clubs entail the presence of an exclusion mechanism; without such a mechanism there would be not incentives for members to join (Cornes & Sandler, 1986).
9. According to this school of thought, technical change may be interpreted and 'stylized' in the following way:

    (a) it is an irreversible, path-dependent and evolutionary process, stemming from the behaviour of the different economic agents which explore only a limited part of the set of theoretically possible actions, strictly linked to previous innovation adoptions and to already acquired know-how;
    (b) it rests therefore on a cumulative learning process, resulting in 'creation' rather than simple adoption or imitation of already existing ideas;

(c) due to its dependence on internal learning processes it cumulatively builds on tacit, firm-specific know-how and on intangible assets: its transfer or imitation is therefore a difficult process.

4 THE RELEVANCE OF THE INDUSTRIAL DISTRICT DEBATE FOR DEVELOPING COUNTRIES

1. For an extensive discussion of SMEs in developing countries see Anderson (1982), Liedholm and Mead (1987), Little (1987), Schmitz (1982) and the classic works of Stanley and Morse (1965) and Hoselitz (1959).
2. For a detailed review of the literature on small firm clusters in LDCs see Nadvi and Schmitz (1994).
3. Stewart (1990) stresses the critical importance played by the macro environment in determining SMEs' technology choice and in offsetting most efforts to promote small-scale enterprises. She strongly supports the necessity to create a favourable 'demand-side' environment for sustaining the growth of small and medium scale enterprises.
4. Concerning policy, this study concludes: 'It follows that the first order of business for SME support policy is to ensure that the private marketplace can work, that liberal rules govern the international flow of technical and marketing resources, and that private banks can go about their business of making and collecting loans, and earning profits in the process'. (Levy, 1994, p. 55)

5 THE ITALIAN DISTRICTS OF BRENTA AND MARCHE

1. ANCI (Associazione Nazionale Calzaturifici Italiani) is the national entrepreneurial association of the footwear sector, which publishes a yearly report with data and comments on the situation of the Italian footwear industry.
2. In September 1992 the Lira left the European Monetary System and was devalued by about 30 per cent. The devaluation allowed the Italian footwear industry to regain some competitiveness in the international market and boosted exports.
3. Following the devaluation of the Lira in 1992, exports to the US increased from about 30 million pairs in 1992 to about 35 million pairs in 1993.
4. ANAC (Associazione Nazionale Accessori e Componenti), UNIC (Unione Nazionale Industria Conciaria) and ASSOMAC (Associazione Nazionale Costruttori Italiani Macchine ed Accessori per Calzature e Pelletteria) are respectively the national entrepreneurial associations of component producers, tanneries and machinery producers. They publish yearly data about their sectors.
5. The data for 1985 and 1991 also include the producers of components and therefore cannot be accurately compared with the data of the industrial census. Anyway, from the comparison we can see an indication of the tendency in the sector towards an increasing weight of small firms.

6. See the case of Mexico where the footwear industry is concentrated in three towns (Leon, Guadalajara and Mexico City) (section 6.2.2) or Brazil where it is concentrated in the Sinos Valley and in two towns (Franca and Birigu) in the state of São Paolo (Schmit, 1995a).

7. The location index is calculated in the following way:

$$L = \frac{Xip \backslash Xmp}{Xin \backslash Xmn}$$

where

L = location quotient;

Xip, Xin = employees in the footwear industry in the province 'i' and in the country 'n';

Xmp, Xmn = employees in the manufacturing sector in the province 'i' and in the country 'n'.

When $L > 1$, it means that the concentration of employment in the shoe industry in the analysed province is higher than the national average.

8. The remaining 23 per cent are shoes which cannot be attributed to any specific consumer category.

9. Our study is focused on firms producing leather street shoes, which are the dominant segment of production both in Italy and in Mexico. As opposed to leather street shoes, synthetic athletic shoes are produced by an injection process which can be fully or semi-automated.

10. In developing countries overheads and raw materials tend to be of greater importance than labour. For instance in India labour costs account for 5 per cent in the cost structure, in Chile 11.5 per cent and in Cyprus 26.5 per cent (UNIDO, 1992).

11. In Santa Croce, one of the most important leather districts, there are 880 tanneries which produce 90 per cent of the leather soles and 35 per cent of the leather tanned skins made in Italy (Moussanet & Paolazzi, 1992).

12. In the study area the density of industrial enterprises is 91.7 per 1000 inhabitants, higher than the regional average of 80.2 firms and the national average of 64.8 (CENSIS, 1993).

13. For a definition of the artisan firm see section 3.2.4, note 4.

14. For a detailed presentation of the methodology adopted in the field work see Appendix 1. The questionnaire used for the sample survey is included in Appendix 2 and the list of questions for the network case studies in Appendix 3.

15. For a discussion about the service centres created at regional level in Italy see section 3.2.4.

16. Four different segments of market are defined according to the quality of products: the high segment (over 60 000 Italian Lira), the medium-high one (40–60 000 Lira), the medium (20–40 000 Lira) and finally the economic one (less than 20 000 Lira). The quality of products is usually defined according to three components: the raw material (high, good or low quality leather, synthetic material or fabric), quality processing and fashion content.

17. The creation of networks of shops, often through franchising agreements, has recently become a strategy common for some of the most successful

enterprises in Marche. For further details on these changes occurring in the footwear distribution system see section 8.3.

18. According to a survey carried out by Nielsen, presented in Gaibisso (1992), the expenditure of the footwear sector in advertising are very low: in 1990 only 185 enterprises (2 per cent of the total number of firms) invested in advertising and 60 per cent of the total investments were concentrated only in 24 firms. Besides, in 59 per cent of the firms the total investment was less than 100 000 US$.

19. It may be worthwhile noting that this centre was created a few years after the failure of a similar initiative sponsored by the Regional Government, which according to the information collected never took off. The most common opinion is that the people who should have managed the centre were not competent and above all they were not familiar with the sector's needs and problems. The general comment of entrepreneurs is that a lot of money was wasted in this initiative, without obtaining any results but generating a diffused mistrust about similar projects.

6 THE MEXICAN CLUSTERS OF GUADALAJARA AND LEON

1. Since 1982 wages per worker declined at an average of 3.2 per cent per year (INEGI, 1991).

2. For the footwear industry the tariff was almost halved from 35 per cent to 17 per cent of import value and all import licences were eliminated (CANAICAL, 1991).

3. Non-official estimates mention 1990 imports at approximately 50 million pairs (Dominguez-Villalobos & Grossman, 1992).

4. CANAICAL – Camara Nacional de la Industrial del Calzado – is the entrepreneurial association of the footwear industry. In Guadalajara and Leon there are two local branches named respectively: CICEJ – Camara de la Industria del Calzado del Estado de Jalisco – and CICEG – Camara de la Industria del Calzado del Estado de Guanajuato.

5. Mexican exports satisfy less than 2 per cent of shoe consumption on the US market, where about 1400 million pairs of shoes are consumed every year and 80 per cent of these are imported (ILO, 1992).

6. The low reliability of the statistics available on the footwear industry and the lack of agreement among figures from different sources are also indicated in other studies about the sector (Comercio Exterior, 1980; Baud, 1992).

7. In Mexico, there are three distinct market segments, defined as follows: (a) high priced segment with leather upper and sole (more than 25 US$); (b) medium priced segment with leather upper and synthetic sole (10–25 US$); and (c) low priced segment with synthetic upper and sole (less than 10 US$).

8. CIATEG – Centro de Investigacion y Asistencia Tecnologica del Estado de Guanajauato – is a centre for research and technological assistance created as an agency of the central government. Its activities are described in greater detail in section 6.3.4.

9. The Dominguez-Villalobos and Grossman study is based on a survey carried out on 18 footwear enterprises.

10. The sample is composed of 54 enterprises of different size.
11. According to the last available census (1990), the population of the metropolitan area of Guadalajara is 2,9 million.
12. Data referred on Guadalajara alone are not available. However, data about Jalisco's industrial structure can be taken as an indicator for Guadalajara, which is the most important industrial town in the state.
13. According to the last industrial census (INEGI, 1989), the number of firms and employees is: in Jalisco 279 shoe enterprises with 15 895 employees and in Guanajuato 1008 firms with 34 605 employees. The sector experts interviewed during the survey agreed that the official statistics strongly underestimated the size of the footwear industry in the two areas analysed (see Table 6.2).
14. Calzado Canadà was not included in our inquiry because it is a completely anomalous case in the footwear industry in Guadalajara, with little relevance for the objective of this work since it is highly vertically integrated (from tanneries to the production of boxes and of the furnishings for its chain of shops), without much interaction with the rest of the local industrial environment. For a study on Calzado Canadà and its history see Arias (1980).
15. In the state of Guanajuato there is also an area specialized in the production of tennis shoes, which includes the two small towns of San Francisco del Rincon and Purisima. The history of this area, which recently transformed its artisan vocation of production of *sombreros* into industrial capability in the footwear sector, is presented in a study by Patricia Arias (1992b).
16. The problem of standardization is particularly relevant for the production of bottoms; it is therefore dealt with greater detail in the next section about suppliers.
17. Referring to the ANPIC directory two aspects have to be emphasized: first, naturally the directory only includes enterprises which are members of the Association, second most of the members of ANPIC are located in Leon. In Guadalajara there is a local association (APICEJ – Asociación de Proveedores de la Industria del Calzado de Jalisco) which does not have a membership directory. APICEJ plans to conduct a census of component producers in Guadalajara.
18. The data reported are estimates based on some communications with sector experts.
19. The *agrupamientos industriales* are groups of firms born from an initiative of the Camara del Calzado of Guadalajara, described in greater detail in section 6.4.3.
20. It is interesting to note that Brazil, a country where the footwear industry is very well developed, plays an important role in the technological development of the Mexican industry, both as one of the countries from which machines are imported and as a supplier of technological consultancy. In the Mexican footwear industry technology and know-how transfer therefore do not necessarily take place only from advanced countries like Italy or Spain but also from an industrializing country like Brazil.
21. Section 6.4.2 shows that there is one Mexican wholesaler who tries to control the quality of its products establishing stable and cooperative re-

lationships with the shoe producers. One of the features of its innovative strategy is the supply of technological assistance.

22. For the definition of the three market segments see note 7, above.

23. A widespread opinion among the sector experts interviewed in the survey is that the increase in imports has recently begun to slow down for two main reasons:

    1. in 1993 a quota on the imports from China was introduced;
    2. Mexican firms have begun to imitate shoes imported from Asia, which they are able to produce in better quality and smaller batches of orders, compensating the higher price in comparison with imports from China or Taiwan. To import from Asian countries in fact Mexican wholesalers or retailers have to buy very large quantities. without the possibility of controlling the quality of the products before delivery.

24. One of these wholesalers, probably the most successful one, has introduced a new way of selling: shoes are sold by non-professional agents, mainly women, house to house. People are encouraged to try this commercial activity because they can return the unsold pairs to the shops, without therefore assuming any risk. Thanks to this strategy in a few years this wholesaler became one of the most important on the Mexico City market.

25. The first two experiments in Mexico were in two small rural towns: San Francisco del Rincon (Guanajuato), mentioned for its specialization in shoe production (see note 14, above), and San Miguel el Alto (Jalisco), specialized in the clothing sector. UNIDO has promoted other projects aimed at the creation of groups of small enterprises also in Bolivia, Honduras, Jamaica and Nicaragua (Rabellotti, 1996).

26. National Financiera (Nafin) finances a number of projects aimed at sustaining small and medium-scale enterprises. Its activity is very broad and reaches manufacturing, service and agricultural enterprises, supplying short, medium and long term credit at easy terms. Firms cannot borrow directly from Nafin, but they have access to its credits through commercial banks and credit unions.

27. Each firm pays according to the number of employees.

28. There are two yearly trade fairs, specialized in women's shoes, in Guadalajara, and two, specialized in men's and children's shoes, in Leon.

29. To become members, firms have to buy a share of the union. Each firm may own from a minimum of one to a maximum of 500 shares. Each share costs about 150 US$.

7 EXTERNAL ECONOMIES AND COOPERATION IN ITALY AND MEXICO

1. For a more detailed analysis of these trends in the Italian footwear industry see section 5.2.

2. There are a few discrepancies in the variables between the Italian and Mexican samples; these are due to differences in the reliability of some of the answers.

3. During the statistical analysis, an attempt was also made to build two loglinear models for summarizing the data collected in Italy and Mexico and potentially forecasting some hypotheses of behaviour of the economic systems analysed. Nevertheless, due to the small size of the two samples the explanatory power of the two models obtained is rather modest and therefore the results are not reported here.

4. For a presentation of factor analysis see Appendix 4.

5. The PROC FACTOR procedure in the SAS system (6.03) was used and the prior communality estimates computed from the maximum value of partial correlation (for further details, see Appendix 4).

6. Table 7.4 represents the rotated matrix of factor loadings, which are the weights used to express the factors as linear combinations of the standardized variables: factors with large coefficients (in absolute value) for a variable are closely related to that variable (see Appendix 4).

7. In this section the term *cluster* is used with a different meaning than in the rest of this book. Generally, the concept of cluster was used to refer to a spatial agglomeration of specialized enterprises. Here, instead, cluster is a group of homogeneous firms resulting from the application of cluster analysis to a sub-set of the survey data. In this section therefore the term cluster is used in the statistical sense; several clusters of firms can be found in what, in the rest of this book, have been defined as the Mexican or the Italian clusters. See Appendix 5 for further details on cluster analysis.

8. Alternatively, the original variables composing the factors could have been used. It was decided to proceed using the factors because it was shown in the literature that differences in results are negligible, and moreover factors allow for a much easier interpretation of the clusters (Everitt, 1983). For running the cluster analysis, the CLUSTER procedure in the SPSS[X] system was used, adopting the method of the average linkage (between groups) for the Italian sample and the median linkage for the Mexican sample, in order to avoid some 'chain effects' (progressive agglomerations of objects which are not homogeneous). For further details on the agglomeration methods see Appendix 5.

9. We must note that the cluster analysis in terms of the second and the third factor is less robust from the statistical standpoint because the total sample variability explained is lower (57 per cent for factors 1 and 3 and 54 per cent for factors 2 and 3) than in the case considered (63 per cent for factors 1 and 2). The same is true in the Mexican sample: 61 per cent for factors 1 and 2, 55 per cent factors 1 and 3 and 38 per cent factors 2 and 3. Both in Italy and Mexico, the cluster analysis was run for the three factors but here we only present the clusters in terms of factors 1 and 2 because, from an interpretative point of view, the other clusters do not add very much to the results discussed in this section.

10. See Appendix 6 for a presentation of correspondence analysis.

11. The MATRIX procedure in the SAS system (6.03) was used for running the correspondence analysis on the Italian and Mexican samples. In the rest of this section the discussion of the results is centred around the interpretation of the graphical outputs.

12. In the Mexican sample small size (*B1N3*) does not appear directly among

the variables which characterize the profile of low performing firms; however, it appears among the variables which identify the second axis as distinguishing *COL3* (firms with decreasing profits) from *COL2* (firms with stable profits). The considerations about the association between small size and low performance among Mexican sample firms were derived from these results.

8 IMPLICATIONS FOR POLICY AND FURTHER RESEARCH

1. The considerations presented in this section on the changes occurring in Brenta and Marche are also based on some interviews with key informers for a research project in the framework of the GREMI (Groupe Européenne de Recherche sur les Milieux Innovateurs). The results of this research project are presented in a paper by Camagni and Rabellotti (1995).

APPENDIX 1 THE METHODOLOGY

1. The inquiry covered two periods: the questionnaire surveys were undertaken in 1991 and in 1993 we did some in-depth network case studies.
2. The first version of the questionnaire adopted for the survey in Marche was improved for the field work in Brenta and Mexico. Nevertheless, most of the data collected were homogeneous and it was therefore possible to analyse them jointly.
3. Due to time and resource constraints this part of the field work could only take place in Brenta. In Marche, although less systematically, we discussed some of the issues addressed in the network case studies with a few firms, during a brief visit in November 1993.
4. See Appendix 3.

APPENDIX 3 NETWORK CASE STUDIES

1. The network analysis is adopted for studying small firm economics, particularly in the Scandinavian literature (see for instance Johanson and Mattsson, 1987 and Rasmussen, 1992). For a general presentation of this technique of analysis see Scott (1991) and for a discussion of its use to study linkages within clusters of firms see Nadvi and Schmitz (1994).

Bibliography

ACRIB, 1980s and 1990s, 'Rilevamenti statistici sulle aziende e sugli addetti nel settore calzaturiero della Riviera del Brenta', Strà: Report.

Alba Vega, C. 1986 'La industrializacion en Jalisco: evolucion y perspectivas', in G. Peña & A. Escobar (eds) *Cambio regional, mercado de trabajo y vida obrera en Jalisco*, Guadalajara: El Colegio de Jalisco, pp. 89–141.

Alba Vega, C. & Roberts, B. 1990 'Crisis, ajuste y empleo en Mexico: la industria manufacturera de Jalisco', *Estudios Sociologicos*, VIII, No. 24, 463–89.

Alessandrini, P. & Canullo, G. 1994 'I distretti marchigiani: evoluzione e prospettive', paper presented at the workshop 'Industrial districts and local economic development in Italy: challenges and policy perspectives', Bologna: May 2–3.

Amsden, A. 1985 'The division of labour is limited by the rate of growth of the market: the Taiwan machine tool industry in the 1980s', *Cambridge Journal of Economics*, 3, 271–84.

ANAC 1994 'Industria dell'accessorio e del componente', ANAC, Milan: Report.

ANCI, 1980s and 1990s, 'L'industria calzaturiera Italiana', ANCI, Milan: Report.

Anderson, D. 1982 'Small Industry in Developing Countries: A Discussion of Issues', *World Development*, 10, No. 11, 913–48.

Arias, P. 1980 'La consolidacion de una gran empresa en un contexto regional de industrias pequeñas: el caso de Calzado Canada', *Relaciones*, Summer, 171–253.

Arias, P., (ed.) 1985 *Guadalajara, la gran ciudad de la pequeña industria*, Zamora: El Collegio de Michoacan.

Arias, P. 1992a *El calzado en la region jalisciense: la industria y la camara*, Guadalajara: Camara de la Industria del Calzado de Jalisco.

Arias, P. 1992b *Nueva rusticidad mexicana*, Mexico City: Consejo Nacional para la Cultura y las Artes.

Arrow, K. 1962 'The economic implications of learning by doing', *Review of Economic Studies*, 29, 155–73.

ASSOMAC 1994 'Rapporto Congiunturale', ASSOMAC, Vigevano: Report.

Axelrod, R. 1984 *The Evolution of Cooperation*, New York: Basic Books.

Aydalot, Ph. (ed.) 1986 *Milieux innovateurs en Europe*, Paris: GREMI.

Bagnasco, A. 1977 *Tre Italie: La problematica territoriale dello sviluppo italiano*, Bologna: Il Mulino.

Bagnasco, A. 1988 *La costruzione sociale del mercato*, Bologna: Il Mulino.

Bagnasco, A. & Trigilia, C. (eds) 1984 *Società e politica nelle aree di piccola impresa. Il caso di Bassano*, Venice: Arsenale.

Bagnasco, A. & Trigilia, C. (eds) 1985 *Società e politica nelle aree di piccola impresa. Il caso Valdelsa*, Milan: Franco Angeli.

Banco de Mexico 1991 *Indicadores Economicos*, Mexico City: Banco de Mexico.

Baud, I.S.A. 1992 *Forms of production and women's labour. Gender aspects of industrialisation in India and Mexico*, New Delhi: Sage Publications.

Bazan, L., Estrada, M., Nieto, R., Sanchez, S., Villanueva, M. 1988 *La situacion de los obreros del calzado en Leon Guanajuato*, Mexico City: Ediciones de la Casa Chata.

Becattini, G. 1975 *Lo sviluppo economico della Toscana con particolare riguardo all'industrializzazione leggera*, Florence: Guaraldi.

Becattini, G. 1978 'The development of Light Industry in Tuscany: An interpretation', *Economic Notes*, 7, 107–23.

Becattini, G. 1979 'Dal 'settore industriale al 'distretto industriale'. Alcune considerazioni sull'unità di indagine dell'economia industriale', *Rivista di Economia e Politica Industriale*, January, 35–48 (reprinted as: 'Sectors and/ or districts: some remarks on the conceptual foundations of industrial economics' in E. Goodman & J. Bamford, (eds) 1989, 123–35).

Becattini, G. (ed.) 1987 *Mercato e forze locali: Il distretto industriale*, Bologna: Il Mulino.

Becattini, G. 1989 'Il distretto industriale marshalliano come concetto socio economico', *Stato e Mercato*, April (reprinted as: 'The Marshallian industrial district as a socio-economic notion' in Pyke F. *et al.*, 1990, eds, 37–51).

Bellandi, M. 1982 'Il distretto industriale in Alfred Marshall', L'Industria (reprinted as: 'The industrial district in Marshall', in E. Goodman & J. Bamford (eds), 1989, 136–52).

Bellandi, M. & Trigilia, C. 1991 'Come cambia un distretto industriale: strategie di riaggiustamento e tecnologie informatiche nell'industria tessile di Prato', *Economia e Politica Industriale*, 70, 121–52.

Bellini, N., Giordani, M.G. & Pasquini, F. 1990 'The industrial policy of Emilia-Romagna: the business service centres', in R. Leonardi, R. Nanetti (eds) *The Regions and European Integration. The case of Emilia-Romagna*, London: Pinter Publishers.

Best, M. 1990 *The New Competition: Institutions of Industrial Restructuring*, Cambridge: Polity Press.

Bianchi, G. 1994 'Requiem for the Third Italy? Spatial systems of small firms and multi-regional differentiation of the Italian development', paper presented at the XXIV European Congress of the Regional Science Association, Groningen: 23–26 August.

Bianchi, P. 1989 'Concorrenza dinamica, distretti industriali e interventi locali', in F. Gobbo (ed.) *Distretti e sistemi produttivi alla soglia degli anni '90*, Milan: Franco Angeli.

Bianchi, P., Bellini, N., Giordani, M.G. & Pasquini, F. 1986 'Servizi reali e politica industriale a livello locale', *Stato e Mercato*, April, 121–46.

Boston Consulting Group 1988 'Industria del Calzado', Mexico City: Report.

Brosio, G. 1993 *Economia e finanza pubblica*, Rome: Nuova Italia Scientifica.

Brugnoli, A. & Porro, G. 1993 'Cooperation and Local Development: Contributions from the Game-Theoretical Approach', paper presented at the VII EADI General Conference, Berlin: 15–18th September.

Brusco, S. 1975 'Organizzazione del lavoro e decentramento produttivo nel settore metalmeccanico', in F.L.M. Bergamo (ed.) *Sindacato e piccola impresa*, Bari: De Donato.

Brusco, S. 1982 'The Emilian Model: Productive Decentralisation and Social Integration', *Cambridge Journal of Economics*, 167–84.

Brusco, S. 1989 'A policy for industrial districts', in E. Goodman & J. Bamford (eds) pp. 259–69.

Brusco, S. 1990 'The idea of the industrial district: Its genesis' in F. Pyke *et al.* (eds), 10–9.

Brusco, S. 1992 'Small firms and the provision of real services', in F. Pyke & Sengenberger, W. (eds) 177–96.

Brusco, S., Garofoli, G., Solinas, G. & Villa, P. 1987 'Struttura Produttiva e Competitività dell'Industria Calzaturiera Italiana', Dipartimento di Scienze Economiche, Università Cattolica, Milan: Report.

Buchanan, J.M. 1965 'An Economic Theory of Clubs', *Economica*, 32, 1–14.

Camagni, R. 1991 'Local "milieu", uncertainty and innovation networks: towards a new dynamic theory of economic space', in R. Camagni (ed.) *Innovation Networks: Spatial Perspectives*, London: Bellhaven-Pinter, pp. 121–44.

Camagni, R. & Capello, R. 1990 'Towards a definition of the manoeuvring space of local development initiatives: Italian success stories of local development – theoretical conditions and practical experiences', in W.B. Stohr (ed.) *Global Challenge and Local Response*, London: Mansell, pp. 328–53.

Camagni, R. & Rabellotti, R. 1995 'Alcune riflessioni sulla dinamica dei milieux calzaturieri in Italia', in G. Gorla & O. Vito Colonna (eds) *Regioni e sviluppo: modelli, politiche e riforme*, Milan: Franco Angeli, pp. 161–84.

CANAICAL 1991 'Estudio tecnico sobre el dano a la industria nacional del calzado por el incremento en las importaciones', Camaras de la Industria del Calzado, Mexico City: Report.

CANAICAL 1994 'Perfil de la Industria del Calzado', Camaras de la Industria del Calzado, Mexico City: Report.

Cawthorne, P. 1995 'Of networks and markets: the rise and rise of a South Indian town: the example of Tiruppur's cotton knitwear industry', *World Development*, 23, 43–56.

CEESP 1993a 'Boletin Informativo', Centro de Estudios Economicos del Sector Privado, Leon: Report.

CEESP 1993b 'Resultados de la encuesta aplicada en el evento SAPICA '93', Centro de Estudios Economicos del Sector Privado de Leon, Leon: Report.

CENSIS 1993, *Il Fermano. Radiografia di un localismo maturo*, Fermo: Andrea Livi Editore.

Cho, M.R. 1994 'Weaving flexibility: large-small firm relations, flexibility and regional clusters in South Korea', in Pederson, P.O. et al. (eds) pp. 111–30.

CIATEG 1992 'Realidades de la Industria del Calzado', Centro de Investigacion y Asistencia del Estado de Guanajuato, Leon: Report.

Colletis, G., Courlet, C. & Pecquer, B. 1990 *Les Systèmes Industriels Localisés en Europe*, Institut de Recherche Economique sur la Production et le Développement, Grenoble: Université des Sciences Sociales.

Comercio Exterior 1980 'Calzado', *Comercio Exterior*, 26, 265–72.

CONCALZADO 1991 'Perfil de la Industria del Calzado', *Calzavance*, September.

Cornes, R. & Sandler, T. 1986, *The theory of externalities, public goods and club goods*, Cambridge: Cambridge University Press.

Dawson, J. 1992 'The relevance of the flexible specialisation paradigm for small-scale industrial restructuring in Ghana', *IDS Bulletin*, 23, 34–8.

Dei Ottati, G. 1986 'Distretto industriale, problemi delle transazioni e mercato comunitario: prime considerazioni', *Economia e Politica Industriale*, 51, 33–121.

Dei Ottati, G. 1987 'Il mercato comunitario', in G. Becattini (ed.) 117–41.

Dijk van, M.P. & Rabellotti, R. (eds) 1997 *Clusters and Networks as Sources of Co-operation and Technology Diffusion for Small Enterprises in Developing Countries*, London: Frank Cass.

Dominguez-Villalobos, L. & Grossman, F. 1992 'Employment and Income Effects of Structural and Technological Changes in Footwear Manufacturing in Mexico', *Working Paper*, World Employment Programme Research, No. 224, Geneva: International Labour Office.

Dosi, G., Freeman, C., Nelson, R., Silverberg, G., Soete, L. (eds), 1988 *Technical change and economic theory*, London: Pinter.

Everitt, B.S. 1983 'Cluster Analysis', in D. McKay, N. Schofield & P. Whiteley (eds) *Data Analysis and the Social Sciences*, London: Frances Pinter.

FAO 1992 *World statistical compendium for raw hides and skins, leather and leather footwear 1972–1990*, Rome: Food and Agriculture Organization of the United Nations.

Ferrucci, L. & Varaldo, R. 1993 'La natura e la dinamica dell'impresa distrettuale', *Economia e Politica Industriale*, December, 73–97.

Fuà, G. 1983 'L'industrializzazione nel Nord Est e nel Centro' in G. Fuà & C. Zacchia (eds) pp. 7–46.

Fuà, G. & Zacchia, C. (eds) 1983 *Industrializzazione senza fratture*, Bologna: Il Mulino.

Gaibisso, A.M. (ed.) 1992 *Struttura e competitività del settore calzaturiero in Italia*, Milan: Franco Angeli.

Garofoli, G., (ed.) 1978 *Ristrutturazione industriale e territorio*, Milan: Franco Angeli.

Garofoli, G. 1981 'Lo sviluppo delle aree periferiche nell'economia italiana degli anni settanta', *L'Industria*, 2, 391–407.

Garofoli, G. 1983 'Le aree sistema', *Politica ed Economia*, XIV, 57–60.

Garofoli, G. 1992 'Industrial districts: structure and transformation', in G. Garofoli (ed.) *Endogeneous Development and Southern Europe*, Aldershot: Avebury, pp. 49–60.

Garofoli, G. 1993 'Economic development, organization of production and territory', *Revue d'économie industrielle*, 22–37.

Goglio, S. 1982 'Sviluppo regionale e dimensione d'impresa' in S. Goglio (ed.) *Italia: centri e periferie*, Bologna: Il Mulino, pp. 175–220.

Goodman, E. & Bamford, J. (eds) 1989 *Small Firms and Industrial Districts in Italy*, London: Routledge.

Gottardi, G. (ed.) 1991 *Trasferimento di tecnologie in un settore maturo*, Padua: CLUEP Editore.

Granovetter, M. 1985 'Economic Action and Social Structure: The Problem of Embeddedness', *American Journal of Sociology*, 91, 481–510.

Graziani, A. 1972 *L'economia italiana: 1945–1970*, Bologna: Il Mulino.

Graziani, A. 1975 'Aspetti strutturali dell'economia italiana nell'ultimo decennio' in A. Graziani (ed.) *Crisi e ristrutturazione nell'economia italiana*, Turin: Einaudi.

Greenacre, M. 1984 *Theory and Applications of Correspondence Analysis*, London: Academic Press.

Hirschman, A.O. 1958 *The Strategy of Economic Development*, New Haven: Yale University Press.

Hoselitz, B.F. 1959 'Small industry in underdeveloped countries', *Journal of Economic History*, 19, 600–18.

Hoffman, D.L. & Franke, G.R. 1986 'Correspondence Analysis: Graphical Representation of Categorical Data in Marketing Research', *Journal of Marketing Research*, 23, 213–27.

Humphrey, J. 1995 'Industrial Reorganization in Developing Countries: From Models to Trajectories', *World Development*, 23, 149–62.

ILO 1972, *Employment, Incomes and Equality: A Strategy for Increasing Productive Employment in Kenya*, Geneva: International Labour Office.

ILO 1992 'Recent developments in the leather and footwear industry', Fourth Tripartite Technical Meeting for the Leather and Footwear Industry, International Labour Office, Geneva: Report.

INEGI 1989 *XII Censo Industrial*, Mexico City: Instituto Nacional de Geografia, Estadistica e Informatica.

INEGI, 1980s and 1990s, *Sistema de Cuentas Nacionales*, Mexico City: Instituto Nacional de Geografia, Estadistica e Informatica.

IRPET 1980 *Il buyer in Toscana*, Florence: Le Monnier.

ISTAT (a) 1980s and 1990s, *Annuario di Contabilità Nazionale*, Rome: Istituto Nazionale di Statistica.

ISTAT (b) 1980s and 1990s, *Annuario di Statistiche Demografiche*, Rome: Istituto Nazionale di Statistica.

Johanson, J. & Mattsson, L.G. 1987 'Inter-organizational relations in industrial systems: a network approach compared with the transaction–cost approach', *International Studies of Management and Organization*, 17, 34–48.

Kim, J. & Mueller, C. 1978 *Introduction to Factor Analysis*, Beverly Hills and London: Sage University Press.

Knorringa, P. 1995 'Economics of Collaboration in Producer-Trader Relations. Transaction Regimes between Market and Hierarchy in the Agra Footwear Cluster, India', D.Phil. thesis, Amsterdam: Free University.

Labarthe, M. 1985 *Notas sobre el proceso de industrializacion de Leon. Autobiografia de un obrero del calzado*, Leon: El Colegio del Bajio.

Lanzara, R. 1988 'I rapporti strategici con le imprese conciarie', in R. Varaldo (ed.) pp. 237–73.

Levy, B. 1991 'Transaction costs, the size of firms and industrial policy: lessons from a comparative case study of the footwear industry in Korea and Taiwan', *Journal of Development Economics*, 34, 151–78.

Levy, B. 1994 'Can Intervention Work? The Role of Government in SME Success', paper presented at the World Bank Conference on 'Successful Small and Medium Enterprises and their Support Systems: A Comparative Analysis of Four Country Studies', Washington: The World Bank.

Liedhom, C. & Mead, D. 1987 'Small scale industries in developing countries: empirical evidence and policy implications', *International Development Paper*, No. 9, East Lancing: Michigan State University.

Little, I.M.D. 1987 'Small manufacturing enterprises in developing countries', *The World Bank Review*, 1.

Marshall, A. 1920 *Principles of Economics*, 8th edn, London: Macmillan (1st edn, 1890).

McCormick, D. 1997 'Industrial District or Garment Ghetto? The Case of Nairobi's Mini-Manufacturers', in M.P. van Dijk & R. Rabellotti (eds) pp. 109–30.

Meyanathan, S.D. & Munter, R., 1994 'Changing Industrial Structures and Small and Medium Enterprise Linkage Development: An Overview' in S.D. Meyanathan (ed.) *Changing Industrial Structures and Small and Medium Enterprise Linkage Development: Some East Asian Examples*, EDI Seminar Series on Industrial Change, Washington: The World Bank.

Mishan, E.J. 1971 'The Postwar Literature on Externalities: An Interpretative Essay', *Journal of Economic Literature*, 9, 1–28.

Mody, A., Suri, R. & Sanders, J. 1992 'Keeping pace with change: organizational and technological imperatives', *World Development*, 20, 1797–816.

Morris, A. & Lowder, S. 1992 'Flexible Specialization: The Application of Theory in a Poor-Country Context: Leon, Mexico', Journal of International Urban and Regional Research, 16, 190–201.

Moussanet, M. & Paolazzi, L., eds, 1992 *Gioielli, bambole e coltelli. Viaggio nei distretti industriali*, Milan: Edizioni Il Sole 24 Ore.

Murray, R. 1991 *Local Space. Europe and the New Regionalism*, Manchester and Stevenage: The Centre for Local Economic Strategies and South East Economic Development Strategy.

Murray, R. 1992 'Flexible specialization in small island economies: the case of Cyprus', in F. Pyke & W. Sengenberger (eds) pp. 255–76.

Nacional Financiera, 1991 *La Economia Mexican en Cifras*, Mexico City: Nacional Financiera.

Nadvi, K. 1992 'Flexible specialization, industrial districts and employment in Pakistan', *Working Paper*, No. 232, Geneva: ILO World Employment Programme.

Nadvi, K. 1995 'Changing Social Networks in Small Firm Clusters: Kinship among Surgical Instrument Producers of Sialkot', Institute of Development Studies, University of Sussex; Brighton: mimeo.

Nadvi, K. & Schmitz, H., 1994 'Industrial Clusters in Less Developed Countries: Review of Experiences and Research Agenda', *IDS Discussion Paper*, No. 339, University of Sussex, Brighton: Institute of Development Studies.

Nelson, R. & Winter, S. 1982 *An Evolutionary Theory of Economic Change*, Cambridge, Mass.: Harvard University Press.

Norusis, M.J. 1985 $SPSS^x$ *Advanced Statistics Guide*, New York: McGraw-Hill.

Nuti, F. 1992 *I distretti dell'industria manifatturiera in Italia*, Milan: Franco Angeli.

Paci, M. 1973 *Mercato del lavoro e classi sociali in Italia*, Bologna: Il Mulino.

Paci, M. (ed.) 1980 *Famiglia e mercato del lavoro in un'economia periferica*, Milan: Franco Angeli.

Parisotto, A. 1991 'The distinctive pattern of non-agricultural self-employment in Italy', *Working Paper*, No. 48, Geneva: ILO World Employment Programme Research.

Pederson, P.O., Sverisson, A. & van Dijck, M.P. (eds) 1994 *Flexible Specialisation. The dynamics of small-scale industries in the South*, London: Intermediate Technology Publications.

Piore, M. & Sabel, C. 1984 *The Second Industrial Divide. Possibilities for Prosperity*, New York: Basic Books.

208 *Bibliography*

Platteau, J.P. 1994 'Behind the Market Stage Where Real Societies Exist – Part I and Part II', *The Journal of Development Studies*, 30, 533–77 and 753–817.

Prochnik, V. 1992 'Spurious flexibility: Technical modernisation and social inequalities in the Brazilian footwear industry', *Working Paper*, No. 22, Geneva: ILO World Employment Programme Research.

Pyke, F. 1992 *Industrial Development Through Small-Firm Cooperation*, Geneva: International Labour Office.

Pyke, F., Becattini, G. & Sengenberger, W. (eds) 1990 *Industrial Districts and Inter-Firm Co-operation in Italy*, Geneva: International Institute for Labour Studies.

Pyke, F. & Sengenberger, W. (eds) 1992 *Industrial Districts and Local Economic Regeneration*, Geneva: International Institute for Labour Studies.

Ragazzi E. 1992 'Profilo del settore calzaturiero', in A.M. Gaibisso (ed.) pp. 15–85.

Rabellotti, R. 1990 'The organization variable in developing countries' industrial development', in E. Ciciotti, N. Alderman & A. Thwaites (eds) *Technological Change in a Spatial Context*, Berlin: Springer-Verlag, pp. 67–84.

Rabellotti, R. 1994 'Small and medium-scale industry in Latin America: Some empirical findings', Inter-American Development Bank, Washington: mimeo.

Rabellotti, R. 1995 'Is There an 'Industrial District Model'? Footwear Districts in Italy and Mexico Compared', *World Development*, 23, 29–42.

Rabellotti, R. 1996 'A strategy to enable the building up of SME's competitiveness: The UNIDO experience in Bolivia, Honduras, Jamaica and Nicaragua', UNIDO; Vienna: Report.

Rasmussen, J. 1991 *The Local Entrepreneurial Milieu: Linkages and Specialization Among Small Town Enterprises in Zimbabwe*, Roskilde University, Copenhagen: Centre for Development Research.

Rasmussen, J. 1992 'The small enterprise environment in Zimbabwe: growing in the shadow of large enterprise', *IDS Bulletin*, 23, 21–7.

Rasmussen, J., Schmitz, H. & Dijk van, M.P. (eds) 1992 'Flexible Specialisation: A New View on Small Industry?', *IDS Bulletin*, 23.

Sabel, C. 1992 'Studied trust: Building new forms of co-operation in a volatile economy', in F. Pyke & W. Sengenberger (eds) 215–50.

Sabel, C. & Zeitlin, J. 1985 'Historical alternatives to mass production: Politics, markets and technology in nineteenth century industrialisation', *Past and Present*, 108, 133–76.

Sandee, H. 1994 'The impact of technological change on inter-firm linkages: A case study of clustered rural small-scale roof tile enterprises in Java', in P. Pederson et al., eds, 84–96.

SARTRA, 1993 *World Footwear Markets* 1992, SARTRA, Kettering: Footwear Technology Centre.

Schmitz, H. 1982 'Growth Constraints on Small-scale Manufacturing in Developing Countries: A Critical Review', *World Development*, 10, 429–50.

Schmitz, H. 1989 'Flexible specialisation – A new paradigm of small scale industrialisation?', *IDS Discussion Paper*, No. 61, University of Sussex, Brighton: Institute of Development Studies.

Schmitz, H. 1992a 'On the clustering of small firms', *IDS Bulletin*, 23, 64–8.

Schmitz, H. 1992b 'Industrial districts: Model and reality in Baden-Wurttemberg', in F. Pyke & W. Sengenberger (eds) pp. 86–121.

Schmitz, H. 1995a 'Small Shoemakers and Fordist Giants: Tale of a Supercluster', *World Development*, 23, 9–28.

Schmitz, H. 1995b 'Collective efficiency: growth path for small-scale industry', *The Journal of Development Studies*, 31, 529–66.

Schmitz, H., & Musyck, B. 1994 'Industrial Districts in Europe: Policy Lessons for Developing Countries?', *World Development*, 22, 889–910.

Scott, A. & Storper, M. 1992 'Regional development reconsidered', in H. Ernste & V. Meier (eds) *Regional Development and Contemporary Industrial Response: Extending Flexible Specialization*, London: Belhaven Press.

Scott, J. 1991 *Social Network Analysis*, London: Sage Publications.

SECOFI, 1992 'Programa para promuover la competitividad e internacionalizacion de la industria de la curtiduria y del calzado', Mexico City: Report.

Secretaria de Promocion Economica, 1993 *Perfil de Jalisco*, Guadalajara: Gobierno del Estado de Jalisco.

Sengenberger, W. & Pyke, F. 1992 'Industrial districts and local economic regeneration: Research and policy issues', in F. Pyke, and W. Sengenberger, (eds) pp. 1–29.

Sforzi, F. 1987 'L'identificazione spaziale', in G. Becattini (ed.) pp. 143–67 (reprinted as: 'The geography of industrial districts in Italy' in E. Goodman & J. Bamford (eds) 1989, pp. 153–73).

Sforzi, F. 1990 'The quantitative importance of Marshallian industrial districts in the Italian economy' in F. Pyke, *et al.*, (eds) pp. 75–107.

Signorini, L. 1992 'The price of Prato, or measuring the industrial district effect', paper presented at the European Conference of the Regional Science Association, Brussels: August.

Stanley, E. & Morse, R. 1965 *Modern Small Industries for Developing Countries*, New York: McGraw Hill.

Stewart, F. 1990 'Macro-policies for small-scale industry and appropriate technology', *Small Enterprise Development*, 1, 4–46.

Stewart, F. & Ghani, E. 1991 'How significant are externalities for development?', World Development, 19, 569–94.

Storper, M. 1990 'A response to Amin and Robins', in F. Pyke, *et al.*, (eds) pp. 228–37.

Storper, M. & Harrison, B. 1991 'Flexibility hierarchy and regional development: the changing structure of industrial production systems and their forms of governance in the 1990s'', *Research Policy*, 20, 407–22.

Sverisson, A. 1992 'Flexible specialisation and woodworking enterprises in Kenya and Zimbabwe', *IDS Bulletin*, 23, 28–33.

Terrasi, M. 1988 'Struttura spaziale e dinamica localizzativa', in R. Varaldo, (ed.) 159–88.

Trigilia, C. 1986 *Grandi partiti e piccole imprese. Comunisti e democristiani nelle regioni a economia diffusa*, Bologna: Il Mulino.

Trigilia, C. 1989 'Small-firm development and political subcultures in Italy', in E. Goodman & J. Bamford (eds) pp. 174–97.

Trigilia, C. 1990 'Work and politics in the Third Italy's industrial districts', in F. Pyke, *et al.* (eds) pp. 160–84.

UNIC, 1994 'L'industria conciaria italiana nel 1993', UNIC, Milan: Report.
UNIDO, 1992 'Internationalization and specialization in product markets', UNIDO, Vienna: Report.
Unioncamere, several years, *I conti economici regionali*, Milan: Franco Angeli.
Varaldo, R. (ed.) 1988 *Il sistema delle imprese calzaturiere*, Florence: Giappichelli.
Villa, P. 1990 'Sistemi territoriali di piccole e medie imprese e lavoro sommerso nel centro-nord e nel mezzogiorno. Uno studio di casi', *Quaderno di Istituto*, No. 33, Naples: ISVE.
Villaran, F. 1993 'Small-scale industry efficiency groups in Peru', in B. Spath, (ed.) *Small Firms and development in Latin America: The Role of Institutional Environment, Human Resources and Industrial Relations*, Geneva: International Institute for Labour Studies.
Visser, E.J. 1997 'The Significance of Spatial Clustering: External Economies in the Peruvian Small-Scale Clothing Industry', in M.P. van Dijk & R. Rabellotti (eds) pp. 61–92.
Weijland, H. 1994 'Trade networks for flexible rural industry', in Pedersen, P. *et al.*, (eds) pp. 97–110.
Webster, L. 1991 'World Bank lending for small and medium enterprises. Fifteen years of experience', *World Bank Discussion Papers*, No. 113, Washington: The World Bank.
Whitaker, J.K. (ed.) 1975 *The Early Economic Writings of Alfred Marshall, 1867–1890*, London: Macmillan.
Wilkinson, F. & You, J. 1992 'Competition and Cooperation: Towards an Understanding of Industrial Districts', *Working Paper*, No. 22, Cambridge: University of Cambridge.
Williamson, O. 1975 *Markets and Hierarchies: Analysis and Antitrust Implications*, New York: The Free Press.
Wilson, F. 1992 'Modern workshop industry in Mexico: on its way to collective efficiency?', *IDS Bulletin*, 23, 57–63.
World Bank, 1990 'Footwear: Global Subsector Study', Industry Series Paper, No. 34, Washington: The World Bank.
Zeitlin, J. 1992 'Industrial districts and local economic regeneration', in F. Pyke & W. Sengenberger (eds) pp. 279–82.

Index